Counselor Education
in the 21st Century

ISSUES AND EXPERIENCES

edited by Jane E. Atieno Okech
and Deborah J. Rubel

AMERICAN COUNSELING
ASSOCIATION
6101 Stevenson Avenue, Suite 600 | Alexandria, VA 22304
www.counseling.org

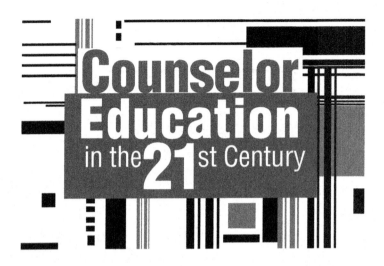

Counselor Education in the 21st Century

American Counseling Association
6101 Stevenson Avenue, Suite 600
Alexandria, VA 22304

Associate Publisher   Carolyn C. Baker

Digital and Print Development Editor   Nancy Driver

Senior Production Manager   Bonny E. Gaston

Copy Editor   Beth Ciha

Cover and text design by Bonny E. Gaston

Library of Congress Cataloging-in-Publication Data
Names: Okech, Jane E. Atieno, editor. | Rubel, Deborah J., editor.
Title: Counselor education in the 21st century : issues and experiences
   / Jane E. Atieno Okech, Deborah J. Rubel, editors.
Description: Alexandria, VA : American Counseling Association, [2018]
   | Includes bibliographical references and index.
Identifiers: LCCN 2018006507 | ISBN 9781556203763 (pbk. : alk. paper)
Subjects: LCSH: Counselors—Training of. | Counseling—Study and
   teaching.
Classification: LCC BF636.65 .C68 2018 | DDC 158.3071—dc23 LC
   record available at https://lccn.loc.gov/2018006507

We dedicate this book to our sons,
Kai Magnus Rubel-Schrier and Maxwell Ochieng Tolo.
You make our work even more purposeful, and
your inspiration knows no bounds.

Table of Contents

Preface

Counselor Education in the 21st Century: Issues and Experiences aims to provide an in-depth exploration of the multidimensional experience of being a counselor educator and the role that institutional characteristics, accreditation status, program models (traditional, online, or hybrid), professional identity, professional development, and diversity and social justice issues play in that experience. The primary purpose of this text is to serve as a resource for doctoral-level students and new professionals in counselor education. Doctoral students and new professionals will understand the diversity of responsibilities, working conditions, role expectations, evaluation criteria, challenges, and benefits experienced by counselor educators. As a resource for master's-level students contemplating a career in counselor education, this book provides a realistic perspective of the career options available in counselor education as well as contextual considerations to keep in mind when exploring postgraduate prospects. Counselor educators exploring career options in academia and career counselors or advisers working with graduate counselor education students will find concrete information about the profession grounded in the experiences of seasoned counselor educators working within a diversity of programs and higher education institutions across the United States. We hope that all readers will benefit from the information provided about the contexts of counselor education programs and the impact of these contexts on the practices and experiences of counselor educators.

Organization of the Text

This book contains 12 chapters. Chapter 1 provides an overview of the current status of the field of counselor education, describes 11 key attributes or elements characteristic of the counselor education profession, and discusses the professional practice domains that influence these attributes. The remaining 11 chapters in this book focus on expanding the conceptualization and understanding of the attributes, domains, and contexts of counselor education in the 21st century.

The 11 key attributes of counselor education addressed in Chapters 2 to 12 are as follows: teaching; supervision; advising and mentoring; admissions and gatekeeping processes; scholarship, research, and grant writing; faculty review, promotion, and tenure processes; adjunct, part-time faculty, and nontenured positions; administration (program coordinator, department chair, associate dean, or dean); professional leadership (state, regional, national, and international levels); service (department, community, college, and university service); and collegiality and wellness.

Within each chapter, the authors provide an overview of contemporary literature on each of these attributes in higher education and then pay specific attention to the role each attribute plays in counselor education. The authors also discuss the experience of being evaluated for each of these attributes and how different institutional contexts affect their experiences. An important highlight of each chapter is an exploration of how counselor educators develop their practice of the aforementioned counselor education attributes. The authors also explore the intersections of the counselor education attributes with the professional practice domains included in every chapter, namely, program accreditation status, professional identity development, professional development, and diversity and social justice issues. In addition, the authors address the distinctions, where relevant, between counselor education practices across the higher education milieu, such as program type (e.g., master's-only or master's and doctoral programs), institution type (e.g., research or teaching intensive), and training modality (e.g., traditional, online, or hybrid models). In every chapter, the authors provide practice and training recommendations relevant to the attributes and contexts discussed in the chapter.

Throughout the book, the authors provide a combination of theory, research, practice, case vignettes, and personal narratives to provide perspectives on the evolution of each attribute of counselor education. Our objective in choosing this format is to ensure that the text remains focused on contextualizing and expanding understanding of the experiences of counselor educators rather than focused exclusively on how the various attributes of counselor education should be enacted. In Chapters 2, 3, and 4 (on teaching, supervision, and advising and mentoring, respectively), for example, the authors explore the experiences of teaching, providing supervision, and advising and mentoring in diverse contexts but do not prescribe how to teach, supervise, or advise and mentor. The same approach can be seen in Chapters 5 and 6, which address admissions and gatekeeping processes and research and grant writing and management, respectively. The author of Chapter 7, on faculty review, promotion, and tenure processes, addresses the paths to success, challenges, and issues related to such processes and the counselor educator's professional life. In Chapter 8, the authors discuss the unique practices, benefits, and challenges of being an adjunct, part-time, or non-tenure-track faculty member in various types of counselor education programs. In Chapter 9, the author provides information useful to doctoral students and new professionals in understanding the roles, responsibilities, and tasks of various types of university administrators and useful to understanding current trends in academia. In Chapter 10, the authors provide valuable information on leadership in counseling and counselor education organizations at the state, regional, national, and international levels. In addition to providing useful information about the roles, responsibilities, challenges, and benefits of specific leadership positions, the authors share compelling narratives on personal/professional growth and the nature of leadership. In Chapter 11, the author provides a detailed discussion of the role of faculty service in academia, with a focus on the benefits and potential pitfalls of service to counselor educators in university settings. The final chapter, on collegiality and wellness, addresses the interpersonal and intrapersonal aspects of being a counselor educator. The author provides valuable information on how faculty and work relationships, student interactions, and personal ways of being can affect job satisfaction and personal wellness. The discussion includes workplace bullying, discrimination, burnout, and compassion fatigue as well as wellness and self-care.

— *Jane E. Atieno Okech and Deborah J. Rubel*

About the Editors

Jane E. Atieno Okech, PhD, NCC, is a professor of counselor education and chair of the Department of Leadership and Developmental Sciences in the College of Education and Social Sciences at the University of Vermont. Before taking on her current administrative role, she served as clinical mental health program coordinator, counseling program coordinator, and interim associate dean for academic affairs and research of the University of Vermont's College of Education and Social Sciences. She is currently an editorial board member of the *Journal for Specialists in Group Work* and was formerly an editorial board member of the *Counselor Education and Supervision*. Dr. Okech's scholarship is anchored in the belief that her teaching, supervision, advising, clinical, and research activities are intertwined and inform one another. At the core of this scholarship is her focus on the practice of group work, guided by an abiding commitment to diversity, multicultural and social justice principles, and the development of the counseling profession. Her scholarly publications have received multiple professional accolades, including the 2017 Article of the Year Award and 2015 Outstanding Article Award from the Association for Specialists in Group Work. She is a 2018 Fellow of the Association for Specialists in Group Work.

■

Deborah J. Rubel, PhD, is an associate professor and past discipline liaison (roughly equivalent to department chair) at Oregon State University, where she teaches in the doctoral counselor education program and designs undergraduate, master's, and doctoral hybrid counseling courses. She is a Fellow of the Association for Specialists in Group Work and also served in the past as the organization's treasurer. Currently in pursuit of full professorship at a doctorate-granting, research-intensive institution, she is gearing up to submit her dossier in fall 2020.

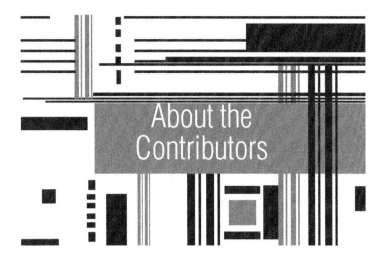

About the Contributors

Ryan G. Carlson, PhD, is an assistant professor of counselor education at the University of South Carolina. He previously worked on four federally funded grants at the University of Central Florida's Marriage & Family Research Institute and currently serves as the lead evaluator for a large randomized controlled trial, Project Harmony. Dr. Carlson is a licensed mental health counselor with clinical experience in community mental health agencies, private practice, and university-based counseling.

Gloria Crisp, EdD, is an associate professor in the College of Education at Oregon State University. Her scholarship focuses on mentoring and related practices and programs designed to support college students' success.

Erin N. Friedman, MS, LPC, NCC, is a counseling and counselor education doctoral student at Syracuse University. She received her master's in clinical mental health counseling from Northern Illinois University.

Susan Furr, PhD, is a professor in the Department of Counseling at the University of North Carolina at Charlotte. She is a former department chair and has served on both departmental and college review committees.

Kristopher M. Goodrich, PhD, LPCC, is an associate professor of counseling in the Department of Individual, Family, and Community Education at the University of New Mexico. He is a past president of the Association for Lesbian, Gay, Bisexual, and Transgender Issues in Counseling and the Rocky Mountain Association for Counselor Education and Supervision. He is the current editor of the *Journal for Specialists in Group Work.*

Danica G. Hays, PhD, is a professor of counselor education and executive associate dean of the University of Nevada, Las Vegas, College of Education. She is past president of the Association for Assessment and Research in Counseling and the Southern Association for Counselor Education and Supervision. Before taking on her current administrative role, she served as a program coordinator and department chair.

Nicole R. Hill, PhD, LPC, is the dean of the College of Education and Human Services at Shippensburg University of Pennsylvania, where she holds the rank of professor in the Department of Counseling and College Student Personnel. She is a former president of the Association for Counselor Education and Supervision, the Rocky Mountain Association for Counselor Education and Supervision, and the Idaho Counseling Association and a former board member for Counselors for Social Justice. She is currently serving as president-elect of Chi Sigma Iota.

Leslie D. Jones, PhD, LPC-S, RPT, is a clinical associate professor in the Department of Counseling and Higher Education at the University of North Texas. She also serves as the director of the Child and Family Resource Clinic at the University of North Texas.

David M. Kleist, PhD, LCPC, is a professor in, and current chair of, the Department of Counseling at Idaho State University. He is a past president of the Association for Counselor Education and Supervision (2008–2009), current editorial board team leader of *The Qualitative Report*, and past editorial board member of *The Family Journal* and *Counseling and Values.*

Jared Lau, PhD, NCC, LPC, is an assistant professor of counselor education in the Department of Counselor Education, School Psychology, and Human Services at the University of Nevada, Las Vegas. Dr. Lau is also a national certified counselor and licensed professional counselor.

Melissa Luke, PhD, LMHC, NCC, ACS, is a dean's professor in the Department of Counseling and Human Services at Syracuse University, where she is associate dean of research and also coordinates both the doctoral program in counseling and counselor education and the master's program in school counseling. Dr. Luke is the president-elect of the Association for Counselor Education and Supervision.

Kok-Mun Ng, PhD, is a professor of counselor education in the College of Education at Oregon State University. His scholarship focuses on multicultural and diversity issues in the theory and practice of counseling, counselor education, and supervision.

Lisa L. Schulz, PhD, LPC-S, NCC, ACS, is a former clinical associate professor of counseling at the University of North Texas in Denton and a former assistant professor at Georgia Southern University in Statesboro. She is currently a practitioner and supervisor.

Heather C. Trepal, PhD, LPC-S, is a professor in and coordinator of the clinical mental health counseling program at the University of Texas at San Antonio. She is a past president of the Association for Counselor Education and Supervision.

Jolie Ziomek-Daigle, PhD, is a professor in the Department of Counseling and Human Development Services at the University of Georgia and a licensed professional counselor. She coordinates the school counseling master's program and advises both master's and doctoral students.

Acknowledgments

Our collaboration began when we were graduate students at Idaho State University. Over the years that collaboration has resulted in multiple conference presentations, publications, and finally this book. Our professional and personal relationship symbolizes the possibilities when two people who admire each other are open to learning from each other's perspectives and experiences. The outcome of our collaboration continues to inspire us to be creative together. We hope that emerging, new, and seasoned counselor educators who read this book are inspired to value the friendships that begin in graduate school and that they continue to believe in the potential of such friendships to blossom into unexpected lifelong personal and professional relationships.

We are grateful for the education and mentoring that we received as graduate students at Idaho State University (ISU) and the United States International University–Africa (USIU-A). From the advising that Jane received from Dr. Ruthie Rono (USIU), the advanced doctoral seminar courses taught by Dr. Arthur Lloyd, the clinical supervision sessions with Dr. Stephen Feit, and the teaching discussions with Dr. David Kleist (ISU), we developed an in-depth understanding of the history and evolution of the field of counselor education and, most important, the value of a well-grounded professional identity. We have gone on to learn from colleagues in our institutions, our students, our clients, and our professional collaborators at state, national, and international levels. We give credit for the strong foundation and understanding of counselor education that we both have today to these individuals and groups and to the unique experiences they enabled.

No one has been as inspiring, challenging, and encouraging to both of us as Dr. William B. Kline, who chaired both of our dissertation committees. We both published articles with him based on our dissertations, and in each case, the collaboration resulted in professional accolades and recognition by peers. Bill saw the potential in both of us long before we individually recognized it. Long after we became leaders and mentors in our own rights, he continued to encourage, support, and celebrate our accomplishments. Bill, we thank you for your unending support, inspiration, and mentorship.

Chapter 1

Introduction to Counselor Education in the 21st Century

Jane E. Atieno Okech and Deborah J. Rubel

Counselor education is a profession with a unique identity supported by a professional organization dedicated to the practice of educating and supervising counselors and an articulated set of standards for counselor preparation, practice, and employment (Association for Counselor Education and Supervision [ACES], 2016; Council for Accreditation of Counseling and Related Educational Programs [CACREP], 2015a; Gibson, Dollarhide, & Moss, 2010; Lloyd, Feit, & Nelson, 2010). The development of the counselor education field is closely associated with the evolution of counseling as a distinct profession.

The counseling profession has distinguished itself among the helping professions, with the master's-level degree accepted as the entry-level requirement for certification and licensure for professional practice (Sweeney, 2001). Professional counselors, the American Counseling Association (ACA) and counselor educators have advocated for the counseling profession, clarified the role of professional counselors among helping professionals, and laid a firm foundation for the role of counselor educators in counselor preparation programs.

ACES has a long history of advocacy for counselor educators and supervisors. By the 1970s, the organization had developed standards for counselor preparation (ACES, 1979, 2016) and advanced "accreditation-related documents that allowed them to conduct voluntary accreditation of counseling programs" (CACREP, 2015a, para.1). The ACES vision statement states in part that it "advances professional counseling through counselor education and supervision" (ACES, 2016, p. 5), reflecting the core role that this organization has in these related professions. It was ACES's efforts at standardizing counselor preparation and establishing accreditation standards and its consultation with the American Personnel and Guidance Association (a precursor to ACA) that led to the creation of CACREP (CACREP, 2015a).

Since its inception in 1981, CACREP's mission has been "to provide leadership and to promote excellence in professional preparation through the accreditation of counseling and related educational programs" (CACREP, 2015a, para. 1). The accrediting body has had a significant impact on the standardization of the counselor education curriculum, the shaping of the professional identity of counselor educators, and the hiring practices in counselor education programs. By 2014, 63% of counselor preparation programs in the United States were accredited by CACREP (Honderich & Lloyd-Hazlett, 2015; Lee, 2013).

The foremost accrediting body for counseling programs has continued to expand and define the field of professional counseling. In 2015, CACREP announced plans to merge with the Council on Rehabilitation Education, an organization that accredits professional rehabilitation programs (CACREP, 2015b). With this merger, the two organizations have formed a powerful body overseeing the accreditation of a broader range of counselor preparation programs.

Over the years, the more the CACREP Standards laid out specific criteria for master's-level counselor training programs, the more its standards evolved to shape the counselor education curriculum at the doctoral level also. Ultimately these evolving guidelines have influenced the identity, role, and function of counselor educators (CACREP, 2015a). This development has intersected with the influence of certification and licensure bodies and the increasing prominence of counselor education programs and counselor educators in shaping the standards and requirements for training, certification, licensure, and professional counseling practice (Bobby, 2013; CACREP, 2015a; National Board for Certified Counselors, 2016).

One result of the widespread acceptance of CACREP Standards is the consistency in focus and content of the doctoral curriculum across accredited programs. The 2009 and 2016 CACREP Standards clearly identify the doctoral degree in counselor education and supervision as the preferred degree for faculty teaching at the master's and doctoral levels. The identity of counselor educators therefore has become deeply entrenched in the training parameters established by the accreditation standards, resulting in the unique academic preparation, professional role, and experiences of counselor educators.

Relationship to Higher Education

Although counselor education is a unique professional and academic field, its practice resides within the larger realm of higher education. Within higher education, the practices commonly engaged in by educators (teaching, research, and service) are affected by the history, evolution, and current status of higher education as well as the standards and traditions of the particular institution within which a program, discipline, or department resides (Altbach, 2016). To understand counselor education faculty practices and experience, it is necessary to understand the higher education context within which counselor education occurs.

Higher education is a high-status field in which faculty maintain relatively high levels of autonomy around their teaching and research activity (Altbach, 2016). Some of the stability of higher education can be attributed to its complex, hierarchical, and culturally entrenched nature (Geiger, 2016). In general, this structure buffers institutions of higher education from external influences, promotes very slow change, and may promote historical inequities (Geiger, 2016). However, higher education is also an evolving field that has experienced profound shifts that affect the professoriate (Altbach, 2016). Although globalization trends place increasing emphasis on the international context of higher education, the American system of colleges and universities remains the gold standard (Finkelstein, Conley, & Schuster, 2016). Thus, the evolving trends that may affect future counselor educators may be usefully informed by examining higher education in the United States.

Trends that are relevant to the context of higher education can be conceptualized as those associated with student characteristics, governmental influence, and actions within institutions (Geiger, 2016). Over time, the students in higher education have become increasingly diverse and focused on preparation for work rather than preparation for entry into academe. Governmental influence can be seen as dual shifts, one from high financial investment to lower financial investment and the other from low regulatory involvement to higher regulatory involvement. At the institutional level, these shifts have resulted in tensions between commitments to teaching and research, with demands for higher productivity in both areas with fewer resources. This has been coupled with a growing focus on accounting for productivity related to student and scholarly outcomes. In addition, these shifts have also resulted in increased financial pressures that have resulted in increased entrepreneurial activity in both teaching (such as growth in for-profit education) and research (such as research collaborations with private companies; Geiger, 2016).

Altbach (2016) interpreted these general trends into more specific effects on the professoriate. Current economic struggles broadly affect pay, program resources, and teaching loads for faculty (Altbach, 2016). And although the valuing of research within higher education remains high, funding for research is increasingly difficult to acquire. This, along with the increased vocational focus of students and the pressure to prioritize teaching, creates a difficult division of purpose for many faculty. This division of purpose has affected the structure of higher education. It has caused declines in tenure-track positions and increases in part-time, adjunct, and full-time nontenured positions while also perpetuating inequality among these positions. Finally, increases in governmental oversight and public calls for the accountability of academic institutions have increased the influence of administrators, decreased the power of faculty, and further shaped their work (Altbach, 2016).

Each of these trends affects counselor education programs and the counselor educators working within them. The effects on teaching and research are obvious and related to productivity and accountability pressures with dwindling resources. The declining emphasis on tenure-track positions and growing use of non-tenure-track faculty and part-time faculty are also changing the face of counselor education faculty. Although this shift is usually in response to universities' teaching mission, it also presents growing issues within faculty, such as pay inequality, marginalization, and shifting expectations about academic careers (Banasik & Dean, 2016). These are but a few ways the current context of higher education may affect the 21st century counselor educator; the effects can be seen in each of the domains discussed in the ensuing chapters. To fully understand what it means to be a part of counselor education, one must understand higher education; consider the specific employment settings within which counselor educators work; and consider institution type, program accreditation status, program model (traditional, online, or hybrid), professional identity, professional development, and social justice and diversity issues.

Counselor Educators' Employment Settings

A quick cross-referencing of accredited counselor education programs (CACREP, 2015a) and institutional characteristics (Indiana University Center for Postsecondary Research, n.d.) provides a useful perspective on the diverse academic settings in which counselor educators work. The academic settings range from research-intensive to teaching-intensive institutions. The settings may offer only master's degree programs or may offer both master's and doctoral degree programs. Counselor education is offered at both nonprofit and for-profit institutions as well as those classified as public and private. In addition, academic settings that house counselor education programs differ in terms of training modality, from online or hybrid to traditional training, in which the majority of training experiences are completed face to face. These contextual differences in the types of institutions in which counselor educators work and the types of delivery models used contribute to the differences and similarities in counselor educators' professional functions and experiences in academia. It is for this reason that the authors of these chapters also address the intersection of the attributes of counselor education and the domains of institutional characteristics, accreditation status, traditional or variations of online models of curriculum delivery, professional identity, professional development, and diversity and social justice issues (see Figure 1.1).

Understanding Counselor Educators' Work Experience in Context

Understanding counselor educators' work experience requires an understanding of the history of and current trends in counselor education and higher education and also an understanding of several domains of

TYPES OF INSTITUTIONS				
Book Chapter Topics	Research Intensive and Others	Teaching Intensive and Others	Traditional Online or Hybrid	PROGRAM TYPE (MASTER'S ONLY OR MASTER'S AND DOCTORAL)
Introduction				
THE PRACTICE OF COUNSELOR EDUCATION — Teaching / Supervision / Advising and Mentoring / Admissions and Gatekeeping Processes / Scholarship, Research, and Grant Writing / Faculty Review, Promotion, and Tenure Processes / Adjunct, Part-Time Faculty, and Nontenured Positions / Administration (Program Coordinator, Department Chair, Associate Dean, or Dean) / Professional Leadership (State, Regional, National, and International Levels) / Service (Community, College, and University Service) / Collegiality and Wellness				
	Professional Identity and Professional Development	Diversity and Social Justice	Program Accreditation Status	
DOMAINS INCORPORATED INTO EACH CHAPTER				

Figure 1.1

An Overview of the Focus of the Book and Each Chapter

counselor education. These domains include institution type, accreditation status, professional identity, professional development, and diversity and social justice issues. What follows is a general introduction to the background, significance, and scope of influence of each of these domains. The interactions between each of these domains and the individual attributes of counselor education are explored in more depth in Chapters 2 to 12.

Institution Type

Counselor educators' work experience is influenced by institutional characteristics. The most familiar way in which universities and colleges are categorized in terms of their institutional characteristics is via the

Carnegie Classification of Institutions of Higher Education. This system originated in 1973 and was intended to facilitate research on institutions of higher education by providing ways to differentiate between institutions (Altbach, 2015). Changes in institutional characteristics have been connected to shifts in stakeholders' priorities over time. Characteristics that are currently tracked include data such as enrollment numbers, type and number of degrees awarded, part-time and full-time faculty numbers, funds generated from intellectual property and research, amount of research conducted, and level of internationalization (Altbach, 2015). Although the classification system has changed over time, at its most basic level it has always separated universities as doctorate, master's, or baccalaureate granting; classified them to denote higher versus lower research and teaching focus; noted whether institutions are publicly or privately owned; and noted whether they are run for profit or are nonprofit (Indiana University Center for Postsecondary Research, n.d.). These are the dimensions that are most closely examined in these chapters.

It is important to explore and understand how an institution's level of focus on research or teaching affects the experiences of counselor educators as they engage in their varied roles and responsibilities. An institution's classification as a doctoral university with very high research activity or as a master's college or university indicates a sociopolitical context and set of priorities that affect overall decision-making processes, including what faculty activities and outcomes are valued, how resources such as finances and time are allocated, and who is hired and retained (Geiger, 2016). These in turn can affect the experience of counselor educators as they engage in the many different activities that may make up their daily work lives. This influence is most often associated with expectations of higher research productivity at institutions with high or very high research activity and the commensurate effect on tenure and promotion processes (Lambie, Ascher, Sivo, & Hayes, 2014) but can also be seen in potentially higher teaching loads and an emphasis on advising and teaching evaluations during promotion processes at master's colleges and universities (Altbach, 2016). The influence can be seen less directly in activities such as service expectations, in the status and treatment of non-tenure-track faculty, and in faculty wellness or job satisfaction.

The status of an institution as private or public may also have implications for counselor educators' experiences in their roles and responsibilities. Historically private colleges and universities have been seen as institutions that provide high-quality education at high prices to the elite of society (Geiger, 2016). Today private colleges and universities run the gamut from a very few large research-oriented institutions that are almost indistinguishable in their operation from large state-funded schools, to smaller high-caliber liberal arts colleges, to denominational colleges, to for-profit institutions that focus on a few sustainable or even lucrative programs (Geiger, 2016). Current trends indicate that whereas older, more prestigious private, nonprofit institutions are stable, experience high demand, and continue to largely represent a privileged dominant culture population, smaller for-profit institutions are financially vulnerable, experience less prestige, and serve a very diverse student body (Hunt, Callender, & Parry, 2016). Most private institutions voluntarily adhere to the same policies as public institutions, and many are required to because they receive public funding of some type. However, the agendas and values of private universities may more freely affect the curriculum, student admission, student evaluation and retention, and faculty hiring and evaluation. An example of this is the inclusion of lifestyle agreements for faculty and students at religiously affiliated colleges (Smith & Okech, 2016a, 2016b).

Within the realm of private universities, the status of an institution as for profit or nonprofit affects the experience of counselor educators. In general, the culture of an institution is affected at all levels by its status as for profit or nonprofit. An institution's status as for profit results in a culture oriented toward the marketplace, employers, and decision making based on business principles, although increasingly traditional nonprofit institutions of higher education are also adopting elements of this culture also (Lechuga, 2008). Although almost all counselor education programs must cut costs and maximize revenue generated via student credit hours, for-profit institutions may feel this pressure even more so. This pressure can affect admissions decisions, course sizes, advising load, general workload, pay, and the stability of job contracts (Hunt et al., 2016; Lechuga, 2008).

Accreditation Status

Given both the prevalence and importance of CACREP to the counselor education field at large, accreditation status may greatly affect the experience of the counselor educator. Accreditation is a status that indicates that the institution, college, department, or program has met the standards set by the accrediting body, and these standards address whether the structures and processes of the institution, college, department, or program will lead to the desired educational outcomes. At the level of individual programs, the outcomes are typically informed by professional standards. For the counseling profession, the most common accreditation is from CACREP.

CACREP's merger with the Council on Rehabilitation Education, an organization that accredits professional rehabilitation programs, has made it a powerful accrediting body. In addition, the endorsement of CACREP Standards by ACA highlights its importance and influence in the field of counselor education and counseling. More recently, counseling programs may be accredited by the Master's in Counseling Accreditation Committee. This newer accrediting body emerged in 2009, partly in response to the 2009 CACREP Standards, which required counselor preparation programs to only hire core faculty who "have earned doctoral degrees in counselor education and supervision, preferably from a CACREP-accredited program, or have been employed as full-time faculty members in a counselor education program for a minimum of one full academic year before July 1, 2013" (CACREP, 2009, Standard I.W.2). This requirement prevents new doctoral-level psychologists from gaining core faculty positions and has led to many counseling and clinical psychologists, long dedicated to counselor preparation, feeling unappreciated and disenfranchised (Kurpius, Keaveny, Kim, & Walsh, 2015). In addition, counselor educators' experiences may also be affected when their programs overlap with or share resources with programs accredited by other bodies, such as the American Psychological Association. This may be a positive effect, such as broader exposure to differently skilled clinicians, or a negative one, such as challenges for students with an undifferentiated professional identity or competition for resources such as clinical placements. More specifically, accreditation status affects almost all of the roles, responsibilities, and experiences of counselor educators. Accreditation both provides counseling programs and counselor educators with resources and benefits and places additional demands on them (Thomas, 1991). Accreditation requirements shape the curriculum, specify student-to-faculty ratios, specify ratios of full-time to part-time faculty, set requirements for faculty professional identity and training, dictate the maximum size of clinical courses, and shape student and program assessment practices (CACREP, 2015a). Because accreditation may be attractive to prospective students, counselor educators can advocate for positive program changes and funding (Honderich & Lloyd-Hazlett, 2015). Conversely, accreditation has been criticized as potentially burdensome to maintain both in terms of faculty workload and in terms of program finances, potentially exclusionary, and detrimental to program innovation and creativity (Thomas, 1991).

Professional Identity

Issues of professional identity have existed since the inception of the counseling profession. With its multiple origins in guidance and psychology, as well as its overlap with other professions such as marriage and family therapy, rehabilitation, psychology, psychiatry, and social work, the counseling profession has struggled yet succeeded in forging a unique professional identity (Dollarhide, Gibson, & Moss, 2013). Professional identity operates at both a profession-wide or collective level and a personal level. At the collective identity level, challenges have included unifying diverse specializations into one counseling profession (McLaughlin & Boettcher, 2009), conflicts between the humanistic values of the profession and the medical model values of the systems that surround it (Eriksen & Kress, 2006), and the multidisciplinary nature of the body of knowledge from which the profession draws (Pistole & Roberts, 2002). These challenges in part spurred efforts by ACA to develop strategies to strengthen the collective identity of counseling (Kaplan & Gladding, 2011) and to develop a unified definition of counseling (Kaplan, Tarvydas, & Gladding, 2014). Despite this unified definition, the collective identity also operates as a professional culture marked by implicit values, language, and norms for behavior. Within the larger profession, professional identity also operates as an individual's relationship to the profession and its formal and informal culture. At a suprasystemic level, other institutions, such as licensing bodies and legislatures, interact with professional identity by allowing activities for identified professionals and by consulting with professionals as experts on policy.

For counselor educators, professional identity is active in several ways. Counselor educators may identify as counselors or may potentially identify with another helping profession, and their level of identification with these professions may vary in intensity and meaning. They may also identify primarily as counselor educators, or they may identify more with a practice specialty, such as school counseling or addictions counseling (Brott & Myers, 1999; Eriksen & Kress, 2006). Regardless, the individual setting in which they work, as well as the particular tone of the institution and locality in which their program resides, may place greater or lesser value on specific professional identities. This valuing may take the form of subtle validation or invalidation (Okech & Geroski, 2015); differential access to resources; and, in the extreme, the inability or struggle to gain employment (Kurpius et al., 2015). Those entering the profession of counselor education should be aware of and receive mentoring on how their professional identity may interact with and affect their employment opportunities and the various roles they will fulfill within their institutions.

In addition to having their own professional identity, counselor educators are also charged with facilitating the development of professional identity in their students (Dollarhide et al., 2013; Okech & Geroski, 2015). Given the variety of ways in which counselor educators may identify and the variety of ways in which those identities may or may not be valued within their institutions or programs, it is clear that facilitation of professional identity is a complex endeavor. The governing body of counseling benefits from students and practicing counselors having a strong identification with the profession, and there is evidence that professional practice and clients may benefit from this identification as well (Granello & Young, 2012). It is in part because of this that the practices of counselor education, including curriculum, clinical experiences, and hiring practices, are shaped by accreditation standards, which are in turn shaped by professional governing bodies. Those moving into counselor education positions should be aware of how their own identification and the processes and practices of their programs can affect the professional identity of their students through the variety of roles faculty engage in. For instance, specific courses within the counseling curriculum are geared toward the professional development of students. Thus, it is imperative that the instructors of those courses understand the professional identity outcomes desired. Similarly, supervisors may play a large role in supervisee professional identity development (Dollarhide et al., 2013; Okech & Geroski, 2015) and thus should be aware of that influence and use it wisely. The leadership and service domains in which faculty choose to become involved, such as leading Chi Sigma Iota chapters, assist in students' professional identity development. Similarly, becoming involved in state, regional, national, or international counseling or counselor education organizations provides professional identity role modeling for counseling students.

Professional Development

Another factor that affects the roles, responsibilities, and experiences of counselor educators is counselor educators' professional development. In this text, we conceptualize professional development as the gaining of skills and knowledge, formal and informal, to earn or maintain professional credentials. In the context of counselor education, professional development may be seen as gaining the experience, knowledge, and skills needed to maintain necessary credentials such as counselor licensure or supervision certification; to perform typical tasks such as teaching; or to develop personal or interpersonal skills such as self-care, assertive communication, or stress management. Each domain of counselor educator roles, responsibilities, and experiences comes with its own set of knowledge and skills, both formal and informal, that enable its practice.

Several issues are present in terms of counselor educator professional development. One is the initial training and mentoring of doctoral students who will fill counselor education positions, whether the positions are tenure-track, clinical or instructor, part-time, or term-to-term positions. The course work and experiences that are part of doctoral counselor education should provide a sound foundation of knowledge and skills for new professionals to build on. In addition, doctoral students should have the opportunity to connect with experienced mentors who share their specific counselor education interests and can provide guidance at a more personalized level. Although accreditation provides a framework for doctoral programs, how skills, knowledge, and experiences are imparted is still highly dependent on the program or institution.

Another issue is the professional development that must occur after the doctoral degree is completed and a position has been secured. Counselor educators are charged with keeping their clinical skills and licenses current, developing supervision skills to match students who are interning in a variety of settings, and gaining the content knowledge and pedagogical skills to teach a variety of courses. They must also further develop their research and writing skills and potentially develop the knowledge and skills needed to move into administrative positions such as program coordinator, department chair, associate dean, or dean (Magnuson, 2002; Sangganjanavanich & Balkin, 2013). The acquisition of skills and knowledge at this level is essential but very often not formally supported.

The roles, responsibilities, and experiences of counselor educators change as they become more experienced and gain knowledge and skills. In addition, the institutional culture rooted in higher education's history also affects the experience of faculty as they become more proficient. In some institutions, new faculty are mentored in their new responsibilities and protected through course releases or funding to assist them in establishing a research agenda. In these institutions, more experienced faculty who have gained skills, knowledge, and the protection of tenure share the load, in particular taking on tasks that may prove risky for new faculty, such as administration. In other institutions, new faculty, as they attempt to establish themselves, may become the bearers of unwanted courses, bearers of heavy advising loads, and authors of accreditation reports, and they may be responsible for administrative duties that more senior faculty do not want.

Diversity and Social Justice Issues

Beyond the boundaries of the institution and program, the experience of counselor educators is also affected by issues of diversity and social justice.

Higher education, as noted before, is a system affected by its history and hierarchical structure. It is also a system that exists within society, and although it is often seen as a driver of social progress, higher education also operates as a microcosm of society (Geiger, 2016). Racism, sexism, classism, ableism, heterosexism, and other forms of marginalization and oppression exist within higher education, its institutions, and programs within those institutions. Institutions struggle to equitably serve students from diverse groups, and both female faculty and faculty of color, in particular Hispanic or Black/African American faculty, suffer disproportionately from low pay and promotion rates (Ali, 2009; Altbach, 2016).

Counselor education programs are not immune to the effects of the history and hierarchical structure of higher education. Counselor education faculty, staff, students, and clients are affected by various forms of marginalization and oppression in ways that can be blatant and more dangerously, in ways that can be nearly invisible, unintentional, and damaging (Constantine, Smith, Redington, & Owens, 2008; Henfield, Woo, & Washington, 2013). The insidious nature of these dynamics implies that each role, activity, and experience of the counselor educator is affected in some way. This requires prospective and current counselor educators to be vigilant. Although counselor educators may be the target of marginalization and discrimination based on social identity (Constantine et al., 2008), counselor educators with the dominant group or positions of relative safety and power have the responsibility and opportunity to effect change at the microlevel with students and colleagues and at the macrolevel within the institution, community, and beyond. They should be prepared to do so.

The counseling profession has increasingly identified itself with social justice values. It has long sought to update its practice and training to provide better training and treatment across cultural and identity differences and to position counselors of all specialties to be advocates and agents of social change. Thus, the widely varying roles and practices of counselor educators should be not only examined but also envisioned as opportunities for positive change.

Conclusion

Many people enter the counseling profession for very idealistic reasons. They want to help others and also enjoy and value working with people. Some become inspired and intrigued during their own training or when they take on clinical supervision duties with the training and development of counselors. They may be fascinated by the diverse and evolving knowledge base associated with counseling and its specialties. They may also feel compelled to add to that knowledge base. Such people become counselor educators. However, just as counselors' professional experiences are not limited to direct work with clients, counselor educators' professional experiences are not limited to teaching, supervision, and research. The life of a counselor educator is made of many roles and responsibilities, and they are subject to a variety of relationships and stressors (Magnuson, 2002). Although doctoral programs strive to educate and mentor students to thrive in these environments, there are many things to accomplish during doctoral education, and students may feel surprised or unprepared in their first position (Magnuson, 2002).

The many influences mentioned previously hint at some of the benefits and challenges of being a counselor educator. In addition to the material effect of these influences on work and working conditions, the complexity of the influences themselves can add to the overwhelming experience of beginning work as a counselor educator, whether part time or full time. It is not unusual for new faculty to feel somewhat helpless, confused, overwhelmed, or disappointed (Magnuson, 2002). And it is not unusual for both new and more experienced counselor educators to experience burnout (Sangganjanavanich & Balkin, 2013). Yet the counselor educator has many opportunities within these roles and responsibilities both to personally prosper and to effect positive change that can benefit colleagues, students, and clients. New professionals who have an understanding of the reality of these roles and responsibilities and the broader context of higher education and their specific institution will be better able to cope, thrive, and make positive changes.

Additional Online Resources

American Counseling Association's endorsement of the Council for Accreditation of Counseling and Related Educational Programs Standards for accreditation
　　https://www.counseling.org/accreditation
Association for Counselor Education and Supervision
　　https://www.acesonline.net
Carnegie Classification of Institutions of Higher Education®
　　http://carnegieclassifications.iu.edu/
Council for Accreditation of Counseling and Related Educational Programs
　　www.cacrep.org
National Board for Certified Counselors
　　www.nbcc.org

References

Ali, P. (2009). Job satisfaction characteristics of higher education faculty by race. *Educational Research Reviews, 4,* 289–300. Retrieved from www.academicjournals.org/journal/ERR/article-full-text-pdf/C83012F4120

Altbach, P. G. (2015). The Carnegie classification of American higher education: More and less than meets the eye. *International Higher Education, 80,* 21–23.

Altbach, P. G. (2016). Harsh realities: The professoriate in the twenty-first century. In M. N. Bastedo, P. G. Altbach, & P. J. Gumport (Eds.), *American higher education in the 21st century: Social, political, and economic challenges* (4th ed., pp. 84–109). Baltimore, MD: Johns Hopkins University Press.

Association for Counselor Education and Supervision. (1979). *Standards for preparation in counselor education.* Falls Church, VA: American Personnel and Guidance Association.

Association for Counselor Education and Supervision. (2016). *Association handbook.* Retrieved from https://www.acesonline.net/sites/default/files/October%202016%20ACES%20Handbook%20Revision%20FINAL.pdf

Banasik, M. D., & Dean, J. L. (2016). Non-tenure track faculty and learning communities: Bridging the divide to enhance teaching quality. *Innovation in Higher Education, 41,* 333–342. doi:10.1007/s10755-015-9351-6

Bobby, C. L. (2013). The evolution of specialties in the CACREP standards: CACREP's role in unifying the profession. *Journal of Counseling & Development, 91,* 35–43. doi:10.1002/j.1556-6676.2013.00068.x

Brott, P. E., & Myers, J. E. (1999). Development of professional school counselor identity: A grounded theory. *Professional School Counseling, 2,* 339–349.

Constantine, M. G., Smith, L., Redington, R. M., & Owens, D. (2008). Racial microaggressions against Black counseling and counseling psychology faculty: A central challenge in the multicultural counseling movement. *Journal of Counseling & Development, 86,* 348–355. doi:10.1002/j.1556-6678.2008.tb00519.x

Council for Accreditation of Counseling and Related Educational Programs. (2009). *2009 standards.* Retrieved from www.cacrep.org/wp-content/uploads/2017/07/2009-Standards.pdf

Council for Accreditation of Counseling and Related Educational Programs. (2015a). *CACREP 2016 standards.* Alexandria, VA: Author.

Council for Accreditation of Counseling and Related Educational Programs. (2015b). *For immediate release.* Retrieved from www.cacrep.org/wp-content/uploads/2017/05/Press-Release-on-Merger-7-20-15.pdf

Dollarhide, C. T., Gibson, D. M., & Moss, J. M. (2013). Professional identity development of counselor education doctoral students. *Counselor Education and Supervision, 52,* 137–149. doi:10.1002/j.1556-6978.2013.00034.x

Eriksen, K., & Kress, V. E. (2006). The *DSM* and the professional counseling identity: Bridging the gap. *Journal of Mental Health Counseling, 28,* 202–217.

Finkelstein, M. J., Conley, V. M., & Schuster, J. H. (2016). *The faculty factor: Reassessing the American academy in a turbulent era.* Baltimore, MD: Johns Hopkins University Press.

Geiger, R. L. (2016). The ten generations of American higher education. In M. N. Bastedo, P. G. Altbach, & P. J. Gumport (Eds.), *American higher education in the 21st century: Social, political, and economic challenges* (4th ed., pp. 3–34). Baltimore, MD: Johns Hopkins University Press.

Gibson, D. M., Dollarhide, C. T., & Moss, J. M. (2010). Professional identity development: A grounded theory of transformational tasks of new counselors. *Counselor Education and Supervision, 50,* 21–38. doi:10.1002/j.1556-6978.2010.tb00106.x

Granello, D. H., & Young, M. E. (2012). *Counseling today: Foundations of professional identity.* Upper Saddle River, NJ: Prentice Hall.

Henfield, M. S., Woo, H., & Washington, A. (2013). A phenomenological investigation of African American counselor education students' challenging experiences. *Counselor Education and Supervision, 52,* 122–136. doi:10.1002/j.1556-6978.2013.00033.x

Honderich, E. M., & Lloyd-Hazlett, J. (2015). Factors influencing counseling students' enrollment decisions: A focus on CACREP. *The Professional Counselor, 5*, 124–136. doi:10.15241/emh.5.1.124

Hunt, S., Callender, C., & Parry, G. (2016). *The entry and experience of private providers of higher education in six countries.* Retrieved from http://www.researchcghe.org/publications/the-entry-and-experience-of-private-providers-of-higher-education-in-six-countries/

Indiana University Center for Postsecondary Research. (n.d.). *News and announcements.* Retrieved from http://carnegieclassifications.iu.edu/

Kaplan, D. M., & Gladding, S. T. (2011). A vision for the future of counseling: The 20/20 principles for unifying and strengthening the profession. *Journal of Counseling & Development, 89*, 367–372. doi:10.1002/j.1556-6676.2014.00164.x

Kaplan, D. M., Tarvydas, V. M., & Gladding, S. T. (2014). 20/20: A vision for the future of counseling: The new consensus definition of counseling. *Journal of Counseling & Development, 92*, 366–372. doi:10.1002/j.1556-6676.2014.00164.x

Kurpius, S. E. R., Keaveny, M. K., Kim, C. S., & Walsh, K. J. (2015). MCAC and state counselor licensure laws: David and Goliath. *The Counseling Psychologist, 43*, 1008–1033. doi:10.1177/0011000015575393

Lambie, G. W., Ascher, D. L., Sivo, S. A., & Hayes, B. G. (2014). Counselor education doctoral program faculty members' refereed article publications. *Journal of Counseling & Development, 92*, 338–346.

Lechuga, V. M. (2008). Assessment, knowledge and customer service: Contextualizing faculty work at for-profit colleges and universities. *Review of Higher Education, 31*, 287–307. doi:10.1353/rhe.2008.0004

Lee, C. C. (2013). The CACREP site visit process. *Journal of Counseling & Development, 91*, 50–54. doi:10.1002/j.1556-6676.2013.00070.x

Lloyd, P. A., Feit, S. S., & Nelson, J. (2010). The evolution of the counselor educator. *Counseling Today, 11*, 58–59.

Magnuson, S. (2002). New assistant professors of counselor education: Their 1st year. *Counselor Education and Supervision, 41*, 306–320. doi:10.1002/j.1556-6978.2002.tb01293.x

McLaughlin, J. E., & Boettcher, K. (2009). Counselor identity: Conformity or distinction? *The Journal of Humanistic Counseling, 48*, 132–143. doi:10.1002/j.2161-1939.2009.tb00074.x

National Board for Certified Counselors. (2016). *Understanding certification and licensure.* Retrieved from http://www.nbcc.org/Certification/licensure

Okech, J. E. A., & Geroski, A. (2015). Interdisciplinary training: Preparing counselors for collaborative practice. *The Professional Counselor, 5*, 458–472. doi:10.15241/jeo.5.4.458

Pistole, M. C., & Roberts, A. (2002). Mental health counseling: Toward resolving identity confusions. *Journal of Mental Health Counseling, 24*, 1–19.

Sangganjanavanich, V. F., & Balkin, R. S. (2013). Burnout and job satisfaction among counselor educators. *The Journal of Humanistic Counseling, 52*, 67–79. doi:10.1002/j.2161-1939.2013.00033.x

Smith, L. C., & Okech, J. E. A. (2016a). Ethical issues raised by CACREP accreditation of programs within institutions that disaffirm or disallow diverse sexual orientations. *Journal of Counseling & Development, 94,* 252–264. doi.10.1002/jcad.12084

Smith, L. C., & Okech, J. E. A. (2016b). Negotiating CACREP accreditation practices, religious diversity, and sexual orientation diversity: A rejoinder to Sells and Hagedorn. *Journal of Counseling & Development, 94,* 280–284. doi:10.1002/jcad.12084

Sweeney, T. J. (2001). Counseling: Historical origins and philosophical roots. In D. C. Locke, J. E. Myers, & E. H. Herr (Eds.), *The handbook of counseling* (pp. 3–26). Thousand Oaks, CA: Sage.

Thomas, K. R. (1991). Oedipal issues in counseling psychology. *Journal of Counseling & Development, 69,* 203–205. doi:10/1002/j.1556-6676.1991.tb01487.x

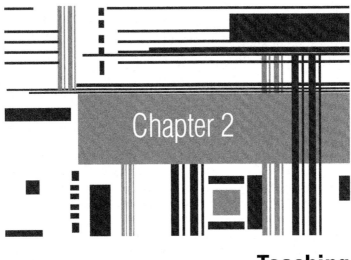

Teaching

David M. Kleist

I never teach my pupils, I only attempt to provide
the conditions in which they can learn.
—Albert Einstein

The Current State of Teaching in Counselor Education

Teaching, in the service of educating students, is central to the function of higher education (Fabrice, 2010). For Aristotle, "The educated differ from the uneducated as much as the living from the dead" (Laertius, 1942, p. 463). Teaching students, traditional and nontraditional, serves to enhance society. Teaching, although related to advising and mentoring, is different in its focus. Advising seeks "to inform, suggest, counsel, discipline, coach, mentor, or even teach" (Kuhn, 2008, p. 3). Compared with advising, mentoring involves a less formal relationship that develops between faculty and graduate students, serving to socialize students to the academic profession (McWilliams & Beam, 2013). Life, quite simply, thrives through the education of its members. Although this function of teaching has existed for hundreds of years, forms of teaching, and the manner in which learning is facilitated, have changed dramatically. Gone are the days of immense classrooms with blackboards and chalk and the days of skilled teachers as orators of knowledge lecturing to a sea of students eagerly writing notes with paper and pencil. Teaching or instruction in higher education today increasingly emphasizes developing the learner as a skilled contributor to the workforce (Hénard & Roseveare, 2012).

Quality teaching has firmly moved toward the measurement of student learning outcomes and associated key performance indicators that relate to the application of knowledge and skills to a work setting.

Today teachers may still be in large venues but now they stand amid a plethora of technologies that assist in the delivery of educational material and experiences. Smart boards, Elmo visualizers, and computer stations allow teachers to monitor students' own activities on computer stations. Instead of notes, faculty can simply show a picture of a QR code and ask students to download the day's notes via their QR reader app. A recent study by Carlisle, Hays, Pribesh, and Wood (2017) examined educational technology used in distance supervision. Teachers have a dizzying array of applications at their disposal not just for supervision but also for teaching: WebCT, Wimba, Zoom, Box, Kaltura, TK20, Taskstream, and so forth. Teachers can now teach from home, sitting in bed in pajamas participating in an online discussion group with hundreds of students from Pocatello, Idaho, to Chiang Mai, Thailand. Faculty can be stationed in front of a camera uploading a video to their classes' YouTube channel.

Students recording classes through their iPads or using digital pens to write notes has become the norm. Clicks, sometimes imperceptible on the surface of a digital screen with touch capabilities, are being made to create notes, highlight notes in the moment, or organize information via a conceptual mapping application. Technology also brings unique challenges for those engaged in teaching. Today's student can be listening and taking notes while also listening to a Podcast on Bluetooth earbuds or maybe to some old Bob Dylan classic (more likely the Chainsmokers, but I still hold out hope for today's student). Or the student may be connecting to friends and family across the globe by checking Facebook, playing with the latest Snapchat filter, and sending selfies to Instagram. Technology has changed the context for teachers and students and, more specifically, the relationship between them.

Our current place in history serves as the context for what is expected or demanded of the teacher–student relationship and its outcome (Hénard & Roseveare, 2012). We as teachers are steeped in a culture of accountability across professions, and higher education is not excluded from its impact. Funding for higher education has decreased significantly over the decades. Conversely, the financial burden on students and their families is rising dramatically. With these changes comes the need for teachers—be they tenure-track or contingent faculty—to be more accountable to their institutions, students, and employers. Tenure-track faculty may attend more to institutional needs, say, meeting accreditation standards (e.g., measuring student learning outcomes) and system values, whereas contingent faculty serve more exclusively the needs of students and their employers (i.e., the specific programs that hire them for contractual teaching assignments). Attention to the evaluation of teaching effectiveness has increased. Students and employers demand skilled teachers who can meaningfully teach skills and content directly linked to quality job opportunities and employees on graduation. Meaningful learning now consists of greater community-based or service-based learning opportunities in which students put their learning into action beyond the confines of their higher education experience. How the monies that come into higher education are dispersed and used in the service of quality teaching and preparation of the workforce is now evaluated more critically.

The diversification and internationalization of higher education are further contextual influences on teaching practices and experiences. Within the United States, decades of efforts to increase access to higher education for historically disenfranchised populations have diversified the college environment and classroom. Add to this the dramatic increase in the number of international students seeking higher education experiences in the United States, and today's teacher faces a teacher–student relationship far different from that of 50 years ago. This requires that pedagogical practices be firmly rooted in meeting students' diverse learning styles and cultural preferences.

Teaching in higher education has evolved dramatically over the decades, yet the broad expectations for university faculty have not. The three primary pillars of faculty duties remain teaching, research, and service. Beyond the changing context of teaching in higher education, the need to produce knowledge via research is still of primary, if not greater, import to institutions of higher education. Research for the sake of knowledge generation continues, but now research is more connected to securing grant funding to support research endeavors. Thus, with the decrease in public funding of higher education, faculty have the additional responsibility not only to generate revenue for their own research activities but also to support overall institutional operations. In some institutions, this aspect of faculty life is held in higher regard or considered a greater burden. This shift in the significance of research productivity has affected the service responsibilities of faculty. Faculty have always served the university via committee assignments and served the surrounding communities through their particular area of skill and expertise. Service now also means increasing attention to involvement with leadership positions in regional and national organizations linked to one's discipline. However, the purpose of such links is not solely to promote the learned society's goals but to network with like-minded faculty and make links for further research and grant procurement goals.

Within the current cultural climate, the populace may view education with some suspicion and see faculty actions as political acts that may not always be parallel to the everyday experience of citizens. These slowly developing changes in society further complicate the historical and newly culturally sensitized goals of teaching in higher education. Amid these changes within the higher education context sits the profession of counseling and field of counselor education and supervision. The field of counselor education is not immune to such influences. In many ways, the flow of curricular activities, from day-to-day class planning to measuring student learning outcomes to meeting accreditation standards, rides along with these larger societal processes.

Interest in the role of the teacher or educator within the counseling profession goes back at least to the origins of the Association for Counselor

Education and Supervision (ACES) journal *Counselor Education and Supervision (CES)* in 1961. Calls for better understanding of counselor educators' effectiveness (Bixler, 1963; Litwack, 1964), the development of a conceptual framework (i.e., philosophy and theory) to guide educators' actions (Kiesow, 1963; Landsman, 1963), and descriptions of teaching techniques used with counselors-in-training (Cheney, 1963) have been voiced for nearly as long. Yet in 2016, the editor of *CES* stated that "the one topic remarkably absent in the literature published in *CES*, a journal about counselor education, is pedagogy" (Korcuska, 2016, p. 156). A recent study by Barrio Minton, Wachter Morris, and Yaites (2014) examined 10 years of articles on pedagogy in *CES* from 2004 to 2014. They found that approximately 75% of these articles on pedagogy focused on technique, not philosophy and theories of instruction. Clearly, research on the context within which counselor educators teach and the related impact on teaching is lacking. Here, however, I discuss the experience of teaching within counseling programs and the various variables that affect its delivery.

Master's-Level Program Context

The role of teaching in counselor training programs is influenced by whether a program has a master's program or both master's and doctoral programs. The counseling profession views the master's degree as the terminal clinical degree (Council for Accreditation of Counseling and Related Educational Programs [CACREP], 2015a). Even if a program is not accredited, which I speak to below, this stance has influenced the development of counselor licensure laws across the states. Master's-level training for counselors leads first and foremost to a clinical degree. Despite recent conceptualizations of the role of master's-level counselors as encompassing a scholarly component (Balkin & Kleist, 2016), direct counseling is still the foundational role of counselors. This emphasis has an impact on the scope and function of a counselor educator's teaching role. One's role as an educator within a master's-only program is focused on the clinical development of master's-level practitioners. Although educators may connect to the professional society for counselor educators and supervisors (i.e., ACES, a division of the American Counseling Association), this work context will naturally direct attention toward the day-to-day clinical practice of counselors, so much so that faculty may very well have thriving part-time clinical practices alongside their role as teachers (Ray, Jayne, & Miller, 2014). Such a dynamic creates a symbiotic relationship for counselor educators, as their work informs their clinical practice and their clinical practice informs their role as teachers. Over the years, I have repeatedly heard students say that they value a counselor educator who can weave clinical examples into the teaching of a particular subject. This symbiotic relationship may be seen as mutually beneficial to the educator and student. Real-world examples from teachers' own clinical practices bring curriculum materials to life for students. Many instructional theories within the constructivist camp support such practices (McAuliffe & Eriksen, 2011; Snowman & McCown, 2015). And not only will educators hold students' attention with rich, real-world clinical examples (while maintaining confidentiality, of course), but they will experience heightened attention to their own clinical practices, furthering the axiom "Practice what you preach." One's role as an educator within a master's-only counselor education program may well enhance one's roles as teacher and counselor, which in turn will affect one's relationship with one's students.

For counselor educators teaching in master's-only programs, relationships with students will be experienced as having greater valence due to the shared identity as counselor. This shared identity can facilitate mentorship opportunities with students. Attending clinically focused conferences with students (e.g., conferences at national, regional, or state levels sponsored by the American Mental Health Counselors Association, the American School Counselor Association, or the International Association of Marriage and Family Counselors) provides great opportunities to assist students in becoming the future leaders of these divisions and the counseling profession as a whole. Mentorship into the practitioner-scholar role can also take place. Counseling-oriented presentations can include counselors-in-training as coinvestigators and copresenters. Now mentorship includes role-modeling a counselor's responsibility to contribute to the body of knowledge and skills informing the profession. Such contributions need not be formal journal publications (although they could be), as professional presentations are another significant pathway for disseminating knowledge into the clinical marketplace. The counselor educator working within a master's-only program has a great opportunity to significantly affect the direction not only of clinical practice but also of the profession. However, a counselor educator in a master's-only program will still be obligated to attend to his or her own development as a counselor educator.

Attending to a counselor educator's own development will contribute to various degrees of involvement with organizations related to counselor education and supervision (e.g., ACES, National Council on Rehabilitation Education). Professional development, specifically the enhancement of one's role as teacher, is furthered by more than simply engaging in the practice of counseling as mentioned previously. The teacher, as counselor educator, has a responsibility similar to that of a counselor to enhance his or her skills and knowledge related to the education of master's-level counselors (American Counseling Association, 2014). This requires involvement with fellow counselor educators at conferences and with potential research activities that inform the field of counselor education and supervision. Such varied networking activities and relationships enhance the master's-level teacher's development as an educator and contributor to the knowledge base of counselor education and supervision.

Through this type of development, an awareness of one's place in the counseling profession's circle of life may be piqued. Teachers in master's-only programs who are connected to both the development of master's-level counselors and their own development as counselor educators also see their role as a bridge, both training their students to be master's-level clinicians and mentoring their students into doctoral study and the field of counselor education and supervision. Many counselors-in-training have the goal of becoming professional counselors. Although some may have had their sights on doctoral study from the outset of their graduate programs, many more will be enticed into doctoral study by their faculty as role models and by direct faculty encouragement to become a counselor educator. The impact of master's program faculty as educators on the profession of counseling and the field of counselor education and supervision is immense. They not only hone the clinical skills of the next generation of professional counselors but also plant the seeds for the advancement of the field of counselor education. They do this by role-modeling the enriching impact of being a counselor educator as well as identifying those master's students with interests and capacity for advancing their careers through doctoral study in counselor education and supervision.

Doctoral-Level Program Context

The complexity of work roles only increases when one is working within a counseling program that educates both master's-level counselors and doctoral-level counselor educators and supervisors. Imagine all of the roles assumed when working with master's-level counseling students and now factor in the primary responsibility of doctoral-level programs: developing counselor educators and supervisors. The task of educating counselor educators and supervisors builds off the primary focus of master's-level counselor training: clinical competence. As the doctoral-level CACREP Standards articulate, advanced clinical development is still an emphasis at the doctoral level (CACREP, 2015a). Research on counselor development (Skovholt & Ronnestad, 1995) clearly supports this continued attention to furthering the clinical skills of the post-master's graduate, as clinical development continues for years, even decades, beyond the master's degree. Here certain roles that counselor educators enact with master's students continue, as the need for clinical supervision and training is still present and required. What is different is the amount of time given to advanced clinical skill development in a doctoral-level counselor education program. Although CACREP specifies minimum requirements, doctoral students are free to emphasize advanced clinical counseling skills as much as they wish, even selecting counseling practice as one of their primary domains of focus during doctoral study (CACREP, 2015a). A difference in the relationship between teacher and doctoral student in this context is that, most likely, the doctoral student is already a licensed professional counselor. The role of a supervisor with a doctoral student who is a licensed professional counselor weaves in the role of a peer or colleague serving as supervisor. There may be less focus on gatekeeping, the responsibility of supervisors to intervene with counselor trainees who engage in behavior that could threaten the welfare of those receiving counseling services, and more attention to honing advanced clinical skills. Although degrees of similarity seem present for the teacher in a doctoral program when addressing clinical skill development, more distinctive contextual differences are present, directly impacted by CACREP Standards.

Another set of standards for doctoral-level counselor education programs relate to supervision (CACREP, 2015a). The doctoral-level educator has the task of developing skilled clinical supervisors prepared to supervise either in counselor training programs or out in the community or in private practice. The role and experience of teaching supervision can be viewed as parallel to the experience of teaching master's-level counselors given the obvious educational context. However, the context is different, as educators are now working with their licensed professional counseling peers while in an educational context advancing their development as supervisors. Role complexity is richer, and the evaluative component is evident along with attention to gatekeeping duties for the developing supervisor. Amid these seemingly similar dynamics that faculty may experience while teaching at the master's level, however, are subtle differences.

As teachers responsible for the development of clinical supervisors, faculty educate, mentor, and evaluate their supervisory skill development. They also now supervise the supervisor-in-training's evaluative role with master's students. Most counselor education programs use doctoral students, on some level, as supervisors with counseling master's students. Whether in basic skills courses, individual/triadic supervision during practicum or internship, or group supervision, doctoral students have opportunities to practice and develop their supervision competence within their supervisory relationship with their doctoral-level teacher as supervisor of their supervision. However, the subtle change is that doctoral-level teachers now include, to some degree, doctoral-students-as-supervisor as evaluators of master's-level counselors-in-training. Doctoral students become part of the process of evaluating master's students, providing their assessment of counselor development alongside the faculty member's evaluations. The boundaries between teacher and student are blurred as doctoral students play the dual roles of student and counselor-educator-in-training. To varying degrees, three roles—those of teacher, student, and colleague—are being merged, as the primary goal of doctoral training is to secure employment as a counselor educator and supervisor. These dual or ultimately multiple roles lead to unique ethical dilemmas, which I discuss further below. For now, I shift my attention to the other domains that are the responsibility of a teacher in a doctoral program.

CACREP (2015a) identifies research as a domain necessary to address when educating a doctoral-level counselor educator and supervisor. With this, and the two domains that follow, greater movement away from the everyday notion of teacher emerges toward one that could be called *teacher-colleague* or *teacher as mentor*. The role of teacher, in its classic form, still exists as doctoral students are taught quantitative and qualitative research. But the relationship with students is more complex when it comes to the research domain. Most see the doctoral degree, more than the master's degree, as serving the research needs of the profession (Balkin & Kleist, 2016). ACES set forth a task group to develop research mentorship guidelines, which did emphasize work with doctoral students (Borders et al., 2012). Likewise, the singular, most recognized product of the doctoral degree is the dissertation. The teaching that occurs at the doctoral level regarding research should transition seamlessly into research mentorship, which is embodied by successful completion of the dissertation. Despite efforts to advance the researcher role of master's-level counselors (Michalak, 2013), teaching research at the doctoral level is more extensive and provides a more fluid relationship between teacher and student as eventual coresearchers and colleagues in counselor education.

Another domain of educational standards for doctoral programs in counselor education and supervision is leadership and advocacy (CACREP, 2015a). The crux of this domain is to prepare doctoral students to assume leadership positions within the organizational structure of the counseling profession and to advocate for both clients and the counseling profession itself. Despite the opportunity for teaching roles across doctoral- and master's-level programs to create a culture of leadership, standards and research seem to reify the distinction that doctoral-level counselor educators hold most of the responsibility for leadership within the counseling profession. Reference to *leadership* occurs only three times in the master's-level CACREP Standards (CACREP, 2015a), and then only in school counseling and in college counseling and student affairs specialties. In the doctoral-level CACREP Standards, the word *leadership* appears 14 times. Recent research examining leadership in the counseling profession has tended to emphasize the perspectives of counselor educators rather than counselors (Lockard, 2009; Lyons, 2012; West, Bubenzer, Osborn, Paez, & Desmond, 2006) and place the primary weight of leadership and advocacy at the doctoral level. This emphasis further facilitates the teacher-as-colleague relationship at the doctoral level while maintaining a firmer boundary around the teacher–student relationship at the master's level. Advocacy, in similar fashion, is mentioned only twice in the master's-level CACREP Standards (i.e., once in the "Professional Counseling Orientation and Ethical Practice" and once in the "Social and Cultural Diversity" core areas), five times in the doctoral-level CACREP Standards, and once in Section 1 under "Faculty and Staff" where it describes characteristics and actions expected of core faculty (CACREP, 2015a). Clearly the present conceptualization of training standards contributes significantly to distinctions between the experience of teaching at the master's versus doctoral levels.

The last CACREP domain of educational experiences at the doctoral level is that of teaching. The impact of this domain on the role of the teacher in a counselor education program is self-evident. No aspect of this domain is present in master's-level program accreditation standards. This domain is the essence of the historical role of the counselor educator. Zimpfer (1996) studied faculty as they moved through their fifth year as faculty members in counselor training programs, and the role of educator—of teacher—was the most significant and ongoing duty of a faculty member. ACES recently published a brief, the *ACES Teaching Initiative Taskforce: Best Practices in Teaching in Counselor Education Report 2016* (ACES, 2016), that gave an overview of current trends, research, and issues related to the role of teacher within the field of counselor education and supervision. An educator who has doctoral students in the process of developing teaching skills can frequently be involved in coteaching and mentoring experiences (Baltrinic, Jencius, & McGlothlin, 2016). These experiences facilitate a much more intimate and collegial form of contact between teacher and student than is experienced between a teacher and student in a master's program. In this collegial relationship, faculty themselves learn and grow by observing, supervising, and coteaching with doctoral students. The faculty member, as teacher, in many ways becomes student to the exceptional doctoral student as educator. Simply stated, a faculty member teaching doctoral students is developing relationships that they may very well continue as colleagues upon students' formal graduation and entrance into the professoriate. This is not to say that collegial relationships are not nurtured in master's programs. Master's program faculty commonly serve as supervisors across practicum and internship. Upon graduation, both faculty and graduates are professional counselors who may continue relating as colleagues.

The richness and variety of the multiple roles that a faculty person teaching in a doctoral program has with students (e.g., mentor and colleague in the CACREP domains of research, supervision, teaching, and leadership and advocacy) contribute to multiple relationships with their own unique set of ethical dynamics and benefits (Lloyd, 1992). Lloyd (1992) articulated the need to engage with the ethical dynamics in ways that allow the continuation of these multiple relationships. For Lloyd, there is far too much to gain in these mentoring, collegial relationships between counselor educators and doctoral students in particular to limit them without careful consideration. As said earlier, the crux of doctoral study in counselor education and supervision is to develop the next generation of professional colleagues for the sake of advancing the counseling profession.

The context within which a counselor educator works, whether a master's-only program or a program that offers both master's and doctoral degrees, has a significant impact on the role and experience of teaching. The complexities are clearly evident for faculty working with both master's and doctoral students. A significant challenge is how to balance or navigate one's duties with doctoral students and master's students. However, working in a master's-only program has its own sets of complexities, not necessarily less than but different from working with master's and doctoral students. As one enters a doctoral program in counselor education and supervision or a new job as a counselor educator, these important distinctions require reflection when structuring one's career goals and determining the best fit for work context.

The Influence of Diversity and Social Justice on the Context of Teaching

The diversification of students seeking degrees at the master's and doctoral level, along with that of the faculty who teach them, continues to expand (CACREP, 2012, 2013, 2014, 2015b). Although the call for more social justice–oriented counselor training has been present for more than

40 years (M. D. Lewis & Lewis, 1971), not until 2010 did the ACES journal *CES* develop a special issue titled *Social Justice: A National Imperative for Counselor Education and Supervision.* In this special issue, numerous authors provided examples (e.g., Brubaker, Puig, Reese, & Young, 2010; Dixon, Tucker, & Clark, 2010) and research (Odegard & Vereen, 2010) on how to integrate social justice into the counseling curriculum. This is not to say that publications on infusing social justice into counselor education were not previously available (e.g., Ratts & Wood, 2011; Stadler, Suh, Cobia, Middleton, & Carney, 2006), simply that so great a statement of need and import was made with the special issue. The turn squarely toward the increased diversity of faculty and students, along with social justice competence and skills, has numerous implications for teaching in counselor education, a sample of which are highlighted in the following paragraphs.

CACREP Standards, along with faculty efforts to promote access to the counseling profession for students who better represent the picture of the United States, have led educators as teachers to attend to diverse student characteristics and their impact on pedagogy/instructional theory. Numerous instructional theories have been developed and researched (see Snowman & McCown, 2015), but they are limited in their attention to application with students from diverse backgrounds. Research on student characteristics, be it ethnic diversity or preferred learning styles, and their impact on teaching and learning has focused predominantly on the K–12 learner (Snowman & McCown, 2015). Such a gap in the knowledge base for educating adult learners overall and diverse adult learners in particular within counselor training programs leaves teachers at both the master's and doctoral levels to continuously and consciously reflect on the relevance of their selected instructional theory. The context of teaching at such a moment in time requires active engagement in assessing the effectiveness of one's teaching while trusting the relational skills of counseling and their transferability to the educational environment. Counselor educators on a day-to-day basis are truly sitting with great opportunities for research that could further the field of counselor education's understanding of research-informed practices for promoting learning with diverse learners.

Another implication of increasing attention to the diversity of students and greater infusion of social justice principles across the curriculum relates to the curriculum materials taught to students. As mentioned previously, there are less than a handful of references to the skills of advocacy and leadership in the master's-level CACREP Standards. The majority of master's-level counselor training standards target remedial counseling skills and interventions. On a related note, the symbiotic impact on doctoral-level training will mean greater attention to learning how to teach, supervise, and research remedially oriented counseling skills, theories, and their clinical applications. This implication has at a minimum a twofold consequence for counselor educators attending to their roles as teachers.

First, the philosophy of the counseling profession is rooted in a preventive perspective and values with connections to social justice and advocacy (Kleist & White, 1997). To better align master's- and doctoral-level teaching with the historical values of counseling, counselor educators will have to exceed current CACREP Standards in their curricula and programs as a whole. This can readily be seen as a daunting task, as merely meeting CACREP Standards is a worthy accomplishment. However, for educators and programs that sincerely seek to infuse attention to diversity and social justice across all aspects of their programs, the skills of preventive counseling (Conyne, 2010) and multicultural and social justice counseling (Ratts, Singh, Nassar-McMillan, Butler, & McCullough, 2015) must be a focus of curricular attention. The most powerful preventive intervention is legislative action (Gullotta, 1994). Teachers aspiring to more fully embody the core philosophy and values of the counseling profession need institutional interventions and the required skills to do so. As stated by Ratts et al. (2015) in the Association for Multicultural Counseling and Development's Multicultural and Social Justice Counseling Competencies, traditional, remedially oriented individual counseling must be balanced with systems-level intervention with social institutions that impede mental health and wellness. Similarly, counselors and counselor educators must learn and teach the skills of community intervention. The skills necessary for these systemic interventions exceed the present core and specialty skill standards of CACREP, which are mostly related to confidential, office-based, clinical practice. The aforementioned Multicultural and Social Justice Counseling Competencies can serve as foundational knowledge and skills to fill this gap in the current CACREP Standards.

The second consequence requires meta-advocacy. Counselor educators who teach in CACREP-accredited programs must advocate for richer inclusion of the skills of preventive and social justice–focused counseling, particularly for community and institutional-level interventions. Advocacy must include active engagement with the CACREP revisions process at the individual faculty, department, and professional association levels. CACREP, as the accrediting body for the counseling profession, is composed of counselor educators, supervisors, and practicing counselors. All have a voice and avenue for input on the standard revision process. Ultimately, teachers in accredited programs have an ethical responsibility to participate in these revision processes for current and future clients and their communities. Similarly, counselors and counselor educators can participate in revising the *ACA Code of Ethics* (American Counseling Association, 2014), which occurs approximately every 8 years. My dissertation research (Kleist & White, 1997) found that counselor educators' most agreed-upon reason for not infusing the practice and skills of prevention in counselor training was the lack of demand for such services. The lack of inclusion of prevention and related social justice practices and skills is clearly our responsibility as teachers and counselor educators. Advocacy in this regard will ultimately increase the breadth of services offered to communities.

Case Vignette:
From Theory to Practice and Advocacy

I developed and have taught for the past 17 years a 15-week, two-credit class on parent education primarily for the marital, couples, and family counseling specialty. The objectives of the class include learning the philosophy and practices of prevention in counseling directed at families and community agency service evaluation using the model originally developed by M. D. Lewis and Lewis (1977) and updated to more clearly integrate principles of social justice (J. A. Lewis, Lewis, Daniels, & D'Andrea, 2010). I organize my role as teacher from a social constructionist orientation toward instructional theory, primarily informed by Gowin (1981). The crux of social constructionist theory is that knowledge is emergent in conversation between people. Gowin spoke of a tripartite relationship that is atheoretical and that organizes the process of educating. The three parts are teacher–student/student–teacher, teacher–material, and student–material. From a social constructionist stance, the first relationship is collaborative and values bidirectional input and ideas, with the formal roles of learner and student blurred. The second relationship, that of teacher with curriculum material, is viewed as active, as the teacher is responsible for deconstructing the body of knowledge to be taught; analyzing the relationships between concepts, principles, theories, and so on; and then reorganizing these concepts into meaningful curriculum materials and experiences for students to engage with. Ideally students encounter felt significance between the material and themselves as counselors-in-training. The third relationship is equally as active. Students are held responsible for deconstructing their own knowledge about the topic of (in this case) parenting, parent education, and agency service evaluation for the purposes of integrating the new curriculum material into their previous knowledge on this topic in a process of knowledge construction.

A process very similar to that articulated by Baltrinic et al. (2016) unfurls in which doctoral students engage in a coteaching experience within a mentoring relationship with me as teacher. This relationship is also guided by my social constructionist stance. Similarly, the doctoral students deconstruct for me their evolving understanding of their instructional theory (e.g., concepts, principles, theories, etc.) and how I may see these ideas in action while they are teaching (i.e., the active process of knowledge reconstruction and opportunity for new learning). I require doctoral students to share their evolving instructional theory for the purpose of being able to engage in live supervision and postteaching session feedback. Postteaching sessions are scheduled immediately after a teaching session or, if time does not allow, over the next week.

Weeks 1–3 involve in-class discussion of assigned readings related to the philosophy and practice of prevention, parent education programs, research on characteristics of effective parent education programming, and the J. A. Lewis et al. (2010) model for evaluating the range of services provided by a community-based counseling agency. In addition, we discuss the range of parent education programs offered in the community and contact information to help students find a group to observe over the next 6 weeks. Social justice takes on greater focus with discussion of the array of parent education programs offered or not offered and students' views of the potential reasons why classes are offered or not. Typically students believe that more could be offered to the community at large in terms of parent/family education. It is here that leadership is also discussed as a component of students' duties as members of the mental health community as change agents.

Weeks 4–10 involve students gaining access to and engaging with community-based parent education programs. Students' purpose while attending these groups is to glean what level of preventive intervention a program provides (primary, secondary, remedial); assess at a basic level group leadership skills and styles; and provide, through reflective journals, an overall assessment of the parent education program's process week to week.

Weeks 11–14 involve master's student presentations. Presentations provide a summary of students' observed parent education program, assessment in terms of an effective (or ineffective) prevention program, and a proposal of their own parent education program they would like to implement during internship or after graduation. Included in the program assessment is an environmental assessment of barriers to further program development in the setting and a proposed plan for dissolving such barriers.

Week 15 provides an opportunity for overall class discussion, processing, and thoughts on integrating prevention programming into students' work as marital, couples, and family counselors.

Doctoral student coteacher(s) are integrated into all aspects the class and provide their own level of summary, processing, and thoughts about developing and teaching prevention during their internship, or when formally hired as counselor educators. This vignette has simplified not only Gowin's (1981) social constructionist theory toward instruction but also the nuance and subtleties of the relationships that develop between faculty and student over the course of the semester and the depth of the curriculum material used to influence student learning.

Conclusion

In this chapter, I provided an overview of being a teacher in a counseling program, be it a master's-level program focused on developing professional counselors or a doctoral-level program training the next generation of counselor educators and supervisors. The context of teaching in higher education as a whole has been greatly affected by technology and the potential of hybrid classes or entire programs offered online. The impact is likewise felt in counselor education, but given the contextual nature of a professional program in counseling, these technology issues take on a unique application. Another significant impact on the context of teaching in counselor education—one that I feel is most significant—is CACREP accreditation. I value accreditation and see it as essential for the profession to remain legitimate and extend its professionalism. And across and within the CACREP Standards is a larger discourse toward mental health service delivery and toward the foci of training at the master's and doctoral levels.

The CACREP Standards directly effect the "what" educators teach and in some ways the "how." Moving forward, continued attention toward revising standards to best meet the mental health needs of communities will remain a central ethical duty of counselor educators.

Increasingly present are issues of multiculturalism, social justice and advocacy, and their impact on counselor and counselor educator training. The world in which counseling is provided is increasingly diverse and will continue to become more so. In parallel fashion, the counseling profession will need to continue developing the best preparation standards for practicing counselors and the counselor educators who teach and supervise them. Toward this end, the need exists for research on the education of master's-level counselors and doctoral-level counselor educators and supervisors. This issue is not new and is reiterated within the ACES Teaching Initiative Taskforce's best practices brief (ACES, 2016). ACES has represented counselor educators and supervisors for more than 50 years. Yet it seems that we as counselor educators have focused more on the how-to articles and related research than on larger philosophical and theoretical issues and their related research questions. Herein lies the challenge, as there is also a pull toward evidence-based counseling practice to further legitimize the profession of counseling. As counselor educators, we are stretched thin with the profession's research demands. However, to ensure that we are developing the best trained and most qualified product (i.e., counselor and counselor educator graduates), we must protect research space to engage in research that is directly related to our roles as teachers.

Additional Online Resources

ACES Teaching Initiative Taskforce: Best Practices in Teaching in Counselor Education Report 2016
    https://www.acesonline.net/sites/default/files/ACES%20
    Teaching%20Initiative%20Taskforce%20Final%20Report%20Oct
    %2023%202016%20.pdf

References

American Counseling Association. (2014). *ACA code of ethics*. Alexandria, VA: Author.

Association for Counselor Education and Supervision. (2016). *ACES teaching initiative taskforce: Best practices in teaching in counselor education report 2016*. Retrieved from https://www.acesonline.net/sites/default/files/ACES%20Teaching%20Initiative%20Taskforce%20Final%20Report%20Oct%2023%202016%20.pdf

Balkin, R., & Kleist, D. M. (2016). *Counseling research: A practitioner-scholar approach*. Alexandria, VA: American Counseling Association.

Baltrinic, E. R., Jencius, M., & McGlothlin, J. (2016). Co-teaching in counselor education: Preparing doctoral students for future teaching. *Counselor Education and Supervision, 55*, 31–45. doi:10.1002/ceas.12031

Barrio Minton, C. A., Wachter Morris, C. A., & Yaites, L. D. (2014). Pedagogy in counselor education: A 10-year content analysis of journals. *Counselor Education and Supervision, 53,* 162–177. doi:10.1002/j.1556-6978.2014.00055.x

Bixler, R. H. (1963). The changing world of the counselor: I. New approaches needed. *Counselor Education and Supervision, 2,* 100–105. doi:10.1002/j.1556-6978.1963.tb02099.x

Borders, L. D., Wester, K. L., Granello, D. H., Chang, C. Y., Hays, D. G., Pepperell, J., & Spurgeon, S. L. (2012). Association for Counselor Education and Supervision guidelines for research mentorship: Development and implementation. *Counselor Education and Supervision, 51,* 162–175. doi:10.1002/j.1556-6978.2012.00012.x

Brubaker, M. D., Puig, A., Reese, R. F., & Young, J. (2010). Integrating social justice into counseling theories pedagogy: A case example. *Counselor Education and Supervision, 50,* 88–102. doi:10.1002/j.1556-6978.2010.tb00111.x

Carlisle, R. M., Hays, D. G., Pribesh, S. L., & Wood, C. T. (2017). Educational technology and distance supervision in counselor education. *Counselor Education and Supervision, 56,* 33–49. doi:10.1002/ceas.12058

Cheney, T. M. (1963). Using non-directive techniques in selecting enrollees for counseling institutes. *Counselor Education and Supervision, 2,* 148–151. doi:10.1002/j.1556-6978.1963.tb02107.x

Conyne, R. (2010). *Prevention program development and evaluation: An incidence reduction, culturally relevant approach.* Thousand Oaks, CA: Sage.

Council for Accreditation of Counseling and Related Educational Programs. (2012). *CACREP vital statistics report.* Retrieved from www.cacrep.org/about-cacrep/publications/cacrep-annual-reports/

Council for Accreditation of Counseling and Related Educational Programs. (2013). *CACREP vital statistics report.* Retrieved from www.cacrep.org/about-cacrep/publications/cacrep-annual-reports/

Council for Accreditation of Counseling and Related Educational Programs. (2014). *CACREP vital statistics report.* Retrieved from www.cacrep.org/about-cacrep/publications/cacrep-annual-reports/

Council for Accreditation of Counseling and Related Educational Programs. (2015a). *CACREP 2016 standards.* Alexandria, VA: Author.

Council for Accreditation of Counseling and Related Educational Programs. (2015b). *CACREP vital statistics report.* Retrieved from www.cacrep.org/about-cacrep/publications/cacrep-annual-reports/

Dixon, A. L., Tucker, C., & Clark, M. A. (2010). Integrating social justice advocacy with national standards of practice: Implications for school counselor education. *Counselor Education and Supervision, 50,* 103–115. doi:10.1002/j.1556-6978.2010.tb00112.x

Fabrice, H. (2010). *Learning our lesson review of quality teaching in higher education: Review of quality teaching in higher education.* Paris, France: Organisation for Economic Co-operation and Development.

Gowin, D. B. (1981). *Educating.* Ithaca, NY: Cornell University Press.

Gullotta, T. P. (1994). The what, who, why, where, when, and how of primary prevention. *Journal of Primary Prevention, 15,* 5–14.

Hénard, F., & Roseveare, D. (2012). *Fostering quality teaching in higher education: Policies and practices.* Paris, France: Organisation for Economic Co-operation and Development.

Kiesow, M. A. (1963). A professional approach to the information function in counselor education. *Counselor Education and Supervision, 2,* 131–136. doi:10.1002/j.1556-6978.1963.tb02104.x

Kleist, D. M., & White, L. J. (1997). The values of counseling: A disparity between a philosophy of prevention in counseling and counselor practice and training. *Counseling and Values, 41,* 128–140. doi:10.1002/j.2161-007X.1997.tb00395.x

Korcuska, J. S. (2016). In the spirit of what might be lost: Troubling the boundaries of good fit. *Counselor Education and Supervision, 55,* 154–158. doi:10.1002/ceas.12042

Kuhn, T. L. (2008). Historical foundations of academic advising. In V. N. Gordon, W. R. Habley, & T. J. Grites (Eds.), *Academic advising: A comprehensive campus process* (pp. 3–16). San Francisco, CA: Jossey-Bass.

Laertius, D. (1942). *Lives of eminent philosophers* (Vol. 1, Book 5, Section 19, R. D. Hicks, Trans.). Cambridge, MA: Harvard University Press.

Landsman, T. (1963). Humanistic training for a mechanistic society. *Counselor Education and Supervision, 2,* 112–120. doi:10.1002/j.1556-6978.1963.tb02101.x

Lewis, J. A., Lewis, M. D., Daniels, J. A., & D'Andrea, M. J. (2010). *Community counseling: A multicultural-social justice perspective.* Boston, MA: Cengage Learning.

Lewis, M. D., & Lewis, J. A. (1971). Counselor education: Training for a new alternative. *Journal of Counseling & Development, 49,* 754–758.

Lewis, M. D., & Lewis, J. A. (1977). *Community counseling: A human services approach.* New York, NY: Wiley.

Litwack, L. (1964). Counselor educator—Redundancy or dichotomy? *Counselor Education and Supervision, 4,* 42–45. doi:10.1002/j.1556-6978.1964.tb02154.x

Lloyd, A. P. (1992). Dual relationships in counselor education. In B. Herlihy & G. Corey (Eds.), *Dual relationships in counseling* (pp. 59–64). Alexandria, VA: American Association for Counseling and Development.

Lockard, F. W. (2009). *Perceived leadership preparation in counselor education doctoral students who are members of the American Counseling Association in CACREP-accredited programs: A survey examining the next generation of leaders in the profession* (Doctoral dissertation). Retrieved from http://utdr.utoledo.edu/theses-dissertations/

Lyons, M. (2012). *Leadership in the counseling profession: A qualitative study of CACREP counselor education programs* (Doctoral dissertation). Retrieved from http://ohiolink.edu/etd

McAuliffe, G., & Eriksen, K. (2011). *Handbook of counselor preparation: Constructivist, developmental, and experiential approaches.* Thousand Oaks, CA: Sage. doi:10.4135/9781452230498

McWilliams, A. E., & Beam, L. R. (2013). Advising, counseling, coaching, mentoring: Models of developmental relationships in higher education. *The Mentor.* Retrieved from https://dus.psu.edu/mentor/2013/06/advising-counseling-coaching-mentoring/

Michalak, M. B. (2013). *The scholarly process: A grounded theory exploring how counselor educators promote scholarship of counselors-in-training* (Unpublished doctoral dissertation). Idaho State University, Pocatello.

Odegard, M. A., & Vereen, L. G. (2010). A grounded theory of counselor educators integrating social justice into their pedagogy. *Counselor Education and Supervision, 50,* 130–149. doi:10.1002/j.1556-6978.2010.tb00114.x

Ratts, M. J., Singh, A. A., Nassar-McMillan, S., Butler, S. K., & McCullough, J. R. (2015). *Multicultural and social justice counseling competencies.* Retrieved from https://www.counseling.org/docs/default-source/competencies/multicultural-and-social-justice-counseling-competencies.pdf?sfvrsn=20

Ratts, M. J., & Wood, C. (2011). The fierce urgency of now: Diffusion of innovation as a mechanism to integrate social justice in counselor education. *Counselor Education and Supervision, 50,* 207–223. doi:10.1002/j.1556-6978.2011.tb00120.x

Ray, D., Jayne, K., & Miller, R. (2014). Master counselors as teachers: Clinical practices of counselor educators. *Journal of Mental Health Counseling, 36,* 78–94. doi:10.17744/mehc.36.1.r71044x11x44tn5p

Skovholt, T. M., & Ronnestad, M. H. (1995). *The evolving professional self: Stages and themes in therapist and counselor development.* Oxford, UK: Wiley.

Snowman, J., & McCown, R. R. (2015). *Psychology applied to teaching.* Melbourne, Australia: Cengage.

Stadler, H. A., Suh, S., Cobia, D. C., Middleton, R. A., & Carney, J. S. (2006). Reimagining counselor education with diversity as a core value. *Counselor Education and Supervision, 45,* 193–206. doi:10.1002/j.1556-6978.2006.tb00142.x

West, J. D., Bubenzer, D., Osborn, C., Paez, S., & Desmond, K. (2006). Leadership and the profession of counseling: Beliefs and practices. *Counselor Education and Supervision, 46,* 2–16. doi:10.1002/j.1556-6978.2006.tb00008.x

Zimpfer, D. G. (1996). Five-year follow-up of doctoral graduates in counseling. *Counselor Education and Supervision, 35,* 218–229. doi:10.1002/j.1556-6978.1996.tb00225.x

Chapter 3

Supervision in the Counselor Education Context

Melissa Luke

Supervision is recognized as ubiquitous and essential in counselors' education and development (Bernard & Goodyear, 2014), often bridging the divide between training and practice. As the signature pedagogy of the field (Shulman, 2005), the Council for Accreditation of Counseling and Related Educational Programs (CACREP; 2015) requires participation in counselor supervision as part of education and training procedures in all counselor education programs. Furthermore, CACREP demarks the importance of education in supervision, as it is one of five core areas of foundational knowledge in doctoral preparation. In addition, state licensure boards and professional credentialing bodies are in general agreement on the dispositions, knowledge, and skills necessary to be a competently trained supervisor (Bernard & Goodyear, 2014). Nonetheless, even best practices in supervision do not explicitly stipulate training in how the systemic context of supervision can relate to its practice (Association for Counselor Education and Supervision Taskforce on Best Practices in Clinical Supervision, 2011; Borders et al., 2014). Therefore, it is not surprising that the historic literature in counselor education and its sister fields has largely approached supervision as if it were "the same in whatever context it occurs" (Luke, Ellis, & Bernard, 2011, p. 338). On a related note, few scholars have explored how the "context and configuration" (p. 328) of supervision can contribute to differences in how supervision takes place. It is this gap that the current chapter seeks to begin to fill by expanding the conceptualization of supervision across counselor education contexts and by better understanding how the attributes, domains, and contexts of counselor education in the 21st century affect the supervision taking place.

Thus, this chapter begins with a review of the literature on the practice of supervision, with a focus on the diverse academic settings across counselor education. The first section of the chapter explores diverse factors that contribute to similarities and differences in the practice of supervision across these settings. This is followed by a section that highlights both the challenging and facilitating conditions related to this supervision. The next section discusses the systemic factors associated with how supervision in counselor education contexts affects and is affected by accreditation, professional identity, and social justice issues. The chapter concludes by identifying the relationship between the evolution of supervision in counselor education in the 21st century and the recommended preparation and professional development for effective supervision practice. Professional observations are synthesized with conceptual and empirical literature throughout the chapter to help supervisors conceptualize the varied ways in which supervision can be enacted within the higher education context. The chapter highlights how distinctive aspects of and structures within counselor education affect experiences and the practice of supervision in an effort to support doctoral students and new counselor education professionals in their decision making and practice of supervision.

Supervision

Although there is a growing and abundant literature related to the theory and practice of supervision (Bernard & Luke, 2015), there has been far less discussion of how the systemic context of supervision affects the practice (Garvis & Pendergast, 2012; Holloway, 1995) and even less that aims to assist supervisors to prepare for or navigate how their practice of supervision can vary across counselor education contexts. In fact, none of the hundreds of peer-reviewed articles published in counseling and supervision journals over the past 15 years and included in Bernard and Luke's (2015) and Borders's (2005) content analyses of the supervision literature have addressed this topic. That said, a review of this literature reveals consensus on the basic definition of supervision and an understanding of its role within the profession. In what is frequently recognized as the most cited definition of supervision within counselor education and across allied fields, Bernard and Goodyear (2014) noted that *supervision* is

> an intervention provided by a more senior member of a profession to a more junior colleague or colleagues who typically (but not always) are members of that same profession. This relationship is evaluative and hierarchical, extends over time, and has the simultaneous purposes of enhancing the professional functioning of the more junior person(s); monitoring the quality of professional services offered to the clients that she, he, or they see; and serving as a gatekeeper for the particular profession the supervisee seeks to enter. (p. 9)

Accordingly, scholars have recognized that supervision can serve as a mechanism for professional socialization (Goodrich & Luke, 2011; Gordon & Luke, 2015, 2016; Luke & Goodrich, 2012) and the acculturation of professional mores, attitudes, values, thinking patterns, and problem-solving strategies (Auxier, Hughes, & Kline, 2003). What has not yet been fully explicated is the more isomorphic potential for the differing systemic contexts of supervision in higher education to similarly influence the professional practices of supervisors and their experiences in providing supervision.

The supervision literature carefully differentiates clinical supervision from consultation and administrative supervision (Bernard & Goodyear, 2014; Kreider, 2014). Likewise, it is imperative that when discussing supervision in counselor education, one distinguishes supervision from the other roles that counselor educators may be simultaneously fulfilling. As a supervisor for clinical course work, a counselor educator is typically also identified as the faculty person of record. In these instances, in addition to providing individual, triadic, and/or group supervision (Bernard & Goodyear, 2014), the counselor educator is typically also responsible for evaluating students and providing a course grade. Different from supervising in a practice context, this supervisory role may also be concurrent with the supervisor serving as faculty adviser, program coordinator, or instructor for other course work to the same students supervised. Less frequent but still possible is the chance that the supervisor has, is, or will be also overseeing a student as a teaching assistant or serving as a research mentor or employer if the student supervisee holds a graduate assistant position in the department or is working on a faculty-led grant-funded research project (Garvis & Pendergast, 2012). Goodrich (2008) has described how a comparable multiplicity of professional functions in the counselor education training setting can lead to role confusion that in turn can contribute to boundary violations and ethical dilemmas (Goodrich & Luke, 2012). Although counselor educators are familiar with ethical guidelines (see American Counseling Association, 2014) that address the potential of multiple relationships and inform the delineation of their supervisory and other roles at any given point, the fluid boundaries in higher education and unanticipated changes in them over time (e.g., from semester to semester) can exacerbate role confusion.

It has been recommended that one proactive way to ameliorate the challenges associated with boundary confusion within counselor education is for supervisors to use professional disclosure statements and supervision contracts (Herlihy & Corey, 2015). It has, however, been observed that these are more frequently used in a clinical context, wherein the syllabus or program handbook often serves to explicate the roles and responsibilities within supervision taking place in counselor education. That said, research has supported the importance of counselor educators' ability to manage multiple professional and life roles and their capacity to use strong interpersonal skills when communicating these (Niles, Akos, & Cutler, 2001), especially when these roles change or evolve. Even if the supervisory roles and functions, supervision models, and methods and techniques used in supervision are clearly articulated and remain fairly constant across counselor education settings, what follows identifies and unpacks aspects of how supervision can be affected by particular aspects of the counselor education context and their influence on the supervisor and supervision itself.

Institutional Context

All counselor education programs are housed within higher education institutions. That said, a plethora of differences across institutional contexts can directly and indirectly influence the supervision taking place. For example, counselor education programs may be housed within departments offering counseling course work at the undergraduate, master's, and doctoral levels or some combination thereof. Accordingly, this can change the ways in which the supervisor approaches supervision. For example, if the supervisor is working with undergraduate students, it is more likely that the skills under development are being enacted and practiced with classmates or mock clients. Although student welfare is always the responsibility of the supervisor, the mock nature of such practice sessions often diminishes the proportion of supervisory focus on the protection of client welfare or gatekeeping. However, when the supervisor works with master's-level students, there is a point in training when supervision of classroom skill development shifts, and the supervisor is then responsible for the supervision of counseling students working with real clients in practice settings. Thus, it is expected that the increased responsibilities associated with acculturating to a counseling practice context and building a caseload can present new challenges and opportunities to be addressed in supervision. It can be helpful for the supervisor not only to be cognizant of this but also to anticipate how this might affect his or her approach to supervision. This is especially salient if the supervisor has worked with these same supervisees previously and assumes that continued growth will be linear. Supervisors should monitor and respond to the developmental needs of their supervisees (Stoltenberg & McNeill, 2010) across the education level of students.

Concurrently, it is almost always the case that supervision of doctoral students also involves supervision of real-world counseling, as their counseling work begins in practice settings. Nevertheless, in many counselor education programs, doctoral supervision also encompasses supervision of doctoral students' supervision and doctoral students' teaching, as both are part of the doctoral internship (CACREP, 2015). Given that doctoral students' self-efficacy and competence often vary across the counseling, supervision, and teaching domains that may be supervised, supervisors are advised to differentiate doctoral students' developmental level and subsequent needs (Stoltenberg & McNeill, 2010). In addition, Luke and Bernard (2006) suggested that supervision of counseling duties beyond individual and group counseling may involve additional supervisory skills and that supervisors may benefit from supplementary models, frameworks, and supports to accomplish this work. Thus, future scholarship in counselor education can address the gap in the literature on supervision of supervision (more recently identified as meta-supervision; Bernard & Goodyear, 2019) and supervision of teaching, as the publications in these areas are quite limited.

Carnegie Classification

Clearly, some counselor education programs are housed within teaching-focused institutions and others in research-intensive institutions. The Carnegie classification of an institution not only relates to organizational structure and culture (Altbach, 2015) but also contributes to whether supervision activity is considered to be part of teaching or service responsibility. At some institutions, supervision, especially when associated with a clinical class, is accounted for as part of the faculty teaching load. Alternatively, supervision may be an expected aspect of department service across all faculty separate from or in addition to an assigned teaching load. Although teaching, service, and scholarly engagement are expected parts of the work in all higher education contexts, institutional expectations for the proportion and amount of these experiences vary (Altbach, 2016). Not only does this affect the workload of counselor educators, but it can also present unique demands on the promotion and tenure process, as discussed later in the chapter.

Given that counselor educators have reported dissonance with some of the systemic demands on their time and focus, and they have described challenges in finding balance across the role demands (Magnuson, Norem, & Lonneman-Doroff, 2009), supervisors are encouraged to be reflective about their personal and professional processes. Counselor educators need to understand that planning for, implementing, and documenting supervision can involve a significant investment of their time as well as consume psychosocial-emotional resources. For example, faculty report investing significant amounts of time and experiencing a range of taxing affective and interpersonal challenges when working with a student exhibiting problems of professional competence. When the proportion of time and other resources that counselor educators are investing (or are expected to invest) in supervision pulls from that available for teaching or research (Altbach, 2016), it can interfere with professional development and have negative implications for balance, connection, and perceived success (Wilde, Feit, Harrawood, & Kleist, 2015).

Program Size and Specialty

Additional intersecting institutional contextual considerations are related to supervision in counselor education as well. For example, both institution and program size can affect the expectations for and experiences of counselor educators providing supervision. Although not always the case, a larger institution may be more likely to have resources and a shared infrastructure to support supervision (e.g., software platform for recording transfer and storage), whereas a smaller institution might facilitate more collaborative relationships that encourage student success (Geiger, 2016). Just as both of these types of supports can facilitate the work of the supervisor, a lack of supports may complicate or stymie it. For example, some institutions have caps on overall program enrollment, whereas others have more flexibility and can adapt their course offerings based on the changing enrollment of students. When student enrollment varies significantly, or when program enrollment exceeds the capacity of available supervisory structures, the system can become taxed. In such instances, it is not uncommon for the supervisor to become the initial symptom bearer in a system in which demands outstrip reserves. As mentorship was shown to be an effective proactive and responsive strategy for other counselor education responsibilities (Magnuson et al., 2009), forging mentorship relationships in the area of supervision may prove helpful for counselor educators in buoying stressors as well.

Sometimes the number of counseling specialties offered within a counselor education program is related to program size, and this too can affect supervision. Although there is a concerted movement in the profession to identify as counselor first, area of specialty second (Bobby, 2013), many counselor educators continue to identify by their specialty first. The higher education institutional context may inadvertently contribute to this by crafting position descriptions and program coordination roles that are specialty focused, leading counselor educators to think of themselves and to be viewed by specialty first. As a result, when counselor educators are asked to provide supervision across their area of clinical focus, as they often are, they may feel or be perceived by students or colleagues as less credible.

Although it can be assumed that the majority of counselor educators going into higher education will teach and supervise in a program with degrees across more than one counseling specialty, the current doctoral-level CACREP Standards (CACREP, 2015) do not mandate that doctoral training programs provide a breadth of counseling and supervision training opportunities across counseling specialties. Thus, it is entirely possible for new counselor educators, having yet to establish a clear professional identity, to find themselves facing indirect repercussions of counseling (Woo, Henfield, & Choi, 2014). For example, state licensure boards and educational departments are increasingly placing demands on specialty-related supervisor credentialing for eligibility to supervise (American Counseling Association, Office of Professional Affairs, 2014; National Board for Certified Counselors, 2016), which in turn may result in an unbalanced load of supervisees across counseling faculty who are eligible for such supervision and those who are not. For instance, some counselor education programs have an in-house training clinic serving the university or surrounding community (Bernard & Goodyear, 2014). Whether all counseling students begin their clinical experience in the in-house clinic or only some do, counselor educators can be asked to supervise clinical work with a population with whom they have little counseling experience. One way to address this in training programs is to encourage all counselor education doctoral students to expand their clinical focus and to engage in both course work and clinical practice outside of their master's program specialty.

In-Person, Hybrid, and Online

Twenty years ago, it was assumed that counselor educator programs were part of brick-and-mortar higher education institutions; however, counselor education programs have increasingly become part of hybrid or blended online systems (Renfro-Michel, Rousmaniere, & Spinella, 2016) as well. Even if counselor education programs offer most of the course work within their programs of study in person, contemporary climate and fiscal demands in higher education (Geiger, 2016) may create pressure for them to offer at least some course work online to accommodate student need. This has necessitated that counselor education expand the use of online and computer-mediated technology as part of effective teaching (Malott, Hall, Sheely-Moore, Krell, & Cardaciotto, 2014) and supervision (Rousmaniere & Renfro-Michel, 2016). Although research has associated participation in computer-mediated supervision with positive attitudes toward technology in counselor education and future practice and found no differences between satisfaction with supervision across in-person and online modalities (Conn, Roberts, & Powell, 2009), to date no research has examined supervisors' experiences. Given that technology continues to advance at such a rapid pace and that there are no current training standards for doctoral students in the use of computer-mediated technology in supervision, this may result in counselor educators being unprepared to do this work, being mistaken that all in-person supervisory skills translate to computer-mediated environments, and underestimating the investment necessary to achieve competence (Luke & Gordon, 2016).

Public, Private, For-Profit, and Denominational

Last, counselor education programs may be housed within public, private, for-profit (see Lechuga, 2008), and/or religiously affiliated and denominational institutions (Smith & Okech, 2016). Although these factors may not obviously affect how counselor educators approach supervision in a direct way, they have the potential to indirectly affect supervision through the intersection of institutions', supervisors', and students' cultural religious worldviews (Gilbride, Goodrich, & Luke, 2016; Luke, Gilbride, & Goodrich, 2016; Luke, Goodrich, & Gilbride, 2013a, 2013b). It has been argued that although often not recognized, institutions have cultural religious worldviews just as people do, and these can contribute to decision making within the institutional context (Gilbride et al., 2016; Luke et al., 2013a, 2013b, 2016). For example, institutional values frequently inform institutional policies and practice, including interpretation and implementation of standards and best practices (Smith & Okech, 2016). Therefore, institutional priorities across public, private, for-profit, and religious or denominational contexts may inform the supervisory models, frameworks, and approaches that counselor educators are expected to use. As has been demonstrated in prior research with practicing counselors and those in training, not only can conflicts between institutional and individual cultural religious worldviews contribute to ethical dilemmas, but how they are navigated also informs decision making.

Differences and Similarities

This section explores similarities and differences in two primary areas that can manifest within supervision within counselor education contexts. One area is related to the contractual position of the counselor educator as a supervisor, and the other is related to similarities and differences in the modalities of supervision that are used. Up until now in the chapter, discussion of the counselor educator as a supervisor has referred to a doctoral-level full-time counselor educator with primary employment within the higher education institution. Thus, supervision is one of many components of the broad faculty role. That said, full-time faculty may be employed at the assistant, associate, or full professor rank, with or without tenure (Altbach, 2016), with supervision being one component of their role. Although less common, some counselor education programs within higher education institutions do not ascribe to traditional faculty rank, and others do not offer tenure at all. Regardless, scholarship suggests that it is expected that such institutional structures influence counselor educators' professional identity and career development (Calley & Hawley, 2008; Carlson, Portman, & Bartlett, 2006; Gibson, Dollarhide, & Moss, 2010) and how counselor educators think and feel about their faculty work (Magnuson et al., 2009), including the supervision they provide.

In addition, many counselor education programs employ part-time instructors (e.g., adjuncts) and clinical faculty on a temporary or time-limited basis in response to the contemporary demands of higher education in the 21st century (Altbach, 2016; Geiger, 2016). Furthermore, some programs use doctoral students who have been trained in supervision to supplement the supervision of counseling students. Whether or not (a) the supervisor is a part-time instructor, clinical faculty member, or doctoral student; (b) the supervisor is a full-time counselor educator providing supervision alongside a team of other part-time faculty, clinical faculty, or doctoral students also providing supervision; or (c) the supervisor is collaborating with part-time faculty, clinical faculty, or doctoral students who supervise shared students, there is the potential for differences across the institutionalized hierarchical structures to manifest and affect the supervision provided. As culturally competent and systemically savvy professionals, supervisors need to examine how the endorsed cultural capital embedded in positionality may come to bear in supervision and the counselor education program system in which the supervision is taking place. Just as it has been recommended that supervisors approach their supervision with multiculturally responsive models and methods (Ancis

& Ladany, 2010; Goodrich & Luke, 2011), it is appropriate for supervisors to proactively reflect on and conceptualize their own identity and systemic place in the higher education context with similar multiculturally responsive frameworks to better understand and effectively approach their supervisory work.

Although this chapter does not prescribe how to practice supervision per se, some attention is warranted to discern how the varied modalities of individual, triadic, and group supervision (Bernard & Goodyear, 2014), which can each be delivered in person, by email, or through synchronous online platforms (Rousmaniere & Renfro-Michel, 2016), can affect the supervisor. Although supervisors may generally approach the goals and procedures within supervision similarly across individual, triadic, and group supervision and perhaps even adapt similar models for their practice, there are a few fundamental differences for the supervisor. The amount of direct contact time necessary to enact supervision differs across individual, triadic, and group supervision modalities. If a supervisor is working with six supervisees total and seeing each individually, that will most typically involve scheduling 1 hour of supervision with each supervisee. However, because triadic supervision can accommodate two supervisees at a time, even if the triadic supervision sessions were scheduled for 90 minutes each, this would require less time for the supervisor. Following this pattern, group supervision could accommodate all six supervisees at once, and as a result, even if group supervision were scheduled for a full 3 hours, it would require the least amount of direct contact time for the supervisor.

In addition to efficiency in terms of the supervisor's time, the supervisor also needs to determine the level of effectiveness of the supervisory modality in meeting the specific needs of the supervisees and furthermore how the level of effectiveness can affect the work of supervision. Given the simultaneous goals of supervision, the supervisor will always be assessing how the selected supervisory modality is meeting the developmental needs of his or her student supervisees (Stoltenberg & McNeill, 2010), protecting client welfare (Bernard & Goodyear, 2014), and serving to fulfill the gatekeeping commitment to the profession (Brear, Dorrian, & Luscri, 2008; Hutchens, Block, & Young, 2013). However, if the supervisor does not balance these considerations when making the initial decision about the supervisory modality and carefully attend to how the modality is working to respond to the supervisee's varied needs (Goodrich & Luke, 2011), it can result in inadequate supervision and the supervisor needing to change course midway through the supervisory experience. Not only can this type of unanticipated transition require significant logistical demands for the supervisor to manage, which can contribute to a stressful process for both the supervisor and supervisees, but such a lack of clarity around associated expectations has been implicated in negative supervisory outcomes as well (Ellis, Siembor, Swords, Morere, & Blanco, 2008).

In the past decade, there have been significant advances in the development and use of technology to support the practice of supervision (Rousmaniere & Renfro-Michel, 2016). Given that most supervisors now use some technology (e.g., email) as part of their supervision (Luke & Gordon, 2016), and many use advanced computer-mediated platforms (McAdams & Wyatt, 2010), it has expanded some of their responsibilities. Not only must supervisors be concerned with the efficiency and effectiveness of in-person, email (e.g., asynchronous), and other synchronous computer-mediated supervision modalities, but they also need to consider whether their own supervisory preparation and practice adequately informs their use of the modalities and whether their counselor education institutional context affords access and support for this use. Scholars have cautioned against the erroneous assumption that what is known about supervision from face-to-face formats transfers directly to online and computer-mediated ones (McAdams & Wyatt, 2010; Rousmaniere & Renfro-Michel, 2016). Similarly, counselor educators who are supervising across computer-mediated platforms need to ensure that they have institutional access to Health Insurance Portability and Accountability Act (HIPAA)–compliant video conferencing and other software as well as that they and the program are adhering to the varied state licensure requirements for virtual versus face-to-face supervision (Baldwin, 2018). Therefore, as the literature in this area continues to mature, it is suggested that supervisors keep detailed records and intentionally reflect on the incorporation of such modalities into their supervisory work, seeking consultation, additional training, and supervision when appropriate (Luke & Gordon, 2016). It is surmised that making more intentional decisions about supervisory modalities is associated with greater supervisor agency and self-efficacy.

Challenging and Facilitating Conditions

In addition to what has already been discussed in the chapter, there are factors within the context of higher education in the 21st century that can challenge and facilitate counselor educators' practice of supervision. One such factor is evaluation. Not only do counselor educators need to evaluate the students whom they supervise, but counselor educators often need to provide documentation that evaluates the supervision that they themselves provide. Unlike practice and trainings contexts that have established mechanisms and structures for supervision of supervision, counselor educators' supervision is rarely observed or monitored and is even less frequently examined through a clinical lens. This is perplexing, as the supervision literature notes the importance of ongoing supervision of supervision and direct feedback over time for continued development of the supervisor (Bernard & Goodyear, 2014). Furthermore, as discussed earlier in the chapter, it is not uncommon for new counselor educators in particular to lack a depth and breadth to their supervisory expertise (Halse, 2011). Nonetheless, higher education contexts regularly solicit student feedback in the form of course evaluations. Whether including supervision as a component of an overall course evaluation or developing a supervisory evaluation form of its own, supervisors should be aware that such evaluations are in effect satisfaction measures. Like any perception measure, this type of assessment provides access to a particular type of data and is an incomplete measure of supervisory effectiveness. It has been observed that many of the positive and negative attributions within course evaluations correspond to students' perceptions of their pending grades. Thus, supervisors may wish to include a question within the evaluation asking supervisees to note their expected grade and then use this in interpreting and making sense of the feedback.

On a related note, and unique to counselor education contexts, supervisors are frequently expected to explain their supervisory work to colleagues across higher education who may not be professionally familiar with the responsibility. For example, counselor educators may be asked to frame and explain supervision as part of the job search process, an annual performance review, or the promotion and tenure process. In doing so, there is an assumption that those within counselor education will have a clearer recognition of what is entailed. Those outside of counselor education, namely, unit heads, promotion and tenure committees composed of faculty from across the institution, and school-level and university leaders from other disciplines, will require a more careful description of the counselor educator's work within supervision. Counselor educators are strongly encouraged to define and explain their supervisory work for these purposes to illuminate supervisory work that might otherwise be invisible. Doing so can minimize the risk of cross-disciplinary misunderstandings that can have profound implications for career development (Carlson et al., 2006). Some supervisors have found it helpful to develop a compendium of resources related to their supervision, including artifacts that can be used as evidence of and data for the evaluation of the supervision provided (e.g., deidentified recordings or transcripts of their supervision sessions, counselor educator peer observation or review of supervision).

Communication with colleagues across the supervisory team can be another factor that affects supervision. Unlike other practice settings, where the entire supervision team is composed of professionals from within the agency, school, or organization, by its nature supervision in a counselor education context almost always involves interinstitutional membership across the supervisory team. Having opportunities to communicate across multiple perspectives can facilitate a vibrant community across the supervisory team in which diverse perspectives are nourished and greater complexity of thought is encouraged. That said, challenges can also arise in communicating across institutions (Zuchowski, 2014). As access to shared supervision-related information is one of the barriers noted in the literature, supervisors within counselor education may wish to use electronic mailing lists (Bjornestad, Johnson, Hittner, & Paulson, 2014) and other software platforms that can store procedural information and then explore HIPAA-compliant technology (Rousmaniere & Renfro-Michel, 2016) that can facilitate more meaningful and clinically rich communication across the supervisory team. Just as supervisors need to be cognizant of their legal and ethical responsibilities with respect to communication, so too do they need to attend to other legal and ethical responsibilities more broadly as well. It has been recommended that counselors and supervisors use ethical decision-making models to support how they navigate complex professional dilemmas (Gilbride et al., 2016; Luke et al., 2013a, 2013b) that can arise in supervision.

Supervisors may also encounter challenges and facilitating conditions related to their work with students with problems of professional competence that are unique to a counselor education context. Although most supervisors will encounter such students at some point in their careers (Bernard & Goodyear, 2014), and many of these students may require collaboration on a student development plan (Jacobs et al., 2011), there may be more opportunities for peer recognition of competency concerns within the evaluative context of higher education (Oliver, Bernstein, Anderson, Blashfield, & Roberts, 2004). Although the literature identifies a range of supervisee situations that can manifest as problems of professional competence (Baldwin, 2018), these same peers report a lack of awareness of the policies or procedures for responding to such within the counselor education context (Oliver et al., 2004) and may experience fear and frustration as a result (Bernard & Goodyear, 2014). To prevent this, Studer (2005) advised that a supervision contract and related programmatic material can be useful in providing clarity and facilitating better understanding, and others have noted the importance of careful documentation (Bernard & Goodyear, 2014).

Systemic Factors

In addition to the range of systemic considerations identified previously in this chapter, a discussion of supervision in counselor education would be incomplete without more exploration of how larger systemic factors such as accreditation, professional identity, and social justice evidence within supervision in a higher education context. As the body responsible for accrediting counselor education and related programs, CACREP has been integral in the standardization of counseling curriculum and thus is widely recognized in counseling credentials and state licensure laws (Foster, 2012). As part of the educational standards related to supervision, CACREP mandates the faculty–student ratios that are part of clinical training (e.g., prepracticum, practicum, internship) and provides guidelines for the format, frequency, and duration of supervisory sessions (CACREP, 2015). On a related note, accreditation standards also set criteria for the qualifications of who can conduct supervision (e.g., trained, credentialed, licensed). Thus, whether or not a supervisor is employed within an accredited counselor education program will affect the supervisory work therein. In addition to increasing the academic rigor of counselor education programs, the standardization of curriculum and training procedures ensured through CACREP shapes the professional identities of both individual practitioners and the counseling field.

The professional identity of an individual supervisor is likely to affect his or her supervisory approach (Halse, 2011). Regardless of whether the supervisor is using a developmental model for his or her supervisory framework (Stoltenberg & McNeill, 2010), the benefits of the supervisor having a more advanced professional identity than the supervisee are understood. At the same time, research has highlighted how the professional identities of the systems in which supervision is taking place are also relevant (Gibson et al., 2010). For example, if a supervisor with a moderately developed professional identity is working within a program that as a whole has a robust professional identity, it may mollify the potential for a negative impact. The opposite applies too, in that if an individual supervisor displays a high level of professional identity development at one point but becomes part of a larger system that is not engaged in professional organizations and activities and with the literature, this can have deleterious effects on supervision. In this way, the systemic relationships related to professional identity can be conceptualized along the lines of the whole being more than the sum of its parts.

In addition, diversity and social justice issues can play a role in supervision within a counselor education context. Not only do the multicultural and advocacy competence of the supervisor and supervisee manifest within the supervisory dynamics and content, but the larger programmatic and institutional commitment to diversity and social justice also contributes to what occurs within supervision. As noted in best practice, it is incumbent on supervisors to recognize how racism, sexism, classism, ableism, heterosexism, and all other forms of marginalization and oppression can be enacted within supervision (Association for Counselor Education and Supervision Taskforce on Best Practices in Clinical Supervision, 2011) and to empower supervisees to do similarly with their counseling. However, depending on the theoretical orientation, development, and context in which the counselor educator is working, the supervisor may or may not conceive of supervision as an explicit mechanism to address institutionalized racism, sexism, classism, heterosexism, and religious or other biases. That said, Inman (2006) noted the importance of supervisors' "awareness, openness, and sincere attention to cultural and racial factors" (p. 74) and went on to explain how evidencing such can provide authentic opportunities for the supervisor and supervisee to explore how interpersonal dynamics related to culture occur with supervision. It has been observed that the ways in which identity, power and privilege, as well as other social justice concerns occur within the supervisory relationship and the larger systemic context can be informative for supervisee development. Thus, supervisors are encouraged to help supervisees connect what is happening in counseling and supervisory relationships to what is happening in the program or institution, the counseling profession, and the culture more broadly.

Conclusion

Supervision is a significant component of the responsibilities of most counselor educators. Although the supervision literature has expanded exponentially over the past 25 years (Bernard & Goodyear, 2014; Bernard &

Luke, 2015), this chapter provides the first codified discussion of how the higher education context in the 21st century influences and is influenced by this supervision.

Additional Online Resources

American Counseling Association
  https://www.counseling.org
American Educational Research Association
  www.aera.net
American Mental Health Counselors Association
  http://connections.amhca.org/home
American School Counselor Association
  https://www.schoolcounselor.org
Approved Clinical Supervisor Credential
  http://cce-global.org/Credentialing/ACS
Association for Counselor Education and Supervision
  https://www.acesonline.net
Council for the Advancement of Standards in Higher Education
  www.cas.edu
Counseling Today, a publication of the American Counseling Association
  http://ct.counseling.org
International Association of Marriage and Family Counselors Code of Ethics
  www.iamfconline.org/public/IAMFC-Ethical-Code-Final.pdf
National Association of Colleges and Employers
  www.naceweb.org
National Association of Student Personnel Administrators
  https://www.naspa.org
National Board for Certified Counselors
  http://nbcc.org

References

Altbach, P. G. (2015). The Carnegie classification of American higher education: More and less than meets the eye. *International Higher Education, 80,* 21–23.

Altbach, P. G. (2016). Harsh realities: The professoriate in the twenty-first century. In M. N. Bastedo, P. G. Altbach, & P. J. Gumport (Eds.), *American higher education in the 21st century: Social, political, and economic challenges* (4th ed., pp. 84–109). Baltimore, MD: Johns Hopkins University Press.

American Counseling Association. (2014). *ACA code of ethics.* Alexandria, VA: Author.

American Counseling Association, Office of Professional Affairs. (2014). *Licensure requirements for professional counselors: A state-by-state report.* Alexandria, VA: Author.

Ancis, J. R., & Ladany, N. (2010). A multicultural framework for counselor supervision. In N. Ladany & L. J. Bradley (Eds.), *Counselor supervision: Principles, process, and practice* (4th ed., pp. 53–95). New York, NY: Routledge.

Association for Counselor Education and Supervision Taskforce on Best Practices in Clinical Supervision. (2011, April). *Best practices in clinical supervision.* Retrieved from www.acesonline.net/sites/default/files/ACES-Best-Practices-in-clinical-supervision-document-FINAL.pdf

Auxier, C. R., Hughes, F. R., & Kline, W. B. (2003). Identity development in counselors-in-training. *Counselor Education and Supervision, 43,* 25–38. doi:10.1002/j.1556-6978.2003.tb01827.x

Baldwin, K. D. (2018). Faculty and supervisor roles in gatekeeping. In A. M. Homrich & K. L. Henderson (Eds.), *Gatekeeping in the mental health professions* (pp. 99–126). Alexandria, VA: American Counseling Association.

Bernard, J. M., & Goodyear, R. K. (2014). *Fundamentals of clinical supervision* (5th ed.). Boston, MA: Allyn & Bacon.

Bernard, J. M., & Goodyear, R. K. (2019). *Fundamentals of clinical supervision* (6th ed.). Boston, MA: Allyn & Bacon.

Bernard, J. M., & Luke, M. (2015). A content analysis of 10-years of the clinical supervision literature in counselor education. *Counselor Education and Supervision, 54,* 242–257.

Bjornestad, A., Johnson, V., Hittner, J., & Paulson, K. (2014). Preparing site supervisors of counseling students. *Counselor Education and Supervision, 53,* 242–253. doi:10.1002/j.1556-6978.2014.00060.x

Bobby, C. L. (2013). The evolution of specialties in the CACREP standards: CACREP's role in unifying the profession. *Journal of Counseling & Development, 91,* 35–43. doi:10.1002/j.1556-6676.2013.00068.x

Borders, L. D. (2005). Snapshot of clinical supervision in counseling and counselor education: A five-year review. *The Clinical Supervisor, 24,* 69–113. doi:10.1300/J001v24n01_05

Borders, L. D., Glosoff, H. L., Welfare, L. E., Hays, D. G., DeKruyf, L., Fernando, D. M., & Page, B. (2014). Best practices in clinical supervision: Evolution of a counseling specialty. *The Clinical Supervisor, 33,* 26–44. doi:10.1080/07325223.2014.905225

Brear, P., Dorrian, J., & Luscri, G. (2008). Preparing our future counselling professionals: Gatekeeping and the implications for research. *Counselling and Psychotherapy Research, 8,* 93–101.

Calley, N. G., & Hawley, L. D. (2008). The professional identity of counselor educators. *The Clinical Supervisor, 27,* 3–16. doi:10.1080/07325220802221454

Carlson, L. A., Portman, T. A. A., & Bartlett, J. R. (2006). Self-management of career development: Intentionality for counselor educators in training. *The Journal of Humanistic Counseling, 45,* 126–137. doi:10.1002/j.2161-1939.2006.tb00012.x

Conn, S. R., Roberts, R. L., & Powell, B. M. (2009). Attitudes and satisfaction with a hybrid model of counseling supervision. *Journal of Educational Technology & Society, 12,* 298–306.

Council for Accreditation of Counseling and Related Educational Programs. (2015). *CACREP 2016 standards.* Alexandria, VA: Author.

Ellis, M. V., Siembor, M. J., Swords, B. A., Morere, L., & Blanco, S. (2008, June). *Prevalence and characteristics of harmful and inadequate supervision.* Paper presented at the 4th Annual International Interdisciplinary Clinical Supervision Conference, Buffalo, NY.

Foster, L. H. (2012). Professional counselor credentialing and program accreditation in the United States: A historical review. *Journal for International Counselor Education, 4*, 42–56.

Garvis, S., & Pendergast, D. (2012). The importance of supervision in higher education: Key lessons learned from a relational approach. In A. Carlie (Ed.), *Whisperings from the corridors: Stories of teachers in higher education* (pp. 25–34). Rotterdam, The Netherlands: Sense.

Geiger, R. L. (2016). The ten generations of American higher education. In M. N. Bastedo, P. G. Altbach, & P. J. Gumport (Eds.), *American higher education in the 21st century: Social, political, and economic challenges* (4th ed., pp. 3–34). Baltimore, MD: Johns Hopkins University Press.

Gibson, D. M., Dollarhide, C. T., & Moss, J. M. (2010). Professional identity development: A grounded theory of transformational tasks of new counselors. *Counselor Education and Supervision, 50*, 21–38. doi:10.1002/j.1556-6978.2010.tb00106.x

Gilbride, D. G., Goodrich, K. M., & Luke, M. (2016). The professional peer membership of school counselors and the resources used within their decision-making. *Journal of Counselor Preparation and Supervision, 8*(2). Retrieved from http://repository.wcsu.edu/cgi/viewcontent.cgi?article=1193&context=jcps

Goodrich, K. M. (2008). Dual relationships in group training. *Journal for Specialists in Group Work, 33*, 221–235. doi:10.1080/01933920802204981

Goodrich, K. M., & Luke, M. (2011). The LGBTQ responsive model for group supervision of group work. *Journal for Specialists in Group Work, 36*, 22–39. doi:10.1080/01933922.2010.537739

Goodrich, K. M., & Luke, M. (2012). Problematic student in the experiential group: Professional and ethical challenges for counselor educators. *Journal for Specialists in Group Work, 37*, 326–346. doi:10.1080/019339 22.2012.690834

Gordon, C. M., & Luke, M. (2015). Metadiscourse in group supervision: How school counselors-in-training construct their transitional professional identities. *Discourse & Society, 18*, 25–43. doi:10.1177/1461445615613180

Gordon, C. M., & Luke, M. (2016). "We are in the room to serve our clients": We and professional identity socialization in email supervision of counselors-in-training. *Journal of Language and Social Psychology, 35*, 56–75. doi:10.1177/0261927X15575577

Halse, C. (2011). "Becoming a supervisor": The impact of doctoral supervision on supervisors' learning. *Studies in Higher Education, 36*, 557–570. doi:10.1080/03075079.2011.594593

Herlihy, B., & Corey, G. (2015). *Boundary issues in counseling: Multiple roles and responsibilities* (3rd ed.). Alexandria, VA: American Counseling Association.

Holloway, E. (1995). *Clinical supervision: A systems approach.* Thousand Oaks, CA: Sage.

Hutchens, N., Block, J., & Young, M. (2013). Counselor educators' gatekeeping responsibilities and students' First Amendment rights. *Counselor Education and Supervision, 52*, 82–95. doi:10.1002/j.1556-6978.2013.00030.x

Inman, A. G. (2006). Supervisory multicultural competence and its relation to supervisory process and outcome. *Journal of Marital & Family Therapy, 32,* 73–85.

Jacobs, S. C., Huprich, S. K., Grus, C. L., Cage, E. A., Elman, N. S., Forrest, L., … Kaslow, N. J. (2011). Trainees with professional competency problems: Preparing trainers for difficult conversations. *Training & Education in Professional Psychology, 5,* 175–184. doi:10.1037/a0024656

Kreider, H. (2014). Administrative and clinical supervision: The impact of dual roles on supervisee disclosure in counseling supervision. *The Clinical Supervisor, 33,* 256–268. doi:10.1080/07325223.2014.992292

Lechuga, V. M. (2008). Assessment, knowledge and customer service: Contextualizing faculty work at for-profit colleges and universities. *Review of Higher Education, 31,* 287–307. doi:10.1353/rhe.2008.0004

Luke, M., & Bernard, J. M. (2006). The school counseling supervision model: An extension of the discrimination model. *Counselor Education and Supervision, 45,* 282–295. doi:10.1002/j.1556-6978.2006.tb00004.x

Luke, M., Ellis, M. V., & Bernard, J. M. (2011). School counselor supervisors' perceptions of the discrimination model. *Counselor Education and Supervision, 5,* 328–343. doi:10.1002/j.1556-6978.2011.tb01919.x

Luke, M., Gilbride, D. G., & Goodrich, K. M. (2016). School counselors' approach to ethical decision making. *Journal of Counselor Leadership & Advocacy, 4,* 1–15. doi:10.1080/2326716X.2016.1223569

Luke, M., & Goodrich, K. M. (2012). LGBTQ responsive school counseling supervision. *The Clinical Supervisor, 31,* 81–102. doi:10.1080/07325223.2012.672391

Luke, M., Goodrich, K. M., & Gilbride, D. D. (2013a). Intercultural model of ethical decision-making: Addressing worldview dilemmas in school counseling. *Counseling and Values, 58,* 177–194. doi:10.1002/j.2161-007X.2013.00032.x

Luke, M., Goodrich, K. M., & Gilbride, D. (2013b). Testing the intercultural model of ethical decision making with counselors-in-training. *Counselor Education and Supervision, 52,* 222–234. doi:10.1002/j.1556-6978.2013.00039

Luke, M., & Gordon, C. M. (2016). Clinical supervision via email: A review of the literature and suggestions for practice. In T. Rousmaniere & E. Renfro-Michel (Eds.), *Using technology to enhance clinical supervision* (pp. 117–134). Alexandria, VA: American Counseling Association.

Magnuson, S., Norem, K., & Lonneman-Doroff, T. (2009). The 2000 cohort of new assistant professors of counselor education: Reflecting at the culmination of six years. *Counselor Education and Supervision, 49,* 54–71. doi:10.1002/j.1556-6978.2009.tb00086.x

Malott, K. M., Hall, K. H., Sheely-Moore, A., Krell, M. M., & Cardaciotto, L. (2014). Evidence-based teaching in higher education: Application to counselor education. *Counselor Education and Supervision, 53,* 294–305. doi:10.1002/j.1556-6978.2014.00064.x

McAdams, C. R., III, & Wyatt, K. L. (2010). The regulation of technology-assisted distance counseling and supervision in the United States: An analysis of current extent, trends, and implications. *Counselor Education and Supervision, 49,* 179–192. doi:10.1002/j.1556-6978.2010.tb00097.x

National Board for Certified Counselors. (2016). *Understanding certification and licensure.* Retrieved from www.nbcc.org/Certification/licensure

Niles, S. G., Akos, P., & Cutler, H. (2001). Counselor educators' strategies for success. *Counselor Education and Supervision, 40,* 276–291. doi:10.1002/j.1556-6978.2001.tb01260.x

Oliver, M. N., Bernstein, J. H., Anderson, K. G., Blashfield, R. K., & Roberts, M. C. (2004). An exploratory examination of student attitudes toward "impaired" peers in clinical psychology training programs. *Professional Psychology: Research and Practice, 35,* 141–147. doi:10.1037/0735-7028.35.2.141

Renfro-Michel, E., Rousmaniere, T., & Spinella, L. (2016). Technological innovations in clinical supervision: Promises and challenges. In T. Rousmaniere & E. Renfro-Michel (Eds.), *Using technology to enhance clinical supervision* (pp. 3–18). Alexandria, VA: American Counseling Association.

Rousmaniere, T., & Renfro-Michel, E. (Eds.). (2016). *Using technology to enhance clinical supervision.* Alexandria, VA: American Counseling Association.

Shulman, L. (2005, February). *The signature pedagogies of the professions of law, medicine, engineering and the clergy: Potential lessons for the education of teachers.* Paper presented at the Math Science Partnerships Workshop "Teacher Education for Effective Teaching and Learning," Irvine, CA.

Smith, L. C., & Okech, J. E. A. (2016). Ethical issues raised by CACREP accreditation of programs within institutions that disaffirm or disallow diverse sexual orientations. *Journal of Counseling & Development, 94,* 252–264. doi:10.1002/jcad.12084

Stoltenberg, C. D., & McNeill, B. W. (2010). *IDM supervision: An integrative developmental model for supervising counselors and therapists* (3rd ed.). New York, NY: Routledge.

Studer, J. R. (2005). Supervising school counselors-in-training: A guide for field supervision. *Professional School Counseling, 8,* 353–359.

Wilde, B. J., Feit, S. S., Harrawood, L. K., & Kleist, D. M. (2015). A phenomenological exploration of beginning counselor educators' experiences developing a research agenda. *The Qualitative Report, 20*(7), 996–1,008. Retrieved from http://nsuworks.nova.edu/cgi/viewcontent.cgi?article=2190&context=tqr

Woo, H., Henfield, M. S., & Choi, N. (2014). Developing a unified professional identity in counseling: A review of literature. *Journal of Counselor Leadership and Advocacy, 1,* 1–15. doi:10.1080/2326716X.2014.895452

Zuchowski, I. (2014). Getting to know the context: The complexities of providing off-site supervision in social work practice learning. *British Journal of Social Work, 46,* 409–426. doi:10.1093/bjsw/bcu133

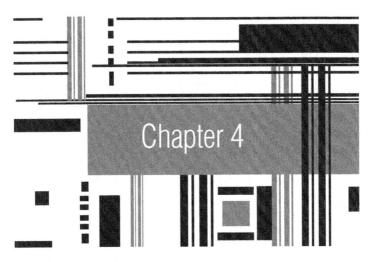

Chapter 4

Advising and Mentoring in Counselor Education

Kok-Mun Ng, Jared Lau, and Gloria Crisp

A 2014 Gallup-Purdue study (Gallup, 2016) examined the long-term success of more than 30,000 college graduates and revealed that graduates who "had a professor who cared about them as a person, made them excited about learning, and encouraged them to pursue their dreams" (p. 4) doubled their odds of being engaged at work as well as "their odds of thriving in their well-being" (p. 4). These findings corroborate the literature that recognizes student experiences of advising and mentoring as significant factors associated with student success in higher education (cf. S. M. Campbell & Nutt, 2008; Crisp & Cruz, 2009). Despite their long-recognized importance and common practice in higher education, advising and mentoring have to date received very limited research attention in counselor education (Chung, Bemak, & Talleyrand, 2007; Schwiebert, 2000). Nevertheless, the importance of advising and mentoring is underscored by their inclusion in the 2016 Council for Accreditation of Counseling and Related Educational Programs (CACREP) Standards (CACREP, 2015), whereby "students in entry-level programs have an assigned advisor at all times during the program" (p. 6) and doctoral training in the teaching domain includes "the role of mentoring in counselor education" (p. 36).

In writing this chapter, we sought to accomplish at least two goals. First, we are hopeful that this chapter will serve as a resource for counselor education students and counselor educators as they consider their roles in and approach to advising and mentoring. Second, we offer this chapter as means of furthering discourse related to mentoring and advising in counselor education. More specifically, our work provides a multisystemic framework for advising and mentoring in counselor education that is grounded in Bronfenbrenner's (1992; Bronfenbrenner & Morris, 2006) ecological systems theory. This chapter includes the following components: (a) a discussion of the definitions of advising and mentoring, (b) an outline of Bronfenbrenner's bioecological framework, (c) a review of relevant research and discussion of the contextual factors pertinent to the practice of advising and mentoring in today's counselor training environment, (d) recommendations for addressing needs for training in the practice of advising and mentoring in counselor education, and (e) illustrations based on personal narratives and observations. We begin by sharing our perspectives regarding the relationship between advising and mentoring. In our discussion, we relate advising and mentoring to student variables (e.g., master's vs. doctoral, cultural background), faculty variables (e.g., teaching and research expectations, relationship dynamics), training program variables (e.g., accreditation status, program culture, instructional delivery environment), and institutional variables (e.g., work culture, Carnegie classification).

Perspectives on Advising and Mentoring

Scholars have differing views about how advising and mentoring are conceptualized and defined. Some argue that advisers are different from mentors because "the primary role of advisors (who are not necessarily faculty members) is to offer degree specific advice, whereas graduate students work closely with mentors (who are faculty members) to enhance their knowledge and skills needed to progress professionally" (Mansson & Myers, 2012, p. 310). Thus, advisers' main responsibilities and priorities are to guide their student advisees through their academic studies, whereas mentors engage with a protégé in a positive developmental relationship (Knox, Schlosser, Pruitt, & Hill, 2006). Others, however, assert that "the advisor-advisee relationship is a type of mentoring relationship and that advisors serve as mentors to their advisees" (Mansson & Myers, 2012, p. 310). The distinction between advising and mentoring is further complicated by inconsistencies in definitions of mentoring in the broader higher education literature (Crisp & Cruz, 2009) as well as empirical evidence that suggests that mentoring relationships are context specific (Paglis, Green, & Bauer, 2006). For instance, some students may consider their adviser to be their mentor, whereas others may not. Furthermore, not all advisers consider their students to be their mentees. Similarly, some advisers may organically develop a stronger relationship with particular students and thus invest additional energy into the advising relationship and transition into the role of a mentor.

Amid the conceptual disagreement, the actual practices of advising and mentoring can take many forms and are experienced to different extents by involved parties because of personal factors of the advisers and the advisees (e.g., background characteristics) and other contextual variables (e.g., institutional financial resources). Conceptually speaking, we believe that graduate-level advising and mentoring should be addressed inclusively rather than separately, as we share the view that the graduate-level adviser–advisee relationship is a type of mentoring relationship. We acknowledge, however, that the advising and mentoring dynamics within graduate counselor education programs can vary depending on the unique characteristics of each program. For instance, advisers who serve only master's students will likely operate differently compared to advisers who work with both master's and doctoral students. For example, advisers in a combined master's/doctoral program may dedicate more of their time to mentoring doctoral students in research and professional development and may have less time to give to mentoring master's students. Nonetheless, we believe that students and programs benefit most when advising and mentoring relationships are intentionally and holistically developed regardless of how the roles and functions of the adviser and mentor are distributed among program personnel. Bronfenbrenner's (1992) ecological systems theory can be used to guide a holistic approach to advising and mentoring.

Bioecological Systems Theory

The bioecological systems theory of human development (Bronfenbrenner & Morris, 2006) contends that attempts to understand a person's development must consider the entire ecological system in which that person's growth occurs. The theory acknowledges the role of biological characteristics and psychological factors, also called the ontogenic system, in a person's interactions with the environment, and consequently his or her development (Bronfenbrenner & Morris, 2006), and presupposes that all human behavior takes place within a multiple systemic context consisting of five nested systems: microsystem, mesosystem, exosystem, macrosystem, and chronosystem. The framework emphasizes person–process–context–time relationships. We define these terms and illustrate them with examples relevant to advising and mentoring counseling students in the next section, which also discusses how to approach advising and mentoring from a bioecological framework.

Researchers have applied the bioecological model to explore human development across the life span and across settings and disciplines (Walls, 2016). In recent years, counseling and related fields have also begun to recognize the theory's utility in understanding and promoting practitioners' development (Chan, Yeh, & Krumboltz, 2015; Heppner, Leong, & Gerstein, 2008; Lau & Ng, 2014). Because counselor education is a discipline whose purpose is to prepare counseling professionals in a multilayered educational environment (multisystem) that involves both direct (microsystem and mesosystem) and indirect (exosystem) interactions with multiple stakeholders such as external accreditors, field placement sites, licensure and credentialing bodies, and consumers of counseling services, Bronfenbrenner's (1992) model provides a holistic and comprehensive framework to guide and understand the practice of advising and mentoring in counselor education. Furthermore, as counselor education's goal is to prepare master's students to enter, and doctoral students to advance in, a profession that is heavily influenced by contextual factors such as social and political movements (macrosystem) and that evolves through time (chronosystem), we argue that Bronfenbrenner's theory can be particularly helpful in addressing the context-dependent advising and mentoring needs of students.

Literature Base and Practice Implications

Although the mentoring literature to date has been largely focused on describing and understanding dyadic relationships between students and mentors (microsystem), evidence suggests that mentoring relationships might be better understood as activities embedded within and shaped by interdependent subsystems described in the bioecological framework (e.g., Chan et al., 2015). Thus, we discuss what is known about the effects of each of the subsystems on mentoring and advising experiences and outcomes as well as offer practical implications. We also discuss an approach to advising and mentoring based on the bioecological framework that accounts for contextual factors such as student variables, training program variables (e.g., master's and/or doctoral, program size, accreditation status, online vs. on campus), and institutional characteristics (e.g., Carnegie classification).

Ontogenic System

The *ontogenic system* refers to physical and psychological traits of a developing person, in this case the counseling student who is receiving advisement and/or mentoring. In recent years, scholars have given increasing attention to understanding how mentoring experiences are shaped by students' ontogenic factors, including but not limited to gender, race/ethnicity, socioeconomic status, openness to mentoring, and prior higher education experiences (e.g., Crisp & Cruz, 2010; Hu & Ma, 2010). Overall, findings indicate that students tend to prefer homogeneous mentoring relationships (Blake-Beard, Bayne, Crosby, & Muller, 2011). Taken together, research findings suggest that students who have different social identities and backgrounds may have varying mentoring needs and perceive and experience mentoring in different ways (Crisp, Baker, Griffin, Lunsford, & Pifer, 2017). For example, Hu and Ma (2010) found that Hispanic students rated the importance of their mentoring experiences higher compared to White students. Findings have also revealed differences in perceptions and expectations of mentoring according to students' generational status, with first-generation students tending to approach mentoring from a utilitarian perspective compared to students who have family members who attended college (Mekolichick & Gibbs, 2012). Although scant, existing qualitative studies in the counseling field support the need to pay attention to how students' cultural identity and sexual orientation influence their mentoring experience (Chung et al., 2007; J. S. Clark & Croteau, 1998).

Collectively, these findings have at least two implications for advising and mentoring practice. When possible, students' and mentors' identities and prior experiences should be considered when one is matching students with advisers/mentors. But it is not necessary for mentors to share students' race, gender, or other identities (Crisp et al., 2017). It is more important that students are matched with an adviser or mentor who is able to affirm and validate the experiences and perspectives they bring to the relationship and program (Reddick & Pritchett, 2015). The matching process should consider the compatibility, shared values, and fit between students and the mentor (Baker & Lunsford, 2016). Findings further highlight the value in providing training to advisers and mentors to help them work effectively given the specific needs of culturally different students (Chan et al., 2015). Also, advisers and mentors should be mindful of gender and ethnic/racial differences in identity formation (Johnson, 2002) and understand that students' expectations and experiences with mentoring are shaped by their identities and prior experiences (Lunsford, Crisp, Dolan, & Wuetherick, 2017). This sensitivity to diversity issues echoes the argument for multiculturally competent supervision in counselor education (Fong, 1994). We recommend that advisers and mentors use Hays's (2001) ADDRESSING framework to help them keep in view the multidimensional personhood and experiences of their advisees as well as their own. The ADDRESSING framework organizes cultural complexities into broad categories: Age and generational influences, developmentally related Disability status, acquired Disability status, Religion and spiritual orientation, Ethnicity, Socioeconomic status, Sexual orientation, Indigenous heritage, National origin, and Gender. Advisers can use the ADDRESSING framework to help them understand how advisees' cultural influences may affect their learning experience and growth and how advising and mentoring can be facilitated in culturally sensitive and responsive ways.

In practice, the ability to match advisees and advisers based on ontogenic factors may be hampered by contextual factors such as the number of faculty members available to advise and mentor in a small program and a lack of minority faculty. One way to address these contextual limitations is for faculty to furnish students with more personal and professional information about themselves so that students can make informed decisions regarding their choice of adviser and mentor, if the program allows such an option. Alternatively, programs can clearly inform students during orientation and in the student handbook that students are welcome to switch advisers and delineate the policy and procedures that guide the process. Clarity of policy and procedure will help prevent unnecessary misunderstanding and relational conflicts among students and faculty.

My colleagues and I (Ng) work in a hybrid program that has a limited number of faculty available to advise and mentor doctoral students. We send emails describing our backgrounds and professional interests to incoming doctoral students before they are matched to faculty advisers. We invite students to contact the faculty for more information to help them choose their adviser and accommodate students' adviser preference as much as possible. We also clearly convey to students that they are welcome to switch advisers later should they believe another faculty adviser better matches their background and needs. However, we are not able to do the same with our master's students because of the limited number of faculty and the workload concerns of a faculty member potentially taking on too many advisees. When I (Lau) entered my doctoral program, all new students were by default assigned as advisees to the doctoral program coordinator. However, during our first semester we were also required to meet individually with the faculty so that we could learn more about them and eventually select our new adviser by the end of the first semester.

Microsystem

The *microsystem* refers to the interpersonal relations and contexts in a person's immediate environment (Bronfenbrenner, 1992). In counselor education, in which the counseling student is the focus of development, the relationship the student has with his or her adviser represents a microsystemic factor. The majority of mentoring research to date has focused on how mentoring is shaped by students' immediate context, including types and sources of relationships; where mentoring takes place; and the various roles, functions, and activities of a mentoring relationship. Research describes mentoring as relational, mutually beneficial, and reciprocal (Johnson, 2002). Successful relationships are developed from clear expectations and mutual respect (Crisp et al., 2017), and both mentors and students are expected to benefit from the relationship (Amaral & Vala, 2009; C. M. Campbell, Smith, Dugan, & Komives, 2012). Mentoring interactions occur in a variety of settings, including classrooms, advisers' offices, on-campus training labs, clinic training locations, and formal mentoring programs. With the growth of online graduate programs, mentoring relationships develop virtually as well. Moreover, findings suggest that the norms and expectations regarding the extent and nature of advisers' and mentors' interactions with students may vary across settings (Paglis et al., 2006), for example, by type of academic program, by discipline, and as a result of the preferences of the student and mentor (Lunsford & Baker, 2016).

Although faculty members commonly serve as counseling students' primary advisers and/or mentors throughout graduate school, mentors may be formal advisers, dissertation chairs, lab supervisors, more experienced graduate students, or peers (Lunsford et al., 2017). In addition, in the context of counseling training programs, mentors may include site/clinical supervisors. Findings reveal that it can be difficult for a single adviser/mentor to provide all of the support needed by a graduate student. Thus, students typically build relationships with several mentors, and this is often referred to as a *developmental network* (Lunsford & Baker, 2016). All three of us have personally developed mentoring relationships with more than one person. We have also mentored students who have established other need-based mentoring relationships. Hence, advisers need to help advisees develop a network of mentoring relationships to help them grow and succeed personally and professionally (Lunsford, 2012). For example, I (Crisp) encourage my graduate students to develop their networks by reaching out to and meeting local practitioners and attending scholarly conferences with the intention of meeting scholars who conduct research in their area of interest. I also make an effort to connect my new advisees with students who are further along in the program to encourage peer mentoring relationships.

Broadly speaking, research indicates that mentoring benefits graduate students by providing them with various types of support, including but not limited to assistance in (a) learning and navigating the university and academic environment, (b) developing strategies and experiences that promote employment opportunities after graduation, (c) completing program requirements, and (d) managing the rigorous workload and expectations of graduate school (Luna & Cullen, 1998). Furthermore, research highlights the value of advisers and mentors serving as role models to students (Crisp et al., 2017). Similarly, although not all supportive advisers and mentors look or act alike, research suggests that effective mentors typically provide encouragement, work to develop students' confidence and identities as scholars and clinicians, are approachable, and regularly collaborate on projects with students (Baker & Lunsford, 2016).

Research findings reveal other ingredients for building a strong mentoring relationship. Mentors should be honest with themselves about the time and commitment they are able to offer to the relationship (Baker & Griffin, 2010). Clear expectations (e.g., desired frequency, preferred means of communication) should be discussed and agreed upon early in the relationship (Baker & Lunsford, 2016). Moreover, advisers and faculty should provide timely, regular, and honest feedback to students (Williams-Nickelson, 2009). It is also important that students articulate their expectations, identify their needs, and acknowledge their role in developing and maintaining the relationship (Crisp et al., 2017). Mentors are encouraged to engage in intentional role modeling (Johnson, 2002), for instance, asking their graduate students to observe their teaching or work together on professional service activities.

For example, I (Ng) have had the privilege of having several mentors who modeled good mentoring. They affected how I advise and mentor my students. I often encourage my advisees to be strategic in their academic pursuits and professional development. I encourage them to attend and present at conferences and submit articles. I also invite advisees to collaborate with me on projects such as course development and publication. I extend similar invitations to students who are not my advisees while focusing my priority on my advisees. I (Crisp) have similar experiences with and perspectives on advising and mentoring students.

Interpersonally speaking, we believe that it is important for both advisers and advisees to practice effective conflict resolution and relationship repair skills because conflicts and misunderstandings are inherent in any human interactions in a microsystem. An example of such conflict is when a counselor educator needs to address gatekeeping issues with his or her advisee and there is a rupture in the advising relationship because the advisee believes that the adviser's expectations are unreasonable. Advisers may also need to help their advisees address relational conflicts they have with other faculty members and students. For example, Jared Lau was my (Ng) doctoral advisee, and we have continued to collaborate professionally after his completion of his doctoral studies. He and I discussed many times the challenges and difficulties he was facing at work.

Factors related to other systemic levels also affect the microsystemic interactions between advisers and advisees. For example, faculty members in online and hybrid training programs understandably do not have the luxury of frequent, regular in-person interaction with their advisees like faculty in traditional on-campus programs. Hence, being an integral part of students' microsystem, faculty in online and hybrid programs should strive to create an environment that promotes quality adviser–advisee interactions, such as intentionally scheduled face-to-face or online advising meetings.

Mesosystem and Exosystem

The *mesosystem* refers to the relationships between microsystemic factors (e.g., relationships among fellow students with whom a counseling student is in direct contact; Bronfenbrenner, 1992). The *exosystem* consists of linkages between subsystems that affect a person indirectly (e.g., an adviser's relationship with other counseling professionals and university policy changes that affect faculty workload). Although scant, there is growing evidence of how the mesosystem and exosystem may influence students' mentoring experiences and outcomes as well as the adviser/ mentor's experience.

In particular, researchers have begun to call for a more holistic conceptualization of mentoring that includes the mesosystemic factors of a student, such as his or her family and community (e.g., Chan et al., 2015). The types of support students need and are expected to receive vary across settings (e.g., field placements, research labs, familial relationships, child care). We encourage faculty to discuss mentoring, develop collaborative efforts when appropriate, and/or share mentoring strategies (Hollingsworth & Fassinger, 2002), as such efforts contribute positively to students' mesosystem. Furthermore, Baker, Pifer, and Flemion (2013) suggest that advisers and mentors work with the institution's graduate school/office to develop workshops for students on how to build developmental networks. Thus, we recommend that mentors take time to recognize and discuss students' family and community (Chan et al., 2015), for example, the challenges and experiences of students who are mothers of school-age children (Trepal & Stinchfield, 2012).

With regard to the mesosystem, we contend that faculty relational dynamics and faculty–student dynamics in a counselor education program also affect students' experience of advising and mentoring. For example, when I (Ng) was in my doctoral program, a fellow doctoral student shared with me that a professor declined to serve on her dissertation committee because this professor did not want to be on the same committee with another faculty member. The mesosystemic conflict between two faculty members affected my friend's learning experience. It is therefore incumbent on advisers to avoid letting office politics and unhealthy relational dynamics (e.g., triangulations) unduly affect students' experience. Students should also avoid letting unhealthy relational dynamics among their peers and faculty members affect their learning experience.

In terms of students' exosystems, our experience working in hybrid programs has taught us the importance of being intentional in advocating for institutional resources and services for online and part-time students, whose needs can be easily overlooked because they are not present in person to be noticed. For example, when we found out that institutional review board application training workshops were available only to on-campus students, we advocated for such training opportunities to be provided to students in online programs as well. Also, when we found out that only full-time students were eligible to apply for the scholarships the college offers, we advocated for change, which resulted in some scholarships being made available to part-time students as well.

Mentors can also facilitate the development of mentoring across and between settings by introducing students to counselor education scholars outside of the institution and by providing students with opportunities to grow both within and outside the institution through teaching, presenting, and publishing (Chan et al., 2015). Mentors may also encourage doctoral students to organize their own research team with undergraduate and/or graduate students (Hollingsworth & Fassinger, 2002). Such efforts will help expand and enrich students' exosystem and mesosystem. From an exosystemic lens, institutional changes that affect faculty members' work environment can also influence advising and mentoring activities students receive. For example, many U.S. counseling programs, like other higher education programs, had to increase faculty workload (e.g., teaching more classes and having more advisees) during and after the recent economic recession. Such increased workloads have likely translated into less advising time and attention that faculty members can devote to each advisee.

Also, faculty members' involvement with the counseling profession and the community may also affect their work with advisees. I (Ng) can attest that my personal and professional growth through the years has positively affected how I teach, supervise, advise, and mentor. I grow by learning from other scholars and practitioners in the field with whom my students have no direct contact (exosystem) when I read their work and attend their conference presentations. My students and advisees benefit from my interactions with other professionals when I apply what I have learned from these individuals to my interactions with them.

Macrosystem

The *macrosystem* is concerned with cultural and ideological aspects of the society a person resides in (Bronfenbrenner, 1992), for example, political ideology, institutional norms, societal trends, and discipline-specific values such as professional identity and program accreditation standards. In our review of the literature, we uncovered a limited amount of evidence to explain how students' macrosystems might shape advising and mentoring experiences. In extant studies, opportunities for mentoring were found to be influenced by broader organizational and sociocultural contexts. Namely, recent findings reveal that mentoring relationships may be negatively affected by societal norms and expectations as well as systemic racism, sexism, and discrimination. For example, research by Rudolph, Castillo, Garcia, Martinez, and Navarro (2015) found that gender-role expectations (i.e., men as workers and providers for the family) limited the time that graduate students were able to commit to a mentoring relationship.

At the same time, findings suggest that interconnections between personal, sociocultural, and professional contexts can be seen as a positive part of a mentoring experience. For example, discussions about race and cultural issues might inspire a mentor and student to collaborate in developing a research project. Several of my (Crisp) collaborative research projects have been born out of conversations with my advisees about how their (negative) experiences as members of a minority group have shaped their identity, perspective, and research interests. Furthermore, students may need assistance in navigating the university context (e.g., academic policy; Chan et al., 2015). Mentors should use their power and position to help students negotiate systems and learn about opportunities in the field (Williams-Nickelson, 2009). This is particularly essential for international students because they often originate from ecosystems that have cultural norms and practices and educational systems that are vastly different from those of their host country. Both domestic advisers and international advisees need to understand the macrosystem factors that affect their cross-cultural relationship. Advisers may also need to pay attention to domestic students who come from social locations that may result in them experiencing difficulties in navigating academia or preparation for the professional world (e.g., first-generation college students, students of other minority groups).

Other research has focused on the role of cultural norms, values, and expectations that may limit a faculty member's willingness or ability to mentor graduate students. Faculty mentors have been shown to experience cultural or organizational obstacles to mentoring, such as a tenure and promotion system that does not reward mentoring and increasing faculty-to-student ratios (Johnson, 2002). In the same vein, we believe that research output expectations contribute to an institutional culture that affects faculty's efforts and time spent on advising and mentoring. Within the Carnegie Classification of Institutions of Higher Education (Indiana University Center for Postsecondary Research, n.d.), doctorate-granting universities are classified by their level of research activity as measured by research and development expenditures, research staff, number of research doctorates awarded, and other indicators. This classification system includes three types of doctoral universities: (a) R1: Doctoral Universities—highest research activity, (b) R2: Doctoral Universities—higher research activity, and (c) R3: Doctoral Universities—moderate research activity.

We believe that the pressure on faculty in R1 and R2 institutions to meet a high level of research output compared to universities with expectations of less research output tends to prevent them from investing their resources in advising and mentoring. Faculty in R1 and R2 institutions likely are more selective in how and when they expend their resources in mentoring students and other junior faculty. Students in R1 and R2 institutions may have good research mentoring experience because their advisers are very involved in research activities. However, these students may not receive the same quality of mentoring in other professional areas, such as teaching and professional service, because their advisers are likely not as involved in teaching and professional services because of high research expectations. Similarly, faculty at liberal arts and teaching-focused institutions are often faced with heavy teaching, clinical supervision, and service requirements that can impede their investment in mentoring their students.

Findings also demonstrate that mentoring is less likely to occur when a department or program fosters a culture of competition (Johnson, 2002). Conversely, mentoring is more prevalent when advising and mentoring are connected to the larger educational mission and goals of the institution and/or recognized and rewarded as a form of teaching (S. M. Campbell & Nutt, 2008). Thus, we recommend that departments/institutions build in support structures to encourage and reward mentoring. For example, mentoring may be considered a criterion in faculty hiring (Johnson & Zlotnik, 2005). In addition, prospective students would be wise to seek information about the extent to which mentoring is valued and an important part of a department's culture when applying to programs (R. A. Clark, Harden, & Johnson, 2000).

At the macrosystem level, we believe that the program delivery format creates norms and a programmatic culture that affect advising and mentoring. For example, faculty and students in online and hybrid programs may rely more heavily on internet-supported communication tools for advising and mentoring activities compared to those in on-campus programs in which in-person interactions are the norm. Furthermore, online and hybrid programs tend to serve students who may be unable to attend on-campus programs and need the degree of flexibility online and hybrid programs offer. It seems obvious that faculty in online and hybrid programs need to be more intentional in advising and mentoring compared to those in on-campus programs. We believe that it takes more time and effort for both advisers and advisees in online programs to work on building a positive working alliance compared to those in on-campus programs, in which formal and informal interactions tend to take place more frequently. I (Crisp) have found that it is particularly important early in the relationship to make an effort to reach out to my students (who are in a hybrid program) rather than wait for my advisees to make the first contact.

Based on our observation and experience, the culture of an academic program that only offers master's-level degrees differs from that of a program that offers both master's and doctoral degrees. Programs that offer both program levels tend to develop a norm that involves doctoral students teaching and supervising master's students alongside faculty members. But this is not so in master's-only programs. In the former, doctoral students have the benefit of working with faculty members as apprentices in advising and mentoring master's students. Also, we believe that the training focus difference is a major systemic factor that can result in master's students not receive advising and mentoring as extensively and intensively as doctoral students. Thus, programs need to avoid neglecting master's students, particularly when it comes to mentoring.

We further believe that a counselor education program's accreditation status is likely to influence the programmatic culture and student expectations that affect the practice of advising and mentoring in that program. For example, CACREP accreditation standards require students to develop a clear counseling identity, and part of that involves being familiar with and participating in counseling organizations. Thus, it is not uncommon for CACREP-accredited programs to encourage their students to participate in professional activities such as attending counseling conferences more than non-CACREP-accredited programs do. With the recent increase in the prominence and importance of CACREP accreditation in counselor education in the United States, we believe that a macrosystem shift in the training environment in counselor education is on its way, leading to a more systematic practice of advising and mentoring that contributes to greater accountability and student success.

Although it has yet to be verified empirically, we believe that current macrosystem issues and trends in higher education affect advising and mentoring. For example, the internationalization of higher education in recent decades has brought many counselor educators into contact with international students from across the world, ranging from countries where professional counseling is well established to those where it is nonexistent. This has resulted in many cross-cultural advising and mentoring opportunities. I (Ng) was an international student and had a few faculty mentors when I was in graduate school and an earlier career counselor educator. I have further advised and mentored domestic and international students. I (Lau), an Asian American counselor educator, have had several cross-cultural advisers and mentors as a student and a counselor educator. I (Crisp), a White faculty member, have had many cross-cultural advising and mentoring experiences as well. Our experiences working with students and advisees, coupled with research findings on the impact of cultural factors on education and training, alerted us to the importance of practicing culturally informed teaching, advising, mentoring, and supervision.

Hence, we recommend that advisers reflect on how the larger culture and society affect the philosophy and practice of counselor education, their students, themselves, and ultimately their advising and mentoring practice. Furthermore, advisers could collaborate with advisees to find ways to capitalize on institutional, programmatic, and professional norms and expectations as well as minimize unwanted effects these macrosystem factors may have on their adviser–advisee relationships.

Chronosystem

The *chronosystem* refers to the temporal dimension and how "the patterning of environmental events and transitions over the life course and effects created by time or critical periods" (Heppner et al., 2008, p. 248) affect a person's behavior and development. In chronosystemic terms, the literature explains that mentoring relationships are long term and complex and often develop gradually and over time (Johnson, 2002). Early work by Kram (1983) identified four stages of mentoring: (a) initiation, (b) cultivation and development, (c) separation, and (d) redefinition. Mentoring relationships are also expected to develop and change as students progress through the various stages of their graduate degree: completing course work, passing candidacy or exams, beginning the dissertation process, and successfully completing the dissertation and job search (Baker et al., 2013). For example, students may rely more heavily on their developmental networks (including mentors outside their institutions) over time as they seek to engage in academic and professional communities (Baker et al., 2013). Thus, mentors' approaches to mentoring should be expected to change and develop as students progress and transition to other stages in their studies. Mentoring relationships will naturally take on new characteristics as students mature professionally (Williams-Nickelson, 2009).

Hence, mentors should focus on providing students with experiences that are appropriate for their stage in the program or learning (Baker et al., 2013). For instance, mentors may offer to hold weekly writing group meetings for students who are working on their dissertation. Similarly, mentors' roles, functions, and priorities may change over time as academic programs develop and evolve (e.g., have an increasingly diverse student population). Programs should also expect to grow and improve their advising and mentoring practice through time. In addition, it is recommended that mentors keep students up to date regarding changes in the landscape of the discipline, including new or emerging areas of research and changing job markets (Williams-Nickelson, 2009). Furthermore, advisers and mentors should also attend to students' personal and social development so that their work with students is informed by and responsive to these developmental changes. We recommend that advisers include discussions with their advisees on issues related to advisees' personal and professional development, for example, when students experience the loss of a loved one, get married, or run for office in a professional organization. Also, advisers should pay attention to cultural differences between them and their advisees that are possibly related to generational gaps (e.g., preferences for using technology as a means of communicating).

Based on our experience, advising and mentoring with doctoral students and master's students in counselor education are qualitatively different. For example, doctoral students get more advising and mentoring experiences than master's students because the former are required to produce a major research project whereas the later are often not required to do so in their curriculum. Also, doctoral students are more often involved than master's students with their adviser/mentor in professional activities (e.g., conference attendance and presentation) because of where they are in their career development. Hence, there is a need to consider how students' program level positively and negatively affects the practice of advising and mentoring so that master's students can still get quality advising and mentoring.

With respect to chronosystemic influences, the current research base on advising and mentoring in counselor education is rather shallow. Therefore, counselor educators attempting to apply research findings from other disciplines to advising and mentoring in counselor education should keep in view limitations related to generalizability. There is a need for counselor education researchers to explore the topics further both quantitatively and qualitatively.

Best Practices for Program-Level Training and Assessment

The following are some recommendations for counselor education programs to consider implementing in hopes of integrating a holistic advising and mentoring practice into their learning ecosystem. Doctoral students may also wish to consider these recommendations for their own student experience and how they can use them when they are in a position to advise and mentor.

Training for Doctoral Students on Advising and Mentoring

Because doctoral students are commonly assigned or asked to select a program adviser at the beginning or by the conclusion of their first term/semester of study before selecting a dissertation adviser, we believe that programs should consider introducing a holistic understanding of advising and mentoring to doctoral students early in their first semester. This is to start students thinking about the purpose and process of advising and mentoring before they select a dissertation adviser and form a dissertation committee. There are many ways in which this can be achieved, for example, by including such topics in one of the introductory doctoral classes or seminars on professional issues or instituting an advising-focused learning activity during an orientation meeting. Programs, particularly online ones, can consider developing an online learning module on the topic.

We believe that the concept of training and mentoring should be developmental and intentional; thus, in addition to simply being told about the mentoring process, students should begin receiving formal training on mentoring during the early stages of their studies. We suggest that this training be intentionally infused throughout the curriculum at appropriate junctures. For example, programs should include such topics in the counseling supervision course, the teaching/instruction design course, and teaching internship classes. Topics relevant to advising and mentoring are readily connected with the role of supervisor and teacher. To achieve this, specific learning objectives that reflect a developmental growth perspective can be explicated in these courses so that by the time students are in their internships, they should be able to demonstrate a higher level of competence related to advising and mentoring. For example, doctoral interns should be able to develop a learning module to help master's-level students understand the importance of advising and mentoring.

Doctoral students and new educators may also want to take a developmental approach to building their exposure to mentoring activities and knowledge by way of consulting with a more advanced/senior student or faculty member. For instance, new doctoral students and educators can seek advice from their senior colleagues on strategies that they found helpful in selecting an adviser as well as strategies that they found helpful in developing their skills and competencies in advising and mentoring.

Training for New Counselor Educators on Advising and Mentoring

Programs should provide systematic training to help all faculty members develop competence in advising and mentoring, particularly the junior ones and the inexperienced ones. The institution should also set up and support a systematic mentoring program to assist young and pretenured faculty to identify mentors for themselves and learn to be effective mentors for their students. Furthermore, we suggest that new counselor educators spend time to better understand the unique dynamics of both their program colleagues and students and to identify connections and shared perspectives and experiences that can lend themselves well to the mentoring relationship. Advising and mentoring training for faculty should be relevant and responsive to the characteristics of the student body (e.g., master's-only or both master's and doctoral programs, online or on-campus environment). Training at the program level should be connected to institutional resources and opportunities (e.g., leadership training and cross-discipline mentoring) and involve students, faculty, staff, site supervisors, and administrators if possible. Such an approach should increase the extent to which advising and mentoring are valued and integrated into the learning environment.

Programmatic Assessment of Advising and Mentoring

Finally, a feedback loop is critical to systems thinking. In an attempt to close the loop, we suggest that programs develop a comprehensive assessment and evaluation plan that is ongoing, fluid, and adaptive and that incorporates feedback and data from a variety of sources. Thus, faculty should develop advising and mentoring goals and objectives for their students and themselves. Next, based on these objectives, faculty members should collaborate to establish a mentoring plan and means of assessing the extent to which the objectives are achieved. Assessments methods should include quantitative and qualitative feedback from students, alumni, and faculty. We recommend that such a plan be part of the program's overall assessment plan targeting student and program improvement.

Conclusion

This chapter has sought to provide an overview of the practice of advising and mentoring in counselor education from a multisystemic framework. We believe that keeping in view the various systemic factors that influence a person's personal, interpersonal, and professional development will help counselor educators and counselor education programs to implement intentional and holistic advising and mentoring components into their learning ecosystems that enhance student success and ultimately result in a stronger counseling profession and better client care. We hope that reading the chapter has helped doctoral students reflect on their advising and mentoring experience and encouraged them to intentionally look for a holistic advising and mentoring experience that will contribute positively to their growth. We also hope that more research on advising and mentoring will emerge in the coming years to give the field of counselor education empirical data to guide its advising and mentoring practices.

Additional Online Resources

Academic Advising Resources, NACADA Clearinghouse
  www.nacada.ksu.edu/Resources/Clearinghouse/View-Articles/
  Advising-Online-Students-Replicating-Best-Practices-of-Face-to-
  Face-Advising.aspx
The Excellence in Mentoring Initiative, The Graduate School of
  Northwestern University
  www.tgs.northwestern.edu/resources-for/faculty/excellence-in-
  mentoring/index.html
Mentoring: A Guide for Faculty, University of Washington
  https://grad.uw.edu/for-students-and-post-docs/core-programs/
  mentoring/mentoring-guides-for-faculty/

References

Amaral, K. E., & Vala, M. (2009). What teaching teaches: Mentoring and the performance gains of mentors. *Journal of Chemical Education, 86,* 630–633. doi:10.1021/ed086p630

Baker, V. L., & Griffin, K. A. (2010). Beyond mentoring and advising: Toward understanding the role of faculty "developers" in student success. *About Campus, 14,* 2–8. doi:10.1002/abc.20002

Baker, V. L., & Lunsford, L. G. (2016). *Mentor well: Quick start guide for PhD advisors.* Retrieved from https://static1.squarespace. com/static/57a36878440243b50f0cb1db/t/57c741f0f7e0aba57 ab14810/1472676338947/LMD+Flyer+for+Faculty+Mentors+Jan+28.pdf

Baker, V. L., Pifer, M. J., & Flemion, B. (2013). Process challenges and learning-based interaction in Stage 2 of doctoral education: Implications from two applied social science fields. *Journal of Higher Education, 84,* 449–476. doi:10.1353/jhe.2013.0024

Blake-Beard, S., Bayne, M. L., Crosby, F. J., & Muller, C. B. (2011). Matching by race and gender in mentoring relationships: Keeping our eyes on the prize. *Journal of Social Issues, 67,* 622–643.

Bronfenbrenner, U. (1992). Ecological systems theory. In R. Vasta (Ed.), *Six theories of child development: Revised formulations and current issues* (pp. 187–249). London, UK: Jessica Kingsley.

Bronfenbrenner, U., & Morris, P. A. (2006). The bioecological model of human development. In W. Damon & R. M. Lerner (Eds.), *Handbook of child psychology: Vol. 1. Theoretical models of human development* (6th ed., pp. 793–828). New York, NY: Wiley.

Campbell, C. M., Smith, M., Dugan, J. P., & Komives, S. R. (2012). Mentors and college student leadership outcomes: The importance of position and process. *The Review of Higher Education, 35,* 595–625. doi:10.1353/rhe.2012.0037

Campbell, S. M., & Nutt, C. L. (2008). Academic advising in the new global century: Supporting student engagement and learning outcomes. *Peer Review, 10,* 4–7.

Chan, A. W., Yeh, C. J., & Krumboltz, J. D. (2015). Mentoring ethnic minority counseling and clinical psychology students: A multicultural, ecological and relational model. *Journal of Counseling Psychology, 62,* 592–607. doi:10.1037/cou0000079

Chung, R. C.-Y., Bemak, F., & Talleyrand, R. M. (2007). Mentoring within the field of counseling: A preliminary study of multicultural perspectives. *International Journal for the Advancement of Counselling, 29,* 21–32. doi:10.1007/s10447-006-9025-2

Clark, J. S., & Croteau, J. M. (1998). Lesbian, gay, and bisexual doctoral students' mentoring relationships with faculty in counseling psychology: A qualitative study. *The Counseling Psychologist, 26,* 754–776. doi:10.1177/0011000098265004

Clark, R. A., Harden, S. L., & Johnson, W. B. (2000). Mentor relationships in clinical psychology training: Results of a national survey. *Teaching of Psychology, 27,* 262–268. doi:10.1207/S15328023TOP2704_04

Council for Accreditation of Counseling and Related Educational Programs. (2015). *CACREP 2016 standards.* Alexandria, VA: Author.

Crisp, G., Baker, V. L., Griffin, K., Lunsford, G. L., & Pifer, M. J. (2017). *Mentoring undergraduate students.* San Francisco, CA: Jossey-Bass.

Crisp, G., & Cruz, I. (2009). Mentoring college students: A critical review of the literature between 1990 and 2007. *Research in Higher Education, 50,* 525–545. doi:10.1007/s11162-009-9130-2

Crisp, G., & Cruz, I. (2010). Confirmatory factor analysis of a measure of "mentoring" among undergraduate students attending a Hispanic serving institution. *Journal of Hispanic Higher Education, 9,* 232–244. doi:10.1177/1538192710371982

Fong, M. L. (1994). *Multicultural issues in supervision* (Report No. EDO-CG-94-14). Washington, DC: Office of Educational Research and Improvement. (ERIC Document Reproduction Service No. ED372346)

Gallup. (2016). *Great jobs great lives: The 2014 Gallup-Purdue Index report: A study of more than 30,000 college graduates across the U.S.* Washington, DC: Author.

Hays, P. A. (2001). *Addressing cultural complexities in practice: A framework for clinicians and counselors.* Washington, DC: American Psychological Association. doi:10.1037/10411-000

Heppner, P. P., Leong, F. T. L. M., & Gerstein, L. H. (2008). Counseling within a changing world: Meeting the psychological needs of societies and the world. In W. B. Walsh (Ed.), *Biennial review of counseling psychology* (pp. 231–258). New York, NY: Taylor & Francis.

Hollingsworth, M. A., & Fassinger, R. E. (2002). The role of faculty mentors in the research training of counseling psychology doctoral students. *Journal of Counseling Psychology, 49,* 324–330. doi:10.1037/0022-0167.49.3.324

Hu, S., & Ma, Y. (2010). Mentoring and student persistence in college: A study of the Washington State Achievers Program. *Innovative Higher Education, 35,* 329–341. doi:10.1007/s10755-010-9147-7

Indiana University Center for Postsecondary Research. (n.d.). *Basic classification methodology.* Retrieved from http://carnegieclassifications. iu.edu/methodology/basic.php

Johnson, W. B. (2002). The intentional mentor: Strategies and guidelines for the practice of mentoring. *Professional Psychology: Research and Practice, 33,* 88–96. doi:10.1037/0735-7028.33.1.88

Johnson, W. B., & Zlotnik, S. (2005). The frequency of advising and mentoring as salient work roles in academic job advertisements. *Mentoring & Tutoring, 13,* 95–107. doi:10.1080/13611260500040443

Knox, S., Schlosser, L. Z., Pruitt, N. T., & Hill, C. E. (2006). A qualitative examination of graduate advising relationships: The advisor perspective. *The Counseling Psychologist, 34,* 489–518. doi:10.1177/0011000006290249

Kram, K. E. (1983). Phases of the mentor relationship. *Academy of Management Journal, 26,* 608–625. doi:10.2307/255910

Lau, J., & Ng, K.-M. (2014). Conceptualizing the counseling training environment using Bronfenbrenner's ecological theory. *International Journal for the Advancement of Counselling, 36,* 423–439. doi:10.1007/s10447-014-9220-5

Luna, G., & Cullen, D. (1998). Do graduate students need mentoring? *College Student Journal, 32,* 322–330.

Lunsford, L. (2012). Doctoral advising or mentoring? Effects on student outcomes. *Mentoring & Tutoring: Partnership in Learning, 20,* 251–270. doi:10.1080/13611267.2012.678974

Lunsford, L. G., & Baker, V. L. (2016). *Great mentoring in graduate school: A quick start guide for protégés.* Retrieved from http://cgsnet.org/ckfinder/userfiles/files/CGS_OPS_Mentoring2016.pdf

Lunsford, L. G., Crisp, G., Dolan, E., & Wuetherick, B. (2017). Mentoring in universities. In D. A. Clutterbuck, F. K. Kochan, L. Lunsford, N. Dominguez, & J. Haddock-Millar (Eds.), *The Sage handbook of mentoring* (pp. 316–334). Thousand Oaks, CA: Sage.

Mansson, D. H., & Myers, S. A. (2012). Using mentoring enactment theory to explore the doctoral student-advisor mentoring relationship. *Communication Education, 61,* 309–334. doi:10.1080/03634523.2012.708424

Mekolichick, J., & Gibbs, M. K. (2012). *Understanding college generational status in the undergraduate research mentored relationship.* Retrieved from the Council on Undergraduate Research website: www.cur.org/assets/1/23/332Mekolichick40-46.pdf

Paglis, L. L., Green, S. G., & Bauer, T. N. (2006). Does adviser mentoring add value? A longitudinal study of mentoring and doctoral student outcomes. *Research in Higher Education, 47,* 451–476. doi:10.1007/s11162-005-9003-2

Reddick, R. J., & Pritchett, K. O. (2015). "I don't want to work in a world of Whiteness": White faculty and their mentoring relationships with Black students. *Journal of the Professoriate, 8,* 54–84.

Rudolph, B. A., Castillo, C. P., Garcia, V. G., Martinez, A., & Navarro, F. (2015). Hispanic graduate students' mentoring themes: Gender roles in a bi-cultural context. *Journal of Hispanic Higher Education, 14,* 191–206. doi:10.1177/1538192714551368

Schwiebert, V. L. (2000). *Mentoring: Creating connected, empowered relationships.* Alexandria, VA: American Counseling Association.

Trepal, H. C., & Stinchfield, T. A. (2012). Experiences of motherhood in counselor education. *Counselor Education and Supervision, 51,* 112–126. doi:10.1002/j.15566978.2012.00008.x

Walls, J. K. (2016). A theoretically grounded framework for integrating the scholarships of teaching and learning. *Journal of the Scholarship of Teaching and Learning, 16,* 39–49. doi:10.14434/josotl.v16i2.19217

Williams-Nickelson, C. (2009). Mentoring women graduate students: A model for professional psychology. *Professional Psychology: Research and Practice, 40,* 284–291. doi:10.1037/a0012450

Chapter 5

Admissions and Gatekeeping Processes

Jolie Ziomek-Daigle

The topics of admissions and gatekeeping processes in counselor education and related fields are critical and complex. Throughout this chapter, I present several domains and contexts related to admissions and gatekeeping, such as the evolution of gatekeeping in general. The chapter also moves from identifying counselor impairment and counselor incompetence as well as identifying the contextual differences between program types and their related gatekeeping challenges.

Gatekeeping in academic preparation programs is not isolated to counselor education. Gatekeeping and working with student impairment issues have long been documented in related fields such as counseling psychology, school psychology, and social work (Gaubatz & Vera, 2002; Jacobs et al., 2011; Rosenberg, Getzelman, Arcinue, & Oren, 2005; Trimble, Stroebel, Krieg, & Rubenstein, 2012). Gaubatz and Vera (2002) referred to *gateslipping,* when students continue to progress in preparation programs when there might be obvious concerns with academic, professional, or personal competence.

Many accrediting bodies and ethical guidelines require some level of gatekeeping, student monitoring, or remediation across disciplines that focus on professional preparation, such as teacher preparation, nursing education, and the medical field. For example, the national accrediting body for teacher preparation is the Council for the Accreditation of Educator Preparation (CAEP). Section 3 of the accreditation standards focuses on candidate quality, recruitment, and selectivity, which speaks to recruiting highly qualified teacher candidates who demonstrate attributes and dispositions beyond academics (CAEP, 2013). Preparation programs such as teacher education, nursing, medicine, psychology, and social work have guiding accreditation standards and codes of ethics that govern the preparation of candidates in professional fields that involve certification and licensure and the provision of services to consumers.

The American Counseling Association (ACA; 2014) and the Council for Accreditation of Counseling and Related Educational Programs (CACREP; 2015) charge counselor educators and counselor education programs with monitoring and assessing student development across multiple domains, providing plans for remediation when necessary, and removing unfit students from academic programs should remediation plans fail. Thus, it is understood that counselor educators serve as gatekeepers for the counseling profession (Homrich & Henderson, 2018; McAdams, Foster, & Ward, 2007).

An increase in counselor educator awareness of gatekeeping issues occurred with a rise in related research and literature in the mid-1990s (Baldo, Softas-Nall, & Shaw, 1997; Frame & Stevens-Smith, 1995; Lumadue & Duffy, 1999). Most literature on gatekeeping focuses on the practices and processes of gatekeeping as well as on litigation that has occurred among counselor educators, counselor education programs, and graduate students. Litigation is mostly focused on counselor educators exercising their role as gatekeepers for the profession and enforcing ACA ethical standards (ACA, 2014) pertaining to discrimination against clients and client welfare. Litigation has challenged faculty members applying gatekeeping practices and procedures that uphold the *ACA Code of Ethics* (ACA, 2014) and ultimately protect marginalized populations, such as persons who identify as lesbian, gay, bisexual, transgender, queer, or questioning (LGBTQ) (*Keeton v. Anderson-Wiley*, 2010/2011; *Ward v. Wilbanks*, 2009). The judicial outcomes of these cases have favored the decisions of the academic training programs based on the profession's ethics codes and standards of practice.

Early research on gatekeeping in counselor education explored the gatekeeping process in general, effective gatekeeping processes, and the formation of effective evaluation policies and procedures (Gaubatz & Vera, 2002; Lumadue & Duffy, 1999; Ziomek-Daigle & Christensen, 2010). Lumadue and Duffy (1999) provided the first set of recommendations and guidelines for gatekeeping and communication with students regarding evaluation procedures. The authors recommended that programs have an open and transparent assessment plan that is clearly communicated to students at admission. Gaubatz and Vera (2002) conducted one of the first quantitative studies on gatekeeping in counselor education and surveyed more than 100 counselor educators. Findings from their study suggested that counselor educators were hesitant to apply gatekeeping practices in programs and that counselor educators in CACREP-accredited programs were more consistent in following through with the gatekeeping process than faculty in nonaccredited programs. Furthermore, Ziomek-Daigle and Christensen (2010) completed the first qualitative study on gatekeeping in counselor education and found that counselor educators applied gatekeeping practices and procedures during four distinct phases: preadmission, postadmission, remediation plan, and remediation outcome.

The gatekeeping research and literature has evolved to include students' perceptions of gatekeeping when reporting their peers and the importance of program faculty response and action when inappropriate student behaviors are reported to faculty (Parker et al., 2014). Another study illuminated counseling students' understanding of the criticality of the gatekeeping process, especially during the admissions process, and the importance of communicating clear and consistent policies regarding gatekeeping to students at admission and throughout program enrollment (Foster, Leppma, & Hutchinson, 2014).

Think back to when you applied to your master's or doctoral program or when you were interviewed. How did faculty assess your fitness for the program and for the counseling profession? Were ethical behaviors or ethical dilemmas discussed? Were specific questions or scenarios presented?

Gatekeeping and Differences Among Academic Programs

In the current age, counseling programs deliver content and provide supervision in many different formats. In addition, differences in delivery can be found at institutions with only master's programs or both master's and doctoral programs. Some programs deliver all course content and supervision in person, whereas in hybrid programs delivery occurs both in person and online. In addition, other programs may only deliver course content and supervision online. These online programs may deliver course content synchronously (i.e., between instructor and student[s] in real time) or asynchronously (i.e., content is loaded and students complete work by a deadline). Most likely, in-person and hybrid programs will offer more opportunities to effectively gatekeep, as there are additional opportunities for in-person interviews, classroom observations, peer-to-peer interactions, clinical site visits, and remediation meetings to occur with present program faculty. Online programs, although providing educational access to students in remote or rural areas or to those needing flexibility, may offer more challenges to faculty in terms of identifying and remediating student issues. It should be noted that online programs often use synchronous virtual learning (i.e., real-time conferencing) more often, enabling faculty to engage in observation of student skills and dispositions. One example of in-person meetings in online programs is the required week-long residencies. Students are required to meet with course instructors and students in person for classes such as counseling techniques, practicum, or internship. These residencies may offer opportunities for student observation, interactions with others, and real-time supervision with tape reviews and ongoing feedback.

Brainstorm the teaching and learning differences among master's and doctoral programs along with in-person, hybrid, and online delivery. Identify dispositions and behaviors related to training counselors that may be more visible through in-person interactions, including class and supervision. In contrast, identify those dispositions or behaviors that may be missed through less contact.

Counselor Impairment Versus Counselor Professional Competence: Terminology

Brown-Rice and Furr (2015) described the distinction between impairment and problems of professional competence and called for the profession to emphasize the use of professional behavior and competence over impairment when referring to counselor behavior. The Americans With Disabilities Act Amendments Act of 2008 describes impairment with a specific legal meaning, one that is associated with legally protected disabilities (Public Law 110–325, ADAAA). Moving away from this problematic terminology proves challenging given the use of the word *impairment* in the profession's ethics code (ACA, 2014) and the frequent use of the term in 20 years of gatekeeping literature. Associating impairment and work performance in the counseling profession may have legal implications, and it is advised that gatekeepers shift the focus from impairment to problematic behavior and also use competency-based models for student evaluation to avoid any legal challenges (Brown-Rice & Furr, 2015).

The limited literature in the area of competency issues among counseling colleagues and peers focuses on cognitive decline and productivity, sexual conduct, mental health issues such as depression and suicide, drug and alcohol abuse, and dual relationships (Brown-Rice & Furr, 2015). More than 75% of counselor educators in one study reported working with colleagues with professional competency issues that interfered with the classroom climate and students' learning (Brown-Rice & Furr, 2015). Only a quick mention of counselor educator competence is included in the *ACA Code of Ethics* (ACA, 2014) and the 2016 CACREP Standards (CACREP, 2015), which address counselor-to-student gatekeeping and exclude any language associated with counselor educator competence. Counselor educators want to know how to deal with incompetent colleagues (Brown-Rice & Furr, 2015) and create healthier and more communicative working environments.

It is estimated that up to 10% of students in counseling programs may be academically or personally impaired or unfit for the profession (Gaubatz & Vera, 2002). Homrich, DeLorenzi, Bloom, and Godbee (2014) reported that problematic behavior centers on a lack of self-awareness and awareness of one's impact on others, a lack of insight and inadequate interpersonal skills, clinical deficiency, professional identity, and a lack of capacity for empathy.

In the past decade, counseling training programs have started to develop contextual or specialty-based standards or learning outcomes. CACREP has been instrumental in providing the impetus to assess in counseling programs with its 2009 and 2016 Standards. Of particular note is that the 2016 CACREP Standards include program and faculty responsibilities to teach, assess, and remediate around professional dispositions (CACREP, 2015). Homrich et al. (2014) emphasized that using only ethical guidelines as the standard of professional and personal conduct is not adequate in assisting student development and addressing potential impairments. Learning outcomes that focus on expected student professional and personal behaviors aid counseling faculty in implementing evaluation and accountability practices and operationalizing student behaviors (Henderson & Dufrene, 2012). However, in some cases student evaluation processes and procedures remain vague and ambiguous. Hesitation on the part of counselor educators to apply gatekeeping policies and procedures may be due to the challenge of differentiating between problematic behavior and typical counseling trainee development.

It can be challenging for counselor educators to apply gatekeeping practices. Many counselor educators develop remediation plans with specific goals listed for improvement in dispositional areas or academics. It can be difficult to assess whether improvement is a quick response to a remediation plan or an actual change in a student's thinking or decision making. Take the example of accepting feedback. Students might be resistant to feedback in a general sense but, to meet the goals of a remediation plan, demonstrate immediately to university and site supervisors that feedback is helpful and they are willing to improve a technique or change a behavior. Ethical violations (e.g., relationships with clients, plagiarism) are more objective and apparent to educators and administrators. It is important to emphasize that any concerns with students' dispositions and behaviors need to be addressed early on and documented. It is also helpful to have multiple forms of student assessments, such as practicum and internship evaluations, university evaluations, academic grades, and so on.

I have discussed gatekeeping across professional fields, including counselor education. I presented the evolution of gatekeeping in counselor education, differences in gatekeeping in reference to degree (i.e., master's or doctoral), strengths and challenges of gatekeeping in the form of course or program delivery, and differences between counselor impairment and professional competence. The next section covers admissions and interview day and provides examples of how counselor education faculty can appropriately assess candidates' academic qualifications and personal dispositions. Then I present accreditation standards that influence gatekeeping and student assessment.

Admissions Protocols

As we further dive into the process of gatekeeping, the first step involves exploring the development and application of admissions protocols and determining the dispositions necessary for and expected of counseling graduate students. Applying stringent gatekeeping procedures during the admissions phase is proactive and may help prevent problematic student behavior and remediation and ultimately safeguard the profession and potential clients. Gatekeeping during the admissions phase should include a thorough review of applicants' academic potential, professionalism, personal dispositions, and overall fit for the profession. Criteria should be clear; visible to the public; and available in different formats, such as on websites and in print (e.g., brochures).

Academics

Most universities and colleges mandate a minimum grade point average (GPA) and scores on the Graduate Record Examination (GRE) or Millers Analogy Examination (MAT) for admission into graduate education. Some universities and colleges may allow programs to appeal or make exceptions for students with a lower than minimum GPA, GRE, or MAT. Programs have been cautioned not to rely on GPA and standardized test scores alone during admissions. These criteria are poor predictors of counselor trainee effectiveness (McCaughan & Hill, 2015), and counselors need to have developed personal qualities (i.e., life experience or work experience) other than academic excellence (Ziomek-Daigle & Bailey, 2011). Smaby, Maddux, Richmond, Lepkowski, and Packman (2005) found that students with high GRE scores have difficulty with skill development and need additional support to "translate their cognitive capacities into empathic understanding" (p. 54).

Furthermore, cultural implications are apparent when a high level of importance is placed on outcomes of standardized testing (McCaughan & Hill, 2015). In one study, Homrich et al. (2014) found that counselor educators maintained that certain conduct must be observed in counseling graduate students, including maintaining confidentiality and ethical behavior, respecting the beliefs and values of others, increasing cultural competence and sensitivity toward others, and being aware of one's personal beliefs and impact on others. The authors hypothesized that the conduct identified as integral for counseling trainees may be in the forefront of counselor educators' thinking, as topics of professional competence, gatekeeping, and adherence to ethics codes are often published in the counseling literature and promoted as behaviors that serve "as the basic building blocks to becoming a competent counselor in training programs" (p. 138).

A review of CACREP-accredited counseling program websites reveals other common admissions requirements beyond the standard GPA, GRE, and MAT scores. Several programs also require a personal statement for admission, with some programs asking questions pertaining to interest in the profession, personal characteristics, or qualities that would make the applicant suitable for the counseling profession. Programs also require letters of recommendation; prerequisite course work (e.g., psychology, communications courses); predetermined majors (e.g., psychology or teacher preparation); and work or volunteer experience, preferably with populations applicants might work with as counselors (e.g., school-age children, agencies).

In terms of doctoral programs, these criteria are listed but additional documentation is needed. Faculty in counselor education doctoral programs also assess applicants for their range of clinical experience and research experience and review a possible portfolio. Students in counselor education doctoral programs will most likely seek positions as faculty members or advancement in their careers, such as becoming the director of a mental health center or school district director of school counseling. Those seeking these positions in leadership, research, and advocacy need to have various clinical experiences; knowledge of conducting research studies and analyzing outcomes; and tangible outcomes of work experience, such as becoming a licensed professional counselor, publishing peer-reviewed journal articles or book chapters, or presenting at the regional and national levels. One study reported that doctoral applicants with a lack of clinical experience and a limited range of counseling work need more support and supervision in a doctoral program (Nelson, Canada, & Lancaster, 2003). Given the norms and expectations of counselor education doctoral programs, this finding seems understandable given the advanced level of course work required, the required supervision of master's students, and the teaching assistance provided to program faculty.

Personal Dispositions

Smaby et al. (2005) defined *personal development* as one's ability to demonstrate the insight and understanding required to be an effective and competent counselor. Through the review of applicant materials, counselor educators should carefully examine the inherent personal dispositions being revealed by the applicant. The 2016 CACREP Standards (CACREP, 2015) indicate that programs and faculty are responsible for teaching, assessing, and remediating students' personal dispositions. A review of the literature provides several examples of personal dispositions that should be discussed or demonstrated by the applicant. Examples include warmth, genuineness, empathy, open-mindedness, and cooperativeness. However, these traits are difficult to assess through a review of a personal statement or during a group interview. Personal dispositions that reveal higher order thinking or decision making should also be examined. Potential counselor trainees should have opportunities to demonstrate traits aimed at dealing with ambiguity; being open to learning; advocating for individuals with different beliefs, lifestyles, or practices; and accepting feedback from peers, faculty, and supervisors. Specifically, formulated questions, well-developed case studies, and in-depth role plays may reveal the personal dispositions so important in developing competent counselors.

In a recent study, master's and doctoral programs used GPA and letters of recommendation more frequently and weighted these criteria more heavily than other requirements (Swank & Smith-Adcock, 2014). It is interesting that another study disputed the credibility of letters of recommendation, as these letters focus on only the positive attributes of the candidate (Nelson et al., 2003). Furthermore, research indicates that both master's and doctoral programs conduct and require interviews more than in the past, along with attending carefully to personal statements (Swank & Smith-Adcock, 2014).

Interviews

Counselor educators have been reporting on interview day practices and decision-making processes for some time (Nagpal & Ritchie, 2002; Swank & Smith-Adcock, 2014). Nagpal and Ritchie (2002) reported that although counselor educators collect and analyze objective data during interview day, many evaluate applicants using subjective processes such as their gut feelings and first impressions. Counselor educators in this study discussed using interviews as a screening tool rather than a selection tool and purposefully honed in on any undesirable or inappropriate characteristics made explicit that day.

Although some counseling programs do not require in-person interviews or interviews conducted in real time, many do. Group or in-person interviews provide applicants and program faculty the time and space to provide a thorough program description, discuss expectations, ask more direct questions regarding counselor fit, and demonstrate beginning counseling skills (such as through role plays). Swank and Smith-Adcock (2014) stipulated that interviews are effective; an important screening process; and an opportunity for applicants to engage in activities similar to what they would expect in counseling classes, such as role plays and group tasks. Researchers recommend that interviews be organized to allow all program faculty and currently enrolled students multiple interactions with candidates (Swank & Smith-Adcock, 2013; Ziomek-Daigle & Christensen, 2010). Activities for interviews should be designed so that assessment for academic potential, professional traits, and personal dispositions can occur.

Swank and Smith-Adcock (2013) discussed the use of creativity during the interview process and certain activities that could assess common dispositional characteristics needed in counseling trainees, such as warmth and acceptance, empathy, flexibility, self-awareness, genuineness, emotional stability, and open-mindedness. These various activities include the use of questions and experiential activities.

Recommendations for the interview process include the following (Swank & Smith-Adcock, 2013):

- Use questions in individual and group interviews.
- Select wording for questions that focuses on the past, present, and future of the individual regarding professional and personal development.
- During the group interview, allow group dynamics to emerge, such as cohesion, disagreement, and so on.
- Provide scenarios if applicants seem confused or unable to respond to questions.
- Provide applicants with counseling-related materials to read before the interview. Counselor educators can ask questions related to these materials to assess for responsibility, critical thinking skills, and fit for the program. Reading materials can include articles related

to the history of the counseling profession, the *ACA Code of Ethics*, multicultural literature, and the program framework/description.

Consider the following activities:

- Work with a partner and construct a list of questions that can be used during the interview process. Consider the following factors as you develop the questions: master's or doctoral interview, academic background and potential, personal dispositions, commitment to diversity and social justice, and work experiences.
- Work with a partner and construct a list of experiential activities that can be used during the interview process. Consider the following factors as you develop your list: master's or doctoral interview (i.e., neophyte vs. experienced counselor), use in small group or large group, duration of the activity, items/props needed, and space/room set up.

Experiential activities can be used during the interview process (Swank & Smith-Adcock, 2013):

- Experiential activities are used frequently in counselor preparation programs; the focus is on the demonstration of skills or dispositions rather than the discussion of them.
- Consider the use of miniatures to allow applicants to introduce themselves, describe themselves, discuss traits they admire, or discuss traits they would like to borrow or aspire to have.
- To assess how applicants may work together, introduce a team-building activity to create something such as a structure or to work through an activity such as solving a problem.
- Distribute counseling scenarios and have applicants work in small groups to identify key issues possibly related to development, the presenting problem, diversity, social justice, systemic influences, ethics codes, and so on.
- Incorporate play media, psychodrama, creative writing, music, or movement to assess applicants for self-expression, comfort with ambiguity, and ability to relate to others.

Accreditation Standards

According the 2016 CACREP Standards (CACREP, 2015) for entry-level programs such as clinical mental health or school counseling programs, three areas should be assessed of applicants during the application review and interview process: academic aptitude, career goals, and the ability to form interpersonal relationships. In most cases, academic aptitude is examined through the applicants' GPA and GRE scores. Applicants' career goals are discussed in personal statements or during in-person interviews. And their ability to form interpersonal relationships can be assessed through letters of recommendation, personal statements, and in-person interviews. Applicants to doctoral programs should be assessed using a different set of criteria, including doctoral-level academic aptitude; professional experience as a counselor; professional fitness for the field; communication skills; and potential for excellence in scholarship, leadership, and advocacy. Doctoral-level applicants in counselor education are assessed on their performance at the master's level and associated GRE score and, in some cases, their analytical writing score, which may reveal their writing level for conducting research and developing the dissertation. Other areas include prior experience as a counselor, fit for the field and a developed professional identity, and strong communication skills. Finally, potential for strong scholarship, leadership in organizations or other entities, and the ability to advocate for clients and the profession are also examined.

The 2016 CACREP Standards (CACREP, 2015) stipulate that applicants need to be assessed in the areas specific to master's and doctoral training (i.e., academic aptitude, professional experience). However, the Standards do not mandate the use of ratings scales or evaluation forms. Swank and Smith-Adcock (2014) found that most counseling programs have formalized procedures for evaluating applicant files or assessing applicants on interview day, such as use of a scoring sheet, but other programs reach agreement on applicant fit for the program through discussion and consensus. Given the recent litigation involving counselor educators and students, thorough student documentation is strongly encouraged.

Examples of admissions criteria across programs include the following:

- Minimum GPA and GRE/MAT scores
- Personal statement
- Letters of recommendation (minimum of three with contact information included)
- Prerequisite course work
- Predetermined major
- Required work or volunteer experience (with potential client population)
- Examination of personal dispositions in all application materials
- In-depth group or individual interview (including the use of specific questions, examination of case studies, and role plays)

Examples of personal dispositions often assessed across programs include the following:

- Warmth
- Genuineness
- Empathy
- Open-mindedness
- Cooperativeness
- Ability to deal well with ambiguity
- Openness to learning and advocating for individuals with different belief systems/practices
- Openness to feedback from faculty and peers

Gatekeeping at Various Assessment Points

Assessment in both K–12 education and higher education has evolved over the past few decades, and best practices stipulate that students should be assessed at multiple points throughout a curriculum. The move is from only assessing academic progress through course grades to undertaking more developmental and competency-based assessment. Many counseling programs housed in colleges and schools of education must work within a larger conceptual framework including broader assessment practices to be compliant with CAEP standards. CAEP mandates documentation of the mastery and collection (i.e., artifacts) of program-specific content knowledge, professional skills, and dispositional characteristics across four transition points: (a) admission, (b) entry to field work, (c) exit from field work, and (d) graduation.

As stated earlier, data should be collected from a variety of sources, including grades, site evaluations, university evaluations, exit examinations, and personal and professional dispositional appraisals. Ziomek-Daigle and Christensen (2010) proposed the first model of gatekeeping that included the phases of preadmission, postadmission, remediation plan, and remediation outcomes. Other literature recommends that assessments of students' academic and personal progress in counseling graduate programs occur at certain evaluation points or gateways (Homrich et al., 2014). These various phases or checkpoints allow faculty to provide oral and written feedback to students regarding their progress in academics, personal and professional growth, inherent strengths, areas that might need additional attention, and possible remediation. Kelly (2011) discussed developing a comprehensive assessment plan within the National Council for Accreditation of Teacher Education transition points framework. The National Council for Accreditation of Teacher Education is the former accrediting body (the current body is CAEP). The transition points at which student-level data were collected and reviewed included (a) program admission (emphasizing the admissions process and new student orientation), (b) entry into clinical work (emphasizing counseling relationships and skills), and (c) prepracticum. In my program (which is accredited by both CAEP and CACREP), counseling master's students are assessed at specific transition points, including admission, prepracticum, preinternship, and graduation. The following sources of data are collected to inform faculty decision making at the transition points: grades, site evaluations, university evaluations, self-evaluations, the counselor preparation comprehensive examination, and the state certification examination.

Student Perspectives on Gatekeeping

Gatekeeping research and literature have evolved to include students' perceptions of gatekeeping when reporting their peers and the importance of program faculty response and action when inappropriate behaviors are reported to faculty (Parker et al., 2014). In one study, researchers compared faculty members' and students' perceptions of peer impairment and found that more students (21%) than faculty (9%) rated their peers as incompetent (Parker et al., 2014). Other studies have illuminated counseling students' understanding of the criticality of the gatekeeping process, especially during the admissions process, and the importance of communicating clear and consistent policies regarding gatekeeping to students at admission and throughout program enrollment, including a clear protocol for reporting incompetent peers (Foster et al., 2014; Parker et al., 2014).

In the few studies focused on student perceptions of gatekeeping (Foster et al., 2014; Parker et al., 2014), students overwhelmingly reported that gatekeeping is important, that gatekeeping and its parameters should be clearly explained during interviews and throughout the program, and that it is the program faculty's responsibility to intervene when needed. Students felt that clear guidelines for appropriate and inappropriate behaviors should be discussed and also noted a gray area present when faculty consider gatekeeping matters (Foster et al., 2014; Parker et al., 2014). Inappropriate behaviors noted by counseling students of their peers included substance use and abuse, poor boundaries, mental health concerns, discriminatory behaviors, rigidity, and an inability to accept feedback (Foster et al., 2014). Students who participated in studies regarding gatekeeping also discussed discomfort with the idea of dismissal for nonacademic reasons, the need for remediation plans with specific goals related to changing behaviors, and the fact that ultimately it is the role and responsibility of counselor educators to gatekeep for the profession (Foster et al., 2014).

Recent Court Cases

In one recent court case at a public university (Hutchens, Block, & Young, 2013; *Keeton v. Anderson-Wiley*, 2010/2011), a counseling graduate student disputed the legal authority of program faculty in developing remediation plans focused on improving competencies to provide services for clients who are LGBTQ. The student, Keeton, expressed views that LGBTQ clients suffer from identity confusion and supported the controversial practice of conversion therapy. Keeton also discussed with classmates approaches to counseling with this population, including expressing that being gay is unacceptable and also morally wrong (*Keeton v. Anderson-Wiley*, 2010/2011). The program faculty found these statements toward potential LGBTQ clients to be in violation of the *ACA Code of Ethics* (ACA, 2005, 2014) and developed a remediation plan. The argument Keeton provided cited her First Amendment rights related to freedom of speech and religion and contended that remediation plans violate these rights. In this specific court case, an appeals court at the federal level upheld the ruling in favor of the university made by a lower court (Hutchens et al., 2013; *Keeton v. Anderson-Wiley*, 2010/2011).

In another recent court case involving students' First Amendment rights and client protection at a different university, a federal appeals court reversed a lower court's decision and determined that the lawsuit should proceed, thus ruling in favor of the student (*Ward v. Polite*, 2012). The student involved in this case, Ward, was assigned a client during practicum who had sought prior counseling services regarding a same-sex relationship (Hutchens et al., 2013). Ward asked the practicum supervisor to assign another client or allow Ward to refer the client to another counselor at the counseling site. Ward's counseling faculty believed that she violated ethical standards against nondiscrimination (ACA, 2014), and Ward was offered a remediation plan and the option to leave the program or participate in a formal hearing. After Ward chose and participated in the formal hearing, program faculty recommended her dismissal after finding Ward in violation of the *ACA Code of Ethics* (ACA, 2005, 2014). Subsequently, Ward challenged the university's decision and filed a lawsuit, resulting in several levels of rulings and appeals, with her case being allowed to proceed (*Ward v. Polite*, 2012).

These two recent court cases illuminate more than two decades of continued research, literature, and litigation in the area of gatekeeping in counselor education. The counseling profession's code of ethics and accreditation standards (ACA, 2014; CACREP, 2015) continue to reinforce program policies and practices concerning student development, progress, and matriculation and support counselor educators as gatekeepers of the profession. Counselor educators must be prepared to defend their decisions, as those who work at public institutions may face First Amendment challenges (Hutchens et al., 2013). Not only should programs demonstrate ongoing systematic evaluation of counseling graduate students from admission through graduation (Ziomek-Daigle & Christensen, 2010), but informed consent and due process must be part of the evaluation process. Engaging in multiple discussions and presentations (e.g., orientation, town halls) and having these processes in print (e.g., on the website, in the student handbook) will demonstrate to students and the general public the institution's commitment to protecting the welfare of clients.

Best practices in gatekeeping policies, procedures, and processes include the following:

- Systematic, ongoing student evaluations are a must. Evaluation begins at admission and goes through graduation. Checkpoints or periodic reviews need to occur throughout the curriculum (e.g., in the semester before practicum, in the semester before internship).
- As stated previously, evaluation begins at admission with careful scrutiny of applications, letters of recommendation, references, and personal statements. Consider running personal statements through software that detects plagiarism. Interview day is key, and group interviews are helpful for observing peer-to-peer behavior and general group interactions. Have applicants role-play with current students or faculty, and have them work through case scenarios focused on

marginalized populations, such as individuals who live in poverty, first-generation college students, children who live in foster care, or individuals in the prison system. Ethics codes and standards of practice need to be discussed early on.

- Standards and expectations regarding academic progress, professionalism, and personal dispositions should be clear, uniform, applied across classes and throughout the program, clearly explained (e.g, on interview day, at orientation, in town halls, at the start and end of each semester), and presented in multiple formats (e.g., on the website, in the student handbook, in syllabi, in evaluations).

- When remediation plans are developed, thorough documentation is necessary. Remediation goals should be clear, concise, and measurable and related to the deficiency (e.g., academic deficits, professional dispositions, personal dispositions). Students should sign remediation plans along with program faculty, and copies need to be included in permanent files.

- Finally, ethical and legal dilemmas need to be infused throughout course work and the curriculum. Students should be offered multiple opportunities to raise ethical concerns in safe and inviting environments, in all counseling course work (including practicum and internship), and from experiences outside of the classroom (such as conferences or informal gatherings; Hutchens et al., 2013; *Keeton v. Anderson-Wiley*, 2010/2011; McAdams et al., 2007; *Ward v. Polite*, 2012; Ziomek-Daigle & Christensen, 2010).

Conclusion

This chapter provided an overview of gatekeeping and summarized two decades of gatekeeping research in counselor education. Academic considerations and personal dispositions were discussed, as were general requirements for entry into master's- or doctoral-level programs in counselor education. Information on interview day formats, including group interviews and the use of creativity during interviews, was presented. Student perceptions of gatekeeping, gatekeeping within accreditation frameworks, and recent litigation in counselor education were also included in this chapter.

As doctoral students in counselor education begin to assume roles as faculty members, as supervisors, and in advanced counseling positions, gatekeeping and protecting both the profession and clients will be their responsibility. Many processes and procedures have been documented and will be in place when they arrive at their new position. Careful screening of applicants; a well-thought-out interview day; the use of multiple assessments; and engaged program faculty, adjuncts, and program stakeholders should be the start of admission. Informed student assessment plans should also include multiple assessments, such as grades, tests, portfolios, and national examinations (e.g., the Counselor Preparation Comprehensive Examination), and faculty and students should discuss progress on a regular basis or at specific checkpoints in the program (e.g., prepracticum, preinternship). Personal dispositions will also need to be included in any assessment plan, as counselors need to be flexible, open to feedback, professional, culturally responsive, and able to work well with others. Should counselor educators have concerns about student progress, they will need to develop and executive remediation plans with goals that are measurable and relevant to the deficiency; all program faculty should be involved in this process and have input into the plan. These practices will guide future counselor educators in developing their own set of gatekeeping or evaluation procedures specific to the context of their work.

I am a midcareer counselor educator and program coordinator, someone who has 13 years of experience and another 20 years ahead of me, and I can attest that student issues will arise. I always feel confident that our detailed student assessment plan, which begins in recruitment and selection, provides checks and balances for both faculty and students. We are a program faculty who discuss student development and progress and meet as a team with students when deficiencies are noted. We have high expectations and expect to see improvement or growth in these areas while continuing to provide both challenge and support. And students involved in the few gatekeeping cases we have had over the years have moved on as counselors with greater awareness, sharper skills, and more knowledge about personality/career fit. Pay attention to your gut, trust your instincts, be proactive, document everything, consult with others, and rely on your team.

Additional Online Resources

ACA Code of Ethics
> https://www.counseling.org/knowledge-center/ethics

Council for the Accreditation of Educator Preparation Standards
> www.caepnet.org/standards/introduction

2016 Council for Accreditation of Counseling and Related Educational Programs Standards
> www.cacrep.org/wp-content/uploads/2017/07/2016-Standards-with-Glossary-7.2017.pdf

References

American Counseling Association. (2005). *ACA code of ethics.* Alexandria, VA: Author.

American Counseling Association. (2014). *ACA code of ethics.* Alexandria, VA: Author.

Baldo, T. D., Softas-Nall, B. C., & Shaw, S. F. (1997). Student review and retention in counselor education: An alternative to Frame and Stevens-Smith. *Counselor Education and Supervision, 35,* 245–253.

Brown-Rice, K., & Furr, S. (2015). Gatekeeping ourselves: Counselor educators' knowledge of colleagues' problematic behaviors. *Counselor Education and Supervision, 54,* 176–188. doi:10.1002/ceas.12012

Council for Accreditation of Counseling and Related Educational Programs. (2015). *CACREP 2016 standards.* Alexandria, VA: Author.

Council for the Accreditation of Educator Preparation. (2013). *Standard 3: Candidate quality, recruitment, and selectivity.* Retrieved from http://caepnet.org/standards/standard-3

Foster, J. M., Leppma, M., & Hutchinson, T. S. (2014). Students' perspectives on gatekeeping in counselor education: A case study. *Counselor Education and Supervision, 53,* 190–203. doi:10.1002/j.1556-6978.2014.00057.x

Frame, M. W., & Stevens-Smith, P. (1995). Out of harm's way: Enhancing monitoring and dismissal process in counselor education programs. *Counselor Education and Supervision, 35,* 118–129.

Gaubatz, M. D., & Vera, E. M. (2002). Do formalized gatekeeping procedures increase programs' follow-up with deficient trainees? *Counselor Education and Supervision, 41,* 294–305.

Henderson, K. L., & Dufrene, R. (2012). Student behaviors associated with remediation: A content analysis. *Counseling Outcome Research and Evaluation, 3,* 48–60.

Homrich, A. M., DeLorenzi, L. D., Bloom, Z. D., & Godbee, B. (2014). Making the case for standards of conduct in clinical training. *Counselor Education and Supervision, 53,* 126–144. doi:10.1002/j.1556-6978.2014.00053.x

Homrich, A. H., & Henderson, K. L. (2018). *Gatekeeping in the mental health professions.* Alexandria, VA: American Counseling Association.

Hutchens, N., Block, J., & Young, M. (2013). Counselor educators' gatekeeping responsibilities and students' first amendment rights. *Counselor Education and Supervision, 52,* 82–95. doi:10.1002/j.1556-6987.2013.000030.x

Jacobs, S. C., Huprich, S. K., Grus, C. L., Cage, E. A., Elman, N. S., Forrest, L., & Kaslow, N. J. (2011). Trainees with professional competency problems: Preparing trainers for difficult but necessary conversations. *Training and Education in Professional Psychology, 5,* 175–184.

Keeton v. Anderson-Wiley, 733 F. Supp. 2d 1368 (S.D. Ga. 2010), *aff'd,* 664 F.3d 865 (11th Cir. 2011).

Kelly, V. (2011). Assessing individual student progress: Meeting multiple accreditation standards and professional gatekeeping responsibilities. *Journal of Counselor Preparation and Supervision, 3,* 110–122.

Lumadue, C. A., & Duffy, T. H. (1999). The role of graduate programs as gatekeepers: A model of evaluating student counselor competencies. *Counselor Education and Supervision, 39,* 101–109.

McAdams, C. R., III, Foster, V., & Ward, T. J. (2007). Remediation and dismissal policies in counselor education: Lessons learned from a challenge in federal court. *Counselor Education and Supervision, 46,* 212–229. doi:10.1002/j.1556-6978.2007.tb00034.x

McCaughan, A. M., & Hill, N. R. (2015). The gatekeeping imperative in counselor education admission protocols: The criticality of personal qualities. *International Journal for the Advancement of Counseling, 37,* 28–40. doi:10.1007/s10447-014-9223-2

Nagpal, S., & Ritchie, M. H. (2002). Selection interviews of students for master's programs in counseling: An exploratory study. *Counselor Education and Supervision, 41,* 207–218.

Nelson, K. W., Canada, R. M., & Lancaster, L. B. (2003). An investigation of nonacademic admission criteria for doctoral-level counselor education and similar professional programs. *The Journal of Humanistic Counseling, 42,* 3–13.

Parker, L., Chang, C., Corthell, K., Walsh, M., Brack, G., & Grubbs, N. (2014). A grounded theory of counseling students who report problematic peers. *Counselor Education and Supervision, 53,* 111–125. doi:10.1002/j.1556-6978.2004

Rosenberg, J. I., Getzelman, M. A., Arcinue, F., & Oren, C. Z. (2005). An exploratory look at students' experiences of problematic peers in academic professional psychology programs. *Professional Psychology: Research and Practice, 36,* 665–673.

Smaby, M. H., Maddux, C. D., Richmond, A. S., Lepkowski, W. J., & Packman, J. (2005). Academic admission requirements as predictors of counseling knowledge, personal development, and counseling knowledge. *Counselor Education and Supervision, 45,* 43–57. doi:10.1002/j.1556-6978.2005.tb00129.x

Swank, J., & Smith-Adcock, S. (2013). Creative group strategies for interviewing applicants for counselor educator programs. *Journal of Counselor Preparation and Supervision, 5,* 38–48. doi:10.7729/51.0039

Swank, J., & Smith-Adcock, S. (2014). Gatekeeping during admissions: A survey of counselor education programs. *Counselor Education and Supervision, 53,* 47–61. doi:10.1002/j.1556-6978.2014.00048.x

Trimble, L. D., Stroebel, S. S., Krieg, F. J., & Rubenstein, R. L. (2012). Problematic students of NASP-approved programs: An exploratory study of graduate student view. *Psychology in the Schools, 49,* 589–605.

Ward v. Polite, 667 F.3d 727 (6th Cir. 2012).

Ward v. Wilbanks, No. 09-CV-11237, Doc. 1 (E.D. Mich., Apr. 2, 2009).

Ziomek-Daigle, J., & Bailey, D. F. (2011). Culturally responsive gatekeeping practices in counselor education. *Journal of Counseling Research and Practice, 1,* 14–22.

Ziomek-Daigle, J., & Christensen, T. (2010). An emergent theory of gatekeeping practices in counselor education. *Journal of Counseling & Development, 88,* 407–415. doi:10.1002/j.1556-6678.2010.tb00040.x

Chapter 6

The Practice of Scholarship, Research, and Grant Writing in Counselor Education

Ryan G. Carlson

Scholarship, research, and grant writing is a complex and multifaceted topic. To fully explore the nuances within the topic, it may help to first clarify differences between the terms *scholarship* and *research*, because these terms are often used synonymously in academia. However, *scholarship* takes many broad forms, such as presenting papers at conferences, writing books or book chapters (such as the chapter you are reading), or writing conceptual (i.e., nonresearch) papers for peer-reviewed publication. In fact, counselor educators frequently engage in many forms of nonresearch (i.e., data-based) scholarship. Although this type of scholarly activity helps to frame many important discussions, as well as bring awareness to relevant topics, it is not typically a grant-funded activity. There are exceptions, as some universities may provide limited funding through summer salary to support faculty time to write a book, for example. *Research* refers to a process of designing and conducting a study, with a supported methodology, that involves collecting qualitative or quantitative data. Data-based research activities are typically what grant funders seek when issuing a call for proposals. Counselor educators engage in diverse types of data-based research practices but often struggle to break the grant research barrier. However, lean federal and state allocations to support public institutions in higher education have increased the emphasis on grant-supported research, motivating many counselor educators to seek grant funding in support of data-based research. Thus, a culture of grant-supported research funding is beginning to emerge in counselor education. More training, development, and support for doctoral students and early career faculty will help support this emerging culture. The purpose of this chapter is to (a) demystify some of the terms and processes associated with research for grant writing and management; (b) describe factors that influence the process of scholarship, research, and grant writing in counselor education (including issues of diversity and social justice); and (c) present strategies to develop research and grant writing self-efficacy.

Diverse academic disciplines, institutional settings, and funders add to the complexity of research and grant writing. Moreover, a specialized discourse accompanies the process of research and grant writing. For example, acronyms such as RFP (request for proposal) and RFA (request for application) or terms such as *funding mechanism, indirect cost rate, preaward, postaward, no-cost extension,* and *carry-forward request* can add to the confusion. Scholars interested in pursuing grants need to understand the difference between funders and funding mechanisms within funding agencies as well as how to find current funding solicitations. Although there are several funding agencies, following is a brief list of examples: National Institutes of Health (NIH; www.nih.gov); National Science Foundation (www.nsf.gov); Institute of Education Sciences (https://ies.ed.gov/); Centers for Disease Control and Prevention (www.cdc.gov); National Institute of Justice (www.nij.gov); and a variety of large foundations, such as the William T. Grant Foundation (www.wtgrantfoundation.org). Each funder has an identified mission, goals, submission process, and review process. It generally takes time and experience to learn the difference between funders and ultimately identify a funding agency that may align with one's research interests. In addition, a federal website (www.grants.gov) serves as a clearinghouse for all federal agencies. Potential investigators can search for grants by funding agency or topic as well as receive regular updates on new solicitations. Pivot, formerly known as Community of Science (https://pivot.cos.com), is another helpful resource that many universities subscribe to on behalf of their faculty. Through Pivot, faculty can filter by topic and receive updates when new funding involving that particular topic is announced.

Factors That Influence Research and Grant Writing in Academia and Counselor Education

In regard to research and grant writing in counselor education, several factors may influence the practice of research through grant writing as well as the types of grants sought. The first such factor to consider is faculty time allocation. Faculty time is typically divided broadly among research, teaching, and service. The time allocated to each category may vary depending on the institution's goals and research classification. Faculty productivity is increasingly measured through scholarly endeavors. This is especially true of faculty employed at research-intensive universities but does not exclude faculty working at primarily teaching universities. (For a breakdown of the criteria used to categorize university research classifications, see http://carnegieclassifications.iu.edu/.) One reason for the emphasis on external funding is that state appropriations to higher education decreased during the Great Recession. State funding allocations to higher education in many states have not returned to prerecession levels. External funding contributes an additional revenue source through indirect cost rates and can help cover faculty salary costs. In addition, faculty may allocate a greater proportion of time to research if they work for universities that place a greater emphasis on research and scholarship to achieve tenure and promotion. Such faculty typically teach smaller course loads to help support time spent conducting research. Conversely, faculty may work in university settings that emphasize teaching and service over research. Thus, faculty in these settings may teach more courses, and their teaching performance may carry greater weight for tenure and promotion. Faculty time allocation may also be influenced by issues of diversity. For example, minority faculty may experience increased service and advising loads, which creates an added burden when developing research skills, resulting in less research productivity and more difficulty obtaining grant funding. The added service and advising loads may result from several factors, such as minority faculty feeling responsible for mentoring underrepresented students because of the scarcity of other minority faculty. In addition, majority faculty may inadvertently add to this burden by directing minority students to minority faculty. Finally, minority faculty may feel the need to work harder than majority faculty to create a stronger case for tenure and promotion.

Institution type and its associated work barriers (e.g., teaching load, service commitment) is a second primary factor that may influence the practice of research through grant writing (Easterly & Pemberton, 2008). Counselor education programs exist in diverse university settings (e.g., research, teaching, online). However, research universities may provide greater support and resources for faculty to pursue external funding as well as manage funding after it has been awarded (e.g., through specific offices within a college supported through indirect costs and designated to support aspects of grant management). This is not to say that faculty from teaching universities do not successfully pursue external funding but that research is typically allocated less time and does not carry as much weight in tenure and promotion decisions.

A third factor that could influence research through grant writing is that counselor educators represent diverse areas of expertise (e.g., school; mental health; marriage, couples, and family counseling) across diverse community and practice settings (e.g., community mental health agencies, hospitals, schools, universities, private practice). Within these areas, counselor educators have a variety of research interests that warrant diverse research methodologies. As a result, counselor educators frequently use quantitative, qualitative, or mixed-methods research designs. Quantitative research methods help identify the occurrence of a phenomenon or whether an intervention has the hypothesized effect. Qualitative methods are frequently used to describe a phenomenon or to more deeply understand the experiences of those under study. However, funding solicitations do not always align perfectly with one's specific research area or methodological specialties. Developing a research agenda that meets a funding agency's mission and goals and includes diverse methodologies requires intentional development through mentorship, understanding one's own biases toward one's research, collaborative learning experiences, and interdisciplinary working relationships. Establishing such relationships is discussed later in this chapter.

A fourth factor influencing the pursuit of research through grant writing is the competitive nature of winning a grant award. More faculty seeking external funding, combined with reduced budgets from funders, has resulted in low funding rates. For example, across 26 institutes and centers in 2015, the NIH reported an 18.3% research project success rate (calculated as the number of investigators who submitted proposals divided by the number of those awarded). Specific institutes within the NIH boast much lower funding rates (e.g., National Cancer Institute = 13.2%, National Institute of Child Health and Human Development = 11.5%; NIH Research Portfolio Online Reporting Tools, n.d.). Moreover, experienced investigators receive 40% of NIH funding; top-tier research institutions receive 60% of funding; and, according to various reports on the NIH's website, the average age of first-time-funded NIH investigators is approximately 42 years (Barr, 2015). Although the NIH has prioritized initiatives to support early career investigators and diversify funding, investigators with more experience and those from top-tier research institutions likely have an edge. This, combined with increased pressure from university administrators to obtain external funding, has resulted in some faculty experiencing a decrease in work satisfaction (Anderson & Slade, 2016). In addition, Hill (2004) identified challenges that new faculty in counselor education may experience, such as (a) multiple time demands, (b) isolation, (c) unrealistic expectations, and (d) a lack of feedback and recognition. Therefore, creating a culture of collaboration, mentorship, and early exposure seems critical to training future faculty, especially counselor education faculty who are often underrepresented in grant proposal submissions and awards.

The published, peer-reviewed literature on research related to grant writing is concentrated in public health disciplines, such as nursing and medicine, as well as psychology and social work (Burrow-Sánchez, Martin, & Imel, 2016; Conn, Porter, McDaniel, Rantz, & Maas, 2005; Jacob & Lefgren, 2011; Savundranayagam, 2014). My search for peer-reviewed publications on grant writing specific to counselor education yielded no results. However, counselor education publications have focused on the development of researcher self-efficacy (e.g., Lambie & Vaccaro, 2011; Okech, Astramovich, Johnson, Hoskins, & Rubel, 2006) in doctoral students and early career faculty as well as on counselor identity development (e.g., Gibson, Dollarhide, & Moss, 2010; Limberg et al., 2013; Moss,

Gibson, & Dollarhide, 2014). Therefore, integrating research, grant writing, and management literature from related disciplines with researcher self-efficacy and identity development literature from counselor education may help provide a platform for conceptualizing how counselor educators can develop in their practice of scholarship, research, and grant writing.

Developing as a Researcher, Grant Writer, and Manager

Developing as a researcher, grant writer, and manager is an intentional process that takes time. Through qualitative interviews, Gibson et al. (2010) identified a process of counselor identity development through which counselors progress over time to eventually arrive at a position of higher self-efficacy. In their model of counselor development, Gibson and colleagues described a process from seeking external validation from professors, peers, and supervisors to achieving self-validation. Counselors in the self-validation phase described a commitment to learning, a sense of professional community, and the ability to integrate their personal and professional identities. Developing an identity as a researcher and grant writer can be conceptualized in much the same way. Many counselor education doctoral students enter doctoral programs as practicing counselors. Thus, they likely have a strong identity as a counselor but have little if any identity as a researcher and grant writer. Mentorship, collaboration, and early exposure are activities doctoral students and early career faculty can engage in to begin developing their research and grant writing identity (Limberg et al., 2013).

Mentorship and Collaboration

Mentorship increases doctoral student and early career faculty research self-efficacy (Lambie & Vaccaro, 2011; Niles, Akos, & Cutler, 2001). Okech et al. (2006) conducted a mixed-methods study identifying doctoral research training in counselor education. Results highlighted mentorship as critical in research training for doctoral students. Savundranayagam (2014) identified the role of sustained mentorship as a result of a project from the NIH's National Institute on Aging designed to support gerontological research by faculty in social work. Savundranayagam identified having senior scientists review a proposal before submission as one of the biggest benefits of participating in this funded mentorship opportunity. Doctoral students and early career faculty who work with a mentor on grant writing and submission are introduced to the complex process of submitting a grant, which helps to demystify the process and increase their likelihood of submitting and obtaining future grant funding.

As a doctoral student, I worked on three federally funded grants. In addition to implementing our grant research, our team regularly applied for funding with the hopes of sustaining this research. These experiences enabled me to learn grant-specific language, such as *indirect cost rate* (the rate charged by universities to funding agencies to cover overhead expenses), *funding mechanism* (the specific mechanism within a funding agency that defines a proposal's expectations), *no-cost extension* (the ability to continue a grant beyond the funding period while using unspent monies), and *carry-over request* (a request by the grantee to carry forward unspent monies from one grant year to the next). Learning grant-specific language and working with a team to ask questions about what funders mean when they use this language can help reduce the anxiety associated with grant writing and management. Our research team developed an internal process for pursuing grants that began with an initial reading of the proposal, followed by a discussion and group read of the grant application. The purpose of the initial read was to determine whether the application was a potential fit for our work. Then, during the group read and discussion, we fleshed out potential ideas and discussed the project's feasibility. An experienced faculty mentor facilitated this grant review process, but each person around the table was treated equally. At the very least, we developed a familiarity with various funders and the structure of grant applications.

In addition, these types of process-oriented research experiences provide an opportunity for researchers to discuss any potential biases toward the research topic that might inherently influence the study. Pack-Brown, Thomas, and Seymour (2008) discussed addressing social justice issues in counseling by helping students to become more aware of their own biases as well as learn to assess clients from a multicultural lens. Diversity among study team members allows for broader perspectives when considering the topic of interest as well as a greater opportunity to consider how the cultural context of the target population should be considered in the study design. Moreover, an additional benefit to including diverse study team members concerns the issue of underrepresented faculty in higher education. As counselor education and other programs in higher education seek to address the immense gap in diverse faculty, counselor educators should be intentional about providing research mentorship. Mentorship and access to experiential research opportunities are essential for the retention of underrepresented students and early career faculty.

Early career faculty may be encouraged to collaborate on grant proposals with more senior faculty or with faculty across disciplines. Such collaborations create opportunities for mentorship from senior faculty. Working with faculty from other disciplines creates a team approach that allows each investigator to contribute in his or her area of expertise. Funding agencies value cross-disciplinary collaborations because complex problems are often better solved with diverse perspectives. Counselor educators bring unique contributions to collaborations because they often have strong partnerships with community agencies, schools or school administrators, and private practitioners. These partnerships create opportunities to develop research that can be tested in real-world applications, with community members who are most likely to use the tested services (e.g., effectiveness studies), resulting in innovative and high-impact results. Mentors and collaborators may work together on grant proposals from external or internal sources. It is also important for mentors to use intentional practices that include underrepresented students or early career faculty. Counselor education faculty from underrepresented groups report feeling as though they have limited mentorship opportunities, particularly at predominantly White institutions, and they are not provided with the same opportunities as their majority counterparts (Salazar, 2005). The variance in mentorship and disproportionate opportunities create a system that continues to favor majority students and faculty. Therefore, mentorship and collaborative opportunities should be intentionally provided for underrepresented students and early career faculty to proactively reduce feelings of alienation.

Internal Seed Funding

Many universities or professional organizations may provide doctoral students or early career faculty with internal seed funding opportunities. Internal proposals are typically broader in scope so that they appeal to diverse faculty within a university setting. Applications from internal sources are generally for smaller dollar amounts, but the primary purpose is to help doctoral students or early career faculty gain experience with writing competitive grant applications and collect preliminary data that can be used to help support a larger application from a federal funding agency. Internal funding may present doctoral students and early career faculty with an opportunity to engage in cross-disciplinary collaborations and to develop community partners. Preexisting community partnerships are often valued by external funders because they demonstrate that the investigator has the capacity and support to implement a proposed investigation.

Internal grant application reviewers may strive to be more developmental in the feedback they provide than reviewers from external funding agencies. For example, during my first year as an assistant professor, I submitted a proposal in response to a university-wide competitive application designed to support nontenured, tenure-track faculty. I was not funded, but I received very helpful feedback from reviewers outside my field of study. Based on the reviewers' feedback, I revised my proposal with more clarity and a stronger research design. I resubmitted my revised proposal the following year and was awarded funding. Although still an intimidating process, the pursuit of internal seed funding demonstrates a trajectory toward external funding, provides an opportunity to collect preliminary data and publish the findings, and helps one establish an identity as a researcher and granter writer.

One final point regarding the benefits of internal seed funding is that it provides early-stage investigators with experience in managing a grant after it has been awarded (e.g., hiring a graduate assistant, purchasing supplies [e.g., computer hardware, software, or assessments], seeking travel reimbursement). Postaward grant management processes vary largely by university and university supports. For example, a large research university may have a budget office dedicated to managing grant-related expenditures, whereas other universities may not. Experiences with smaller grant awards may help an investigator understand how to navigate these logistical procedures. Grant funds support faculty time on related projects through course buyouts; however, grant management is often overlooked when considering the allocation of time to specific grant-related tasks. Time allocation is overlooked because it is difficult to estimate the amount of time spent on unexpected tasks, such as responding to grant-related emails, or planned tasks, such as drafting required quarterly or yearly reports for funders. Managing grants can also be associated with added stress stemming from the responsibility one may feel to ensure that grant deadlines are met and deliverables produced. In addition, the skills used in managing grants are not typically taught in counselor education degree programs. For example, as a project director responsible for hiring and managing a large grant team, I learned the importance of interviewing skills to hire appropriately for a given position as well as developing a training protocol and organizational supervision (which can be quite different from clinical supervision) to help develop staff skills. My learning curve was steep and required external training, but I continue to use these skills on current research projects that involve graduate assistants.

University-Supported Grant Workshops

Early career faculty and doctoral students may benefit from participating in university-sponsored grant writing workshops. Burrow-Sánchez et al. (2016) recommended that doctoral students attend a grant writing workshop. University development offices may provide grant workshop series at no cost for faculty and students. These workshops are often specific to various aspects of proposal writing, such as how to create *specific aims* (a term frequently used in NIH grant applications and included in proposals to highlight the foci of the proposed project), write the narrative in a manner that is concise and minimizes jargon, develop the budget, or manage the grant after it has been awarded. In addition to being a learning opportunity, grant writing workshops may also provide students and faculty with a chance to network and meet other investigators from across the university setting.

Developing an Identity as a Researcher and Grant Writer

Counselor educators represent scholars of diverse clinical backgrounds, training, and ultimately research interests. Not all research topics are of interest to agencies and organizations that fund grants. It is not uncommon to hear people in counselor education state that they do not pursue grant support for their research because there are no grants that align with their research interests. Although this may be true, it is also important for counselor educators to consider how research topics may be relevant to stakeholders (e.g., taxpayers who fund colleges and universities) and how research topics of interest can be adapted to both highlight counselor educators' strengths as well as fit within the scope of the mission and vision of various funding agencies. This process can be referred to as *developing a fundable research agenda.*

Develop a Fundable Research Agenda

I recently attended a regional seminar hosted by the NIH that aimed to teach attendees how to write successful proposals and manage grants after they have been awarded. (Note that the NIH conducts two regional seminars per year; see https://grants.nih.gov/news/contact-in-person/seminars.htm for additional information.) Attendees primarily consisted of scientists from medical and biomedical fields. I was struck by the consistent language and discourse used to describe their research. I cannot recall once hearing the term *research interest* but instead heard *science* or *scientific inquiry.* Although there is no arguing the vast differences between the counselor education and biomedical fields, it is important to remember that the counselor education field exists within the category of social scientists. Thus, it may be helpful for counselor educators to conceptualize research as a type of science and reduce their use of the term *research interest.* As counselors, we are skilled at invoking emotion from our clients and creating cathartic experiences during session. We may rely on these tactics when describing the importance of our research interests and struggle to understand when stakeholders do not seem to value our research. Creating a fundable research agenda does not mean that one abandons passionate topics, but simply means that one seeks to understand how those topics might be integrated into a current grant solicitation or how they may complement another area of science. Doctoral students can be encouraged to have conversations surrounding their research early in their program of study. For example, the professional issues course may provide an opportunity to address grant writing as well as help students begin to identify a fundable research agenda. Developing community partnerships provides another opportunity for counselor educators to create a fundable research agenda. Counselor education programs likely have strong community ties given the experiential nature of graduate students' programs of study. Early career faculty and doctoral students can build on these partnerships and identify opportunities to develop mutually beneficial grant proposals.

Infuse Research and Grant Writing Into Doctoral Curricula

The 2016 Council for Accreditation of Counseling and Related Educational Programs (CACREP) Standards (CACREP, 2015) mandate that doctoral training programs include grant writing (Standard 6.B.4.k.— "grant proposals and other sources of funding") as a form of professional identity. In addition, the learning environment standards address extending knowledge and informing the profession through research (Standard 6.A.2). Therefore, throughout doctoral course work, counselor education faculty should create assignments and activities that may help doctoral students begin to develop an identity as a researcher and grant writer. For example, a logic model is sometimes required by funders in a grant proposal application. Logic models vary in design but typically demonstrate the flow of a proposed research study while identifying short- and long-term goals. Students or early career faculty can complete a logic model with any research idea as a means of helping flesh out study logistics and determine feasibility.

As an activity, use a current research idea and complete a logic model. Logic models typically contain five sections: (a) inputs, or the project participants and strategies for recruiting the sample; (b) activities, or the core activities of the project, such as random assignment and the actual intervention; (c) outputs, or programmatic benchmarks, such as the number of people who will complete the study; (d) immediate outcomes, or short-term goals, such as anticipated findings from the study; and (e) ultimate goals, or long-term goals, such as the contribution of the anticipated findings to the overall goal (i.e., the funder's mission). After completing each section of the logic model, discuss with colleagues or among doctoral students what it was like to develop these goals. How has this process enhanced the initial research idea?

In addition, setting research goals may help the process of developing a research and grant writing identity seem less overwhelming and more intentional. One strategy that I use is to set semester scholarship goals using what I call a *scholarship schedule*. At the beginning of each semester, I update my scholarship schedule with papers that are in progress or anticipated during the current semester as well as grant applications. I set submission goals and then update again at the end of the semester to help monitor my progress. This process may not be helpful for everyone, but students and early career faculty can be encouraged to develop a system that works best for their work style. Figure 6.1 is an example of a growth and goals worksheet that can be used to (a) help identify areas of concern, (b) clarify goals, (c) identify specific tasks related to the goals, and (d) specify benchmarks to serve as indicators of goal achievement. Either during class or through mentorship, doctoral students and early career faculty can be encouraged to complete the growth and goals worksheet to help identify intentional steps in their identity development as a researcher, grant writer, and manager. Goals can be more process oriented, such as working through low self-efficacy and thoughts of "I'm not smart enough for this," or more concrete, such as "I will attend two university-sponsored grant workshops this semester."

Conclusion

Research through grant writing is a competitive process but one that has become a necessity for faculty in higher education. Barriers to and facilitators of research through grant writing vary depending on an institution's goals, faculty time allocation, related supports, and research bias. In addition, counselor educators have typically been underrepresented in gaining external funding. However, creating a counselor educator identity that includes a fundable research agenda is a developmental process. This

Identify an area for growth (e.g., What is the problem?).
What is your subsequent goal for the semester?

What needs to be accomplished to achieve this deliverable?		
Task 1:	S:	Benchmark:
	T:	
	O:	
	R:	
	M:	
Task 2:	S:	Benchmark:
	T:	
	O:	
	R:	
	M:	

Specific = How can you make this task more specific?
Timeline = When, or how frequently, will this task be measured?
Operational = What are the specific steps in meeting this task?
Realistic = How realistic is this task and timeline?
Measurable = How will this be measured and with what tool?

Figure 6.1
Growth and Goals Worksheet

101

developmental process can be facilitated for doctoral students and early career faculty through mentorship, collaboration, early exposure, and participation in grant workshops or other grant-related activities. Counselor educators have much to offer and excel in partnering with community agencies. These partnerships can result in innovative and high-impact research that can help solve social problems and improve client outcomes.

References

Anderson, D., & Slade, C. P. (2016). Managing institutional research advancement: Implications from a university faculty time allocation study. *Research in Higher Education, 57,* 99–121. doi:10.1007//s11162-015-9376-9

Barr, R. (2015). *R01 teams and grantee age trends in grant funding.* Retrieved from https://www.nia.nih.gov/research/blog/2015/04/r01-teams-and-grantee-age-trends-grant-funding

Burrow-Sánchez, J. J., Martin, J. L., & Imel, Z. E. (2016). Applying for grant funding as a counseling psychologist: From thought to action. *The Counseling Psychologist, 44,* 479–524. doi:10.1177/0011000015626272

Conn, V. S., Porter, R. T., McDaniel, R. W., Rantz, M. J., & Maas, M. L. (2005). Building research productivity in an academic setting. *Nursing Outlook, 53,* 224–231. doi:10.1016/j.outlook.2005.02.005

Council for Accreditation of Counseling and Related Educational Programs. (2015). *CACREP 2016 standards.* Alexandria, VA: Author.

Easterly, D., & Pemberton, C. L. A. (2008). Understanding barriers and supports to proposal writing as perceived by female associate professors: Achieving promotion to professor. *Research Management Review, 16,* 1–17.

Gibson, D. M., Dollarhide, C. T., & Moss, J. M. (2010). Professional identity development: A grounded theory of transformational tasks of new counselors. *Counselor Education and Supervision, 50,* 21–38.

Hill, N. R. (2004). The challenges experienced by pretenured faculty members in counselor education: A wellness perspective. *Counselor Education and Supervision, 44,* 135–146.

Jacob, B. A., & Lefgren, L. (2011). The impact of research grant funding on scientific productivity. *Journal of Public Economics, 95,* 1168–1177. doi:10.1016/j.jpubeco.2011.05.005

Lambie, G. W., & Vaccaro, N. (2011). Doctoral counselor education students' levels of research self-efficacy, perceptions of the research training environment, and interest in research. *Counselor Education and Supervision, 50,* 243–258. doi:10.1002/j.1556-6978.2011.tb00122.x

Limberg, D., Bell, H., Super, J. T., Jacobson, L., Fox, J., DePue, M. K., . . . Lambie, G. W. (2013). Professional identity development of counselor education doctoral students: A qualitative investigation. *The Professional Counselor, 3,* 40–53.

Moss, J. M., Gibson, D. M., & Dollarhide, C. T. (2014). Professional identity development: A grounded theory of transformational tasks of counselors. *Journal of Counseling & Development, 92,* 3–12. doi:10.1002/j.1556-6676.2014.00124.x

National Institutes of Health Research Portfolio Online Reporting Tools. (n.d.). *Success rates*. Retrieved from https://report.nih.gov/success_rates/index.aspx

Niles, S. G., Akos, P., & Cutler, H. (2001). Counselor educators' strategies for success. *Counselor Education and Supervision, 40,* 276–291.

Okech, J. E. A., Astramovich, R. L., Johnson, M. M., Hoskins, W. J., & Rubel, D. J. (2006). Doctoral research training of counselor education faculty. *Counselor Education and Supervision, 46,* 131–145.

Pack-Brown, S. P., Thomas, T. L., & Seymour, J. M. (2008). Infusing professional ethics into counselor education programs: A multicultural/social justice perspective. *Journal of Counseling & Development, 86,* 296–302. doi:10.1002/j.1556-6678.2008.tb00512.x

Salazar, C. F. (2005). Outsiders in a White, middle-class system: Counselor educators of color in academe. *The Journal of Humanistic Counseling, 44,* 240–252. doi:10.1002/j.2164-490X.2005.tb00034.x

Savundranayagam, M. Y. (2014). The role of sustained mentorship in grant success. *Educational Gerontology, 40,* 272–277. doi:10.1080/0360 1277.2014.852934

Chapter 7

Faculty Review, Promotion, and Tenure Processes

Susan Furr

You have just landed that first job, and you are excited that you are going to become a counselor educator and join the ranks of academia. After years of studying, writing papers, and reviewing both your own and supervisees' recordings of counseling sessions, you are finally going to put all that you have learned into practice. You arrive at your new destination and move into your office (I hope one with a window) and begin to survey the landscape. What does it really mean to enter the world of the tenure-track professor?

Despite all of your excitement, there may be a growing anxiety about the journey toward tenure. You know that you are expected to fulfill the big three—teaching, research, and service. Although they may carry different labels, the tenure process generally expects faculty members to contribute to a broad array of expectations that are often difficult to juggle. In this chapter, I discuss each aspect of this process along with suggestions for how to navigate this process in a manner that leads to success. Throughout this chapter, I explore the expectations new professors encounter as they seek tenure. I begin by exploring the decision to enter academia, giving consideration to the nature of an academic job. However, the majority of the chapter is devoted to examining that somewhat vague and even mysterious process of obtaining tenure and some of the challenges along the way. Included in this chapter is a discussion of definitions and steps toward tenure, the components of tenure, and the issues faced by diverse job applicants. By becoming familiar with the language of tenure and general expectations, you will be able to formulate your own questions to pose during the interview process.

Are You Ready for Academia?

I must confess that I came to a tenure-track position as a midcareer transition. I worked in the university counseling center for many years and usually taught one graduate course each semester as part of my duties. I did a little publishing, but research was not part of my job duties. But over these years, I realized that preparing the next generation of professional counselors was my aspiration. I had little formal guidance in how to navigate this process but fortunately had supportive colleagues who helped with some aspects of the tenure process. But along the way, I did have some stumbles in terms of making good choices with the use of my time and documenting all that I accomplished. As counselors, we are focused on helping others, whereas in academia we have to stay focused on what will facilitate a successful path to tenure. Unfortunately, I said yes too many times to requests that may have been helpful to the larger community but did not contribute to the goal of tenure. Finding a balance between being a good citizen and keeping a sharp vision of what is required for tenure is a challenge. The purpose of this chapter is to help you become familiar with the tenure journey and potential challenges you will encounter. Each university will have its own well-developed documentation for how tenure is envisioned for its particular faculty. Become familiar with these ideas early in your journey. But also find ways to identify those faculty members who can assist you in the nuances of what these documents actually mean in the cultural context of the university. Think of it as a family system that has both overt rules and rules that are understood but not directly stated. And get guidance when these two sets of rules appear to contradict each other. Institutional expectations around tenure have been described by new counselor education faculty as being "unclear and unrealistic" (Magnuson, Norem, & Lonneman-Doroff, 2009, p. 60). Yet tenure is the doorway to one of the most enjoyable, rewarding, and exciting careers you may ever discover.

Taking the First Steps

After years of being a student, you may believe that you have a good understanding of the academic community. But knowing how to meet the expectations of the classroom as a student is only a portion of the academic demands you will face as a new assistant professor. The tripartite model used in most institutions of higher education includes the areas of teaching, research, and service or community involvement. It is essential that you know the expectations for how you are to divide your time given that time is your most precious commodity. Is there a 40/40/20 split, with the belief that 40% of your time is devoted to teaching, 40% to research, and 20% to service? Or is teaching expected to consume more than 50%

of your time? Once you have this guideline, make decisions judiciously in terms of your commitments.

I hope you have used your years as a doctoral student to begin building credentials in these three areas. Each of these areas is supported in the Council for Accreditation of Counseling and Related Educational Programs (CACREP) Standards (CACREP, 2015), but how does your course work translate to being successful as a counselor educator? What have you done beyond the classroom requirements to position yourself to be a good candidate for your ideal career? The most recent CACREP Standards require that doctoral students complete internships in at least three of five doctoral core areas (counseling, teaching, supervision, research and scholarship, and leadership and advocacy). It is important to make careful choices that will enhance your marketability for the type of position you desire. Once in the position, you will begin the often confusing and complicated journey toward tenure.

One note of caution is needed in terms of readiness for the job market. A growing number of positions that are posted require that the candidate either be licensed or at least be license eligible. You may want to consistently review positions that are posted to examine the expectations. In a recent review of more than 40 positions on HigherEdJobs (www.higheredjobs. com) for which a new graduate would be eligible, I found that 25% required a license, 16% preferred that the candidate be licensed, and 50% required that the candidate be licensed or license eligible. In addition, several positions asked for the candidate to have multiple years of full-time work experience as a counselor. If you entered your doctoral program directly from your master's program, you may want to consider gaining additional experience in the field before graduation. You may find that the more experience you have sitting in the chair as a counselor, the more enriched your teaching will become. Having taught with a large number of doctoral students, I have observed that those who have strong practice backgrounds are able to draw from these personal experiences in a way that adds more credibility to their teaching and supervision.

Research findings indicate that 43% of counselor education doctoral students believe that faculty members have inadequate supervision skills and 28% of faculty members have inadequate clinical skills (Furr & Brown-Rice, 2016). Faculty colleagues also share this view because 49% rated colleagues as having inadequate clinical skills (Brown-Rice & Furr, 2015). Being a strong candidate for faculty positions is the foundation for being a successful faculty member. Any weaknesses in your preparation are likely to show up in the tenure process. Having strong clinical preparation, solid teaching experiences, and in-depth research experiences is a great pathway toward tenure.

The Role of Tenure

Academic tenure is defined as an indefinite appointment that can only be terminated for cause, a concept that has come under fire in recent years because of public assumptions that have not been substantiated. Some of these criticisms of tenure include the belief that once tenured, faculty members cease to teach and have reduced productivity. However, no empirical data support this notion (Allen, 2000). In fact, a recent study indicated that full professors worked more hours than professors at other ranks (Ziker, 2014). Another misconception is that tenure is a guaranteed job for life, when the reality is that tenure is actually a right to due process, which means that a professor who displays incompetence or engages in unprofessional behaviors can be dismissed.

Tenure was put into place to preserve academic freedom; however, new professors may be fearful of propagating ideas that may bring criticism because of the subjectivity of the tenure process. For example, taking on social justice causes that may be controversial in the community could be viewed as a great risk to obtaining tenure, which may present a challenge to new professors from diverse backgrounds who want to speak out about racism or bias but do not know how their actions will be viewed when tenure approaches. As a new professor, you may have to give consideration to how your views and values fit into the principles of the larger college or university system. But even with these limitations, tenure is a benefit of devoting oneself to professional excellence where expectations are high but financial rewards limited. The added elements of job security and a high level of autonomy are often the compensation for the financial constraints.

Know the Terminology

Although tenure is the most central component of the faculty review process, it may be presented in different formats. The two approaches most commonly used are promotion and tenure (P&T) and reappointment, promotion, and tenure (RPT). In systems that use RPT, the reappointment is the first step toward tenure and provides an extension of the original faculty contract. The road to tenure actually spans a 6- or 7-year time frame in both approaches. The difference between the two formats is in how feedback is provided in the middle of the journey toward tenure.

The advantage of a reappointment process is that the faculty member receives feedback on progress toward tenure midway through the tenure process through a formal procedure similar to the one used for tenure. One purpose of such a review is to evaluate how faculty members are displaying their potential for tenure. In this method, the faculty member follows many of the same processes as would be used in the P&T document. Often the materials include sections on teaching philosophy, research agenda, and service activities. Given that this document could be produced as early as the end of the second year, the number of teaching evaluations or published research manuscripts might be limited, but the purpose is to examine whether the pieces are being put in place for tenure. Often language such as *achievement* and *promise* is incorporated into the reappointment document. In universities that use the reappointment process, the documents may be reviewed by the department, department chair, school or college, dean, and provost.

Universities that follow the P&T model will also provide feedback along the way but may limit the number of levels of review. For example, this review may be limited to review by the departmental committee of tenured faculty members, the department chair, and the dean. In this model, the faculty member may be hired under a provisional or probationary process in which there may be multiple reviews, such as second-year and fourth-year provisional tenure reviews. More common is a third-year review that helps the school or college become aware of the progress the faculty member is making in relation to the tenure criteria. There are many variations of this model, so it is important that you become familiar with your institution's tenure process even before accepting a position. Universities provide this information online, so it has become easy to examine the tenure process and criteria before an interview.

Dossier is a term frequently used in the RPT process but may be unfamiliar. In essence, it is your tenure portfolio that contains both your pedagogy of teaching, research agenda, and service activities along with the evidence that supports your achievements in each of these areas. When I made my move from the counseling center to an academic position, I did not recognize the importance of keeping detailed records of everything I did. Having to go back to my weekly planner and recreate all of my activities was a daunting task. By keeping detailed records of all committee meetings, student activities in which you participated, workshops (both ones you facilitated and those you attended), and any other community service, you will be able to create a comprehensive picture of your contributions to the department. Some activities that you can easily lose track of include writing letters of recommendation, completing licensure forms for students, giving guest lectures in classes for other disciplines, and engaging in mentoring activities. One new twist to this evaluation process is looking not only at the activities in which you have been a participant but also at the impact of these activities. It may not be enough to state that you have been a member of the student recruitment and retention committee; you may need to provide a synopsis of strategies developed by the committee, which strategies have been implemented, and the measured outcomes of those strategies. Because you will be so busy actually doing these activities, you may just forget to write them down. It is important that you develop your strategy for recording these events as they occur. Whether you use electronic means or a daily planner, develop your method of tracking activities from day one. One method that I have continued to use (because I figured out I needed to keep track) involves using my university's annual report form. Most universities require some type of annual reporting of activities that may have a template to follow. By recording activities in this format as they occur, you can accomplish two goals with one reporting instrument.

One factor that influences teaching loads and work expectations is the Carnegie classification of an institution. Although there have been changes to the classification system, you will still hear administrators talk about Carnegie's Research 1 and 2. The terminology then changed to doctoral/research *extensive* and *intensive*. The first general category for postgraduate programs is Graduate Instructional Programs, with all counseling programs falling under this category. If there is also a doctoral program, it will be under the Doctoral Universities category. The current terminology for doctoral research universities is divided into three parts: research universities with very high research activity, research universities with high research activity, and research universities with moderate research activity. In 2015 a total of 335 institutions fell into the Doctoral Universities category (Center for Postsecondary Research, 2016). Why is this information important to know? The expectations around research will be congruent with the classification of your university.

Expectations for publication will generally be two or three refereed publications per year, with the higher expectation being at doctorate-granting institutions with very high research expectations. These institutions usually have lower teaching loads to balance the higher research expectations and may (CACREP) even provide more research support, such as graduate assistants. This information is very important to explore when interviewing. If your institution is not a doctorate-granting entity, then it will fall under Master's Colleges and Universities (larger programs, medium programs, and small programs), with 741 institutions belonging to this category (Center for Postsecondary Research, 2016). As you can see from these data, more programs fall into the master's degree areas, which may not place as much emphasis on research or may not even have expectations for publication. According to CACREP (2017), there are 72 accredited doctoral programs in counselor education and supervision and 346 universities with accredited master's programs. In online and for-profit institutions there may be little emphasis on research as well as the possibility that tenure is not an option (Chait, 2002). In these institutions, faculty are not as likely to participate in shared governance or to experience the same degree of academic freedom (Tierney & Lechuga, 2010). At some institutions, there is a possibility for promotion in rank but not an option for tenure. Other institutions have an annual review process and merit-based raises with a primary focus on the quality of teaching but do not have a path to tenure. Research and professional involvement is encouraged, and faculty members often engage in conference presentations and leadership in the field. Thus, carefully examining the contract and terms of employment is essential before committing to a position. In addition, institutions that are totally dependent on student tuition for operation may create pressure to recruit and retain students that may be contrary to the type of faculty role you are seeking. Knowing the classification of the institution as well as the expectations of your program and college will help you craft appropriate questions about research expectations.

Tenure clock is an informal term that is used to denote the timeline for the tenure process. The clock starts ticking as soon as you begin your new position and typically runs continuously until the specified review dates. One of the most important pieces of information you need to know is this timeline. As mentioned previously in the discussion of RPT and P&T guidelines, your first review could come as early as the end of your second year. The review for tenure typically begins at the end of your fifth year. In a few circumstances, the clock can be stopped for events such as the birth or adoption of a child or illness of self or a significant family member. But in reality, not all counseling programs provide positive support for these events (Trepal & Stinchfield, 2012). Trepal and Stinchfield (2012) found that although there was flexibility in the job, some counselor educators experienced discrimination around changing parental status. There was fear that slowing the tenure clock may not be viewed in a favorable light.

As you interview for faculty positions, you may want to investigate university policy around family leave as well as gain insight into how such situations have been handled previously. Although those who conduct job interviews are prohibited from asking personal questions about your family, you are free to ask about their experiences through the tenure process. If younger faculty members have young children, you may be able to explore how they have managed balancing tenure and family.

Why Is Tenure So Difficult?

Awarding tenure to a faculty member implies a lifelong commitment between the institution and the faculty member that could extend 30 or more years. In the long run, your institution could be committing millions of dollars to you throughout your life at the university. Although there are circumstances in which a tenured professor can be terminated, such as disregard of duties, harassment, incompetence, criminal acts, and violation of institutional policy, faculty members generally enjoy a wide range of freedoms not found in other professions. According Euben (2004), who was speaking for the American Association of University Professors, "Tenure is a presumption of competence and continuing service that can be overcome only if specified conditions are met" (p. 2). Tenure does not guarantee employment but does ensure that the professor is protected against arbitrary dismissal and has a right to due process (Scheuerman, 1997).

Decisions about tenure are immensely important because they determine the quality of the institution for many years to come. Not only have you been hired to fulfill certain program needs, but your program should also have a vision of the future and how you fit into those plans. Fortunately for counselor education programs, doctoral graduates are prepared to teach many of the core courses that are necessary to meet CACREP Standards. As much as you may love your specialty courses or electives, you need to be able to contribute to the fundamental mission of the program. If you have not completed your graduate studies, consider what courses you can coteach that would transfer to any counseling program. One bonus of teaching these courses is that you enter your new position with some courses already prepared. In general, your value to the program is increased when you bring a needed specialty such as school counseling, clinical mental health, or addiction counseling. Being able to contribute to both the core and a specialty area provides great value to the teaching mission of the program and enhances your contributions to the teaching aspect of tenure. Be prepared to become the faculty member the program just cannot do without.

However, tenure is more than a simple summing of annual evaluations. Although aggregating the number of activities such as courses taught and articles published is a part of the review, the true meaning of tenure is that the faculty member shows real promise of becoming a scholar who influences the field. It is up to the tenure candidate to make the case for being able to engage in sustained contributions to the field of counseling as well as to the program. One must demonstrate that granting tenure is in the best interest of the university. Tenure allows the faculty member to pursue innovative and even controversial ideas over a period of years without fear of reprisal or upsetting the status quo. Ironically, many of these initially unpopular ideas eventually help reshape how the field views an issue. Freedom to pursue new concepts without fear of losing employment is key to the birth of knowledge.

Fortunately, in today's tenure system, faculty members are not competing against one another for tenure in most settings. In the past, a program might have hired several assistant professors who would vie for the tenured position. In a high-prestige university, new professors were willing to take this risk, knowing that being affiliated with an outstanding institution could help them become attractive candidates at other institutions. That type of competition has largely been eliminated; now if you are hired in a tenure-track position, you do not compete against others for tenure. The competition is relegated to placing oneself against the often confusing and even shifting standards of the college and university.

Know the Steps

As a new professor, you will embark on what is typically a 6-year journey toward tenure—the longest probationary period of any profession. Although you will have a great amount of freedom to determine much of your schedule, you will also face many competing demands with little clear guidance around which voices carry the most weight. Wanting to please everyone, you may find your own goals and purpose not being fulfilled. In the job search process, you may be so eager to get a position (after all, there are those loans to pay) that you may not investigate how well the position fits with your philosophy, goals, and personal values. Research that followed a cohort of new counselor education faculty members for 6 years found that dissatisfaction arose when personal views were incongruent with the program's views (Magnuson et al., 2009).

Be prepared to encounter colleagues who have different views and passions about the field. That is a natural trait of any organization and can even be a strength. The key is whether these differences are handled respectfully with room to accommodate the differences. My own research showed that 75% of respondents who were counselor educators had observed a peer demonstrating problems of professional competency, with the most common types of problematic behavior being unable to regulate emotions, demonstrating unprofessional behavior, and displaying psychological concerns (Brown-Rice & Furr, 2015). Finding a faculty that is a good fit for you in terms of philosophy and values, work expectations, and collegial support provides the underpinnings that will support your tenure journey.

Timeline

Each university has its own timeline for tenure that outlines the levels of review and the components of the tenure document. These requirements are generally easily accessed through published documents. One document may outline the policies, regulations, and procedures of the university as a whole, whereas individual colleges may define the actual content of the dossier you will submit for review. If you are fortunate, the dean of your college will hold regular meetings for tenure-track faculty as a means of keeping everyone informed of both the timeline and the steps regarding what needs to be done. Accessing information from other sources, such as a mentor, department chair, or even colleagues who enter the profession with you, can be helpful. But be careful to rely on the published information about dates and expected content to meet the standards. I have observed tenure-track professors depending on stories of someone who received tenure with few publications only to be dismayed when their own level of research did not meet the expectations of the college.

These timelines are absolute and unforgiving. Many colleges require electronic submission, but you may find that access to the system is blocked at the exact deadline. Planning ahead is essential to producing a quality submission that will showcase your achievements in a way that is easily understood by reviewers outside of your discipline. If you have a tendency to procrastinate, work with your mentor to set review points so that you can stay on track. Rushing to complete your dossier at the last minute may result in an incomplete or unprofessional presentation of your work. Mistakes may distract the reader from the true meaning of your work, and the strength of your contributions may get lost when the work is poorly displayed.

Tenure Data Format

One area you may want to investigate as you interview for positions is the amount of structure in the tenure process at your potential new university. The first type of structure is commonly used at most universities and takes a holistic view of teaching, research, and service. There may be some numerical expectations in terms of the number of classes taught and manuscripts published, but the focus is on how well you have performed in the three areas being reviewed. Although the college's criteria and procedures should be consistent with those defined by the university, the required content of the dossier may be defined by the college in which your program is located. The specific standards and the ways in which these standards reflect the conceptual framework of the college will guide how you construct your dossier. Become familiar with these expectations as early as possible so that you can make wise choices about the commitments you make. Whenever possible, try to find service opportunities that also have the potential for conducting research that can further your research agenda. The more you can accept those projects in which data can be collected, the easier it will be for you to get the maximum benefit from your efforts. One note of caution for faculty who represent diverse groups is to carefully consider all service requests and the impact of these requests on your research. With colleges wanting to emphasize diversity, your involvement in these service activities may overshadow your teaching and research efforts. I have seen demands placed on minority faculty that can detract from the tenure process. Service expectations are often greater in terms of serving the community. For example, faculty members who are native Spanish speakers are expected to serve the Latinx community in ways not expected of majority faculty. Pressure to serve on search committees may be greater for faculty of color because the university wants diversity on all committees but often has not committed to hiring a diverse faculty. This situation leads to a small number of faculty serving on a large number of committees. It is essential for you to have conversations with faculty who are from diverse backgrounds about the support provided for tenure success before accepting a position.

A second type of structure is related to using quantitative data to rate each candidate for tenure. Emphasis has recently been placed on using quantitative metrics that can predict research performance, labeled *moneyball for professors* (Bertsimas, Brynjolfsson, Reichman, & Silberholz, 2015). Although this type of analysis has been conducted outside of the field of counseling, the desire to move tenure decisions away from subjective assessment may be the wave of the future. Data can now be collected in forms not available before, such as the use of Google Scholar to determine how a scholar's publications are influencing the work of other scholars. For example, Hirsch (2005) developed the h-index, which attempts to measure the cumulative impact that a research study may have in a field. This goal is accomplished by examining the number of citations the researcher's work has received. The idea is that if a professor demonstrates good citation metrics by being well cited, then he or she has made a significant impact on the field. You will want to investigate how your college measures the quality of your work. However, counting citations may not be an effective measure in that it can take years for work to be cited, and good work may remain uncited. Journals for very specialized fields may have limited distribution, which may also limit citations. You will have to make the case for the importance of your work. But by knowing how the quality of work is evaluated, you can determine how to divide your efforts among teaching, research, and service and build a positive case for tenure.

Use the Buddy System

Often you will be the only new hire in your program because counseling faculties are often smaller than those in other departments in a college of education. I have had the benefit of observing collaborations that develop between new faculty members in counseling and programs such as educational administration or elementary education. Even if there are not common research interests, having colleagues who are going through the same tenure steps provides a good sounding board as well as a way to keep one another on track.

Why Is the Tenure Process So Confusing?

The awarding of tenure is more than just a compilation of annual reviews. Although it is good to do a lot of different things, review committees are looking at the integration or gestalt of your work. Tenure is expected to reflect excellence in all aspects of performance. The inability to perform well in any of the three areas may be viewed as hindering the program's future ability to excel at a high academic level. It is based not just on the doing of activities but on how well these activities foster the development of students and drive the advancement of the field. One key term that is frequently used is *impact*, which refers to whether your work actually contributes to change. Although it seems like it would be easier to have actual numbers to achieve (produce two publications per year, teach five or six courses per year, serve on three committees, work with advisees), such accounting may fail to capture the essence of your contributions. Although it is important to know whether your college has specific expectations in terms of numbers, the numbers alone may not be enough. Knowing the actual influence your work may have on student achievement or how your research creates new avenues for exploration will add value to your tenure documents.

No matter how much universities try to quantify the contributions of a faculty member, there is always an element of subjectivity. How does one measure the quality of teaching? Student evaluations can measure certain behaviors, such as the teacher being prepared for class and whether work is graded in a timely manner, but these ratings say little about the impact of the course on student outcomes. Colleges that use a faculty peer observation model gain additional information on the quality of classroom interactions that can provide useful feedback in the formative stages of teaching. In counseling programs, scores on assessments such as the Counselor Preparation Comprehensive Examination can evaluate knowledge level, but the results are generally aggregated by the program rather than match outcomes with a particular instructor. Given that content for some topics may span several courses, it would be difficult to state that only one professor is responsible for the growth. For example, students may take a dedicated course on ethics early in the program, but ethics is a topic that is revisited in practicum and internship. If a student performs well on the Counselor Preparation Comprehensive Examination on this topic, it may be difficult to assess which professor had the most influence on this score. As you develop your course assignments, you may want to consider ways to capture the nature of student learning that can be used in your reflections on teaching in your dossier.

You may believe that it is easier to quantify research productivity because you are able to count the number of publications. This area has been subjected to more quantitative methods than teaching but can still be confusing and ambiguous in its evaluation. What is the value of being the first author, second author, or sole author? You will need to know how your college values collaboration versus single authorship. If you collaborate, be sure to keep records of what your contributions were to the publication. Not only must you publish, but your particular program may prefer that you publish in high-impact journals. What does *impact factor* mean, and how does your college use this measure? A general definition of *impact factor* is the frequency with which the average article in a journal is cited in a particular year or period. According to SCOPUS CiteScores from 2016, the highest rated counseling journal was *Journal of Counseling & Development* with a score of 1.70 (Elsevier, 2017). One of the strongest journals for counselor educators is *Counselor Education and Supervision,* which has a score of 0.92. Within your college of education or university, you may be compared to someone publishing in a reading journal with a score of 3.12 or a chemistry journal with a score of 42.79. Making sense of how quantitative scores are used will be part of the challenge you face when building your case for tenure. You will need to be able to articulate why the journals you have chosen for publication have value for the counseling field.

Service activities may be easy to quantify in terms of hours spent or number of activities completed. But tenure reviewers may be looking for the meaning of these activities. If you volunteered to assist elementary students in an after-school program, what difference did your participation make? If you consulted with a community agency, how were clients affected by the changes made as a result of the consultation? Although your annual reports will capture the efforts you made in service, your dossier needs to reflect how these efforts made an impact.

No matter how much information and data you try to collect on your way to your tenure review, you will rarely feel confident about whether you are doing enough. Because most colleges do not use the extensive metrics mentioned earlier, the absence of specific quantitative criteria may lead to a lack of clarity around knowing whether you are meeting the standards. Magnuson (2002) found that new professors in their first year were already encountering challenges related to tenure and promotion. By their third year, some of these same professors expressed scholarship as a source of satisfaction while others continued to have high anxiety because of "double messages" about requirements (Magnuson, Black, & Lahman, 2006, p. 173).

Rather than operate in a vacuum, it is important to seek regular feedback from your chair and mentor. Your annual evaluation needs to include a discussion that gives you fair appraisal of your progress toward tenure. It is not enough to hear the feedback you are given; you need to take it seriously and plan your changes around any suggestions. This may be an even greater challenge for a professor from a diverse background. How can professors determine whether they may have been judged more critically based on their race? Racism among students has been cited as a source of stress for African American faculty members (Bradley & Holcomb-McCoy, 2004). Building a good support network that includes both your chair and mentor can help you decipher any critical subtext of feedback based on gender, race, or other biases.

Perhaps the biggest issue I have seen arise after a reappointment conference has been around the assistant professor not heeding advice. As a member of the college review committee, I have seen faculty members not granted tenure based on deficits in teaching as well as research. In my college, the dean would hold individual meetings with the recently reviewed assistant professors and their chairs to go over the results of the reappointment decision. Very specific feedback was provided in terms of what adjustments were needed for a successful tenure review. Yet when it was time for the tenure review, these same deficits remained.

First Timeline Checkpoint

The value of the reappointment or tenure progress review is that it provides faculty members with guidance about any corrective actions that they need to take before the tenure review. It is imperative for the faculty member to pay close attention to this feedback and work with his or her chair and/or mentors to set specific goals to guide the remainder of the tenure process. In my own experience as a faculty member at the reappointment stage, I was told that although my chair believed that if I completed the research agenda I had created I would earn tenure, the provost had some doubt that I could actually do it. I used this doubt as an incentive to prove her wrong. Even though the criteria for tenure may not always be clear and specific, seeking feedback from appropriate sources gives you a more complete picture of what you need to do.

As mentioned previously, universities vary in relation to reviews before tenure. This is one of the first things you need to learn on taking a position. It might be helpful for you to create a map of all of the steps you must take to achieve tenure, with specific dates for the review processes. The first evaluation may take place in your third year, but what might not be clear at first is that all of your documentation is submitted at the beginning of your third year and really only covers what you have accomplished in your first 2 years. That is why this review is about your promise or potential as a counselor educator. Think about it: You take a new position and are given several new course preparations for the fall. You have moved to a new location, found a place to live, and settled your family into new routines. Often you are just one or two lessons ahead of your students. So getting focused on writing up your dissertation for publication might not be the first thing on your list. Yet you need to be thinking about how you will begin your agendas in teaching, research, and service. Each of these areas is discussed in more detail in the following sections.

Teaching

When you accept this new position, one consideration you may want to negotiate is a reduced course load in your first year or at least in your first semester. Many programs, particularly in universities with high research expectations, want to help you develop a balanced approach that will lead to a successful tenure decision. When teaching loads are overly demanding, then research will suffer. If the teaching load cannot be adjusted, there are several other methods of managing the demands of teaching. If possible, get a commitment from your chair or coordinator about what classes you will be teaching before coming to campus. If the textbook has already been ordered, you can go ahead and procure a copy from the publisher to begin reading ahead of time. Although you are essentially working without pay, your life may become much easier if you can get some preparation completed before classes begin.

Another strategy is to negotiate teaching at least one course that you cotaught as a doctoral student. Many professors are willing to share their course materials with you if you assisted with the class. Although you may still want to revise the materials to make them your own, having a framework for the class will ease some of the burden. It is also helpful to discuss taking on courses that you will be able to teach multiple times over your first 2 years so that every course is not a new preparation. New faculty members are often expected to fill the void left by a departing faculty member, which can lead to their teaching two or three new preparations each semester. This type of teaching load can create significant barriers to meeting research goals, which eventually affects tenure expectations. Finally, volunteer to teach at least one practicum or internship section your first year. Although these courses may have additional time commitments for individual supervision and listening to recorded sessions, the preparation and grading time are significantly reduced from the amount of time needed to prepare and deliver a content course. And do not be fooled by thinking an online course is an easier option. The demands of preparing online material are generally much greater given the complexity of developing engaging online resources.

Teaching Philosophy

During your doctoral program, you may have begun evolving your teaching philosophy, which incorporated instructional design and learning theories. CACREP requires that pedagogy and teaching methods be addressed as part of your curriculum. Early in your career, you need to reflect on and revise your teaching philosophy statement as you gain experience in the classroom. There may be external influences on this document, such as your college's conceptual framework and the program's objectives as derived from the CACREP Standards. You may be asked to show how you have used feedback from student evaluations to adjust and enhance your instruction. If your program has established student learning objectives as part of national accreditation, you may be asked to demonstrate how your classes are meeting these objectives. Ironically, you will be asked to expound on all of these points in just a couple of pages, so your philosophy may go through several revisions as you try to explain these important concepts in a concise way.

Peer Observation

A valuable aspect of the tenure review process is the opportunity to receive feedback from more experienced faculty members on teaching effectiveness. This process often happens in three phases. First, the new faculty member is expected to observe an experienced faculty member and reflect on that experience. Second, the faculty member participates in several formative observations in which experienced faculty members observe the tenure-eligible faculty member, who receives informal feedback on these observations. Third, the tenure-eligible faculty member is observed in summative observations by experienced faculty members who provide evaluative information that becomes part of the reappointment and tenure dossier. One aspect that should receive great emphasis in your tenure document is how you have incorporated this feedback in making constructive changes to your teaching. By incorporating both student and peer feedback into your teaching philosophy document, you will demonstrate your ability to receive feedback and commitment to growing as an instructor.

Quality of Syllabi

You may be surprised by the amount of time it takes to produce a quality syllabus, which may lead you to wonder why you should put so much effort into its design. In some ways, the syllabus is your conceptual map for your course. It outlines the journey your students will take in your course. It also demonstrates how your course will fulfill CACREP Standards when going through the accreditation process. During the RPT process, I have observed that committee members review these documents, which represent how you integrate and synthesize the course content. I recall that during a difficult tenure review, the dean expressed concern about the candidate because she could not find evidence that the course fostered complex thinking, which illustrates the importance of this teaching evidence.

Research

If your new university has high expectations for research, you need to carve out time for this activity right away. Becoming a productive researcher is based on becoming disciplined in your writing. Often you will see language such as *having a research agenda* with the expectation that your research follows defined themes. It is tempting to just jump on any invitation to help with a research study, but it is important to understand whether your university wants a synthesized inquiry. For example, a school counselor may also have an interest in addiction counseling but would need to demonstrate the relationship between research on schools and research on addiction, such as investigating alcohol and drug use and its impact on academic achievement. In addition, certain research topics, particularly those that focus on race, may not be as well received within the university as others (Bradley & Holcomb-McCoy, 2004). Knowing that you have the support of your colleagues to pursue important topics may add to your confidence to tackle areas important to the field of counseling.

One of the biggest challenges around research is not having control over the timeline of a journal. After submitting a manuscript for editorial review, you may wait months to get feedback. Rarely is a manuscript accepted for publication without changes. Early in my career when I worked at the university counseling center, I did not understand this process and so did not revise a manuscript for my dissertation that was not immediately accepted. In retrospect, I realize that there was some interest in the manuscript but much revision was needed. If you do not get an outright rejection, you will receive a letter to revise and resubmit. Such letters often include phrases such as "acceptance for publication is dependent on sufficient accommodation of the reviewers' concerns" accompanied by what seems to be a very long list of concerns. My initial response to this feedback is to shut down for a few days, wondering how I can improve on what I thought was my best effort. But I have found that by going through the comments one by one, I can make the necessary adjustments and produce an even stronger article.

But what do you do with those pieces of work that are rejected? Before you even submit something for publication, it is helpful to have a list of journals that may be a good fit for the content. Everyone aspires to publish in the *Journal of Counseling & Development* or *Counselor Education and Supervision*, but are these journals a good fit for the content? These journals are also very competitive, with low acceptance rates. Yet you may be at a university that values high-impact journals, which makes these journals your first choice for submission. However, you need to identify alternative outlets for your work so that you do not give up too quickly. And while you are waiting to learn the fate of one manuscript, you should have other projects in various stages of completion. Think of it as your research pipeline. As one thing begins to flow through the pipeline, you need to have another project in position to enter the pipeline. This is the type of potential that reappointment committees are seeking.

There are a couple of additional criteria to consider about your research. There is more pressure today to publish data-based research. Whether quantitative or qualitative, research studies seem to carry more weight than conceptual or theoretical pieces. In addition, order of authorship may carry weight in the tenure decision. Find out your university's values concerning single authorship versus collaboration. You will need to be able to quantify your contributions to the research in terms of the roles performed. Areas to consider include conceptualization of the study, writing of the literature review, data collection, data analysis, and discussion of the results. When there are many authors, it can be difficult to assess how much each individual contributed; review committees need to know that your contribution was substantial.

Service

The area of service may also be labeled *outreach* or *community engagement*. The counseling field in particular has extensive opportunities to be involved in service because counselors are trained first as practitioners. These activities, although valuable and meaningful, can become very time consuming. And the rewards in terms of tenure may be minimal; however, the demands may be great, particularly for minority faculty members (Bradley & Holcomb-McCoy, 2004).

Service can occur on many levels, which makes it essential that you know the type of service valued by your institution. Service to your program or department is often manifested by service on committees such as the master's committee or doctoral committee. Your program is also served when you advise student groups or provide continuing education to students. You may become a representative for your department on a college committee, such as a college diversity committee or college faculty council. In some settings, new faculty members are inundated with service opportunities because senior faculty members are ready to leave these positions. In other settings, senior faculty want to protect new faculty from overload and discourage their involvement. It is important that you work with your chair or program coordinator to find the right balance of service involvement at the program, college, and university levels.

Service to professional organizations is also an expectation at many institutions. This type of service can occur at the state, regional, or national levels. Getting involved at the state level can be an excellent precursor to national leadership. The advantages of service to the profession are the connections formed with colleagues across the state or country. Such service can lead to shared research interests and network building. Meaningful relationships that span many years can develop from these types of associations. I have both been mentored by as well as mentored professional colleagues whom I met through service opportunities in the counseling profession.

Perhaps the type of service that can be most demanding yet meaningful is service to the local community. Some state legislatures have an expectation that state-funded colleges of education give back to local schools. Because of the flexibility of university schedules, local schools or organizations view professors as being an endless supply of labor. Their causes are worthy, which leads to difficulty saying no. Once again, those in leadership positions can help you sort through the requests and make choices that both help the community and foster your journey to tenure.

By recognizing the interconnectedness of the spheres of teaching, research, and service, you will be able to maximize your efforts in achieving tenure. This approach will take some careful planning on your part. Having open discussions with your chair or mentor about your goals is an important step. You may need to request this type of guidance if it is not offered. Colleagues are often willing to listen and offer suggestions but may not know your needs unless you ask for support.

By this time in the process, you will also have an idea of whether this position is a good fit for you. Perhaps you realize that you want to be in a position where you can focus on teaching because that is where your heart is. To be a good researcher, you may recognize that you need to be in a climate that supports research by providing the necessary resources. Magnuson et al. (2006) found that during Year 3 of their cohort study, some counselor educators made the decision to leave for other positions that offered a better fit than their first position out of graduate school. Changing positions may lead to a restart of the tenure process.

The Case for Tenure

The tenure review may be very similar in form to earlier reviews, with sections on teaching, research, and service. But after a successful reappointment review, you should have a pretty solid idea of what is expected for tenure. There may be a sense of additional stress given the limited time to get research in press. There will be a lag of as long as a year before you get feedback on your RPT review. During this time, it is essential that you continue being productive. As soon as the review document is completed, set your focus on your next tasks. Even without formal feedback, just completing this review will provide you with a good idea of your strengths as well as areas that need attention.

The tenure review is more about accomplishments than promise. You will be asked to continue to develop your teaching, research, and service activities, but there are higher expectations to meet. The tenure document is about demonstrating your evolution from beginner to accomplished professional.

Teaching

By now you have several courses prepared and may be feeling more comfortable with the content, which enables you to be more creative with the delivery. At this point it is important that you attend to the feedback on your teaching from the sources discussed previously. Your teaching observations may become more evaluative in nature (summative), and you have received student feedback over a number of semesters. It is key that you listen to the feedback and find ways to incorporate it into your class delivery. Review committees will be looking for evidence that you used this feedback to make changes. If your teaching evaluations continue to raise the same concerns, the reviewers will question your ability to evolve as an educator. For example, if students frequently complained about assignments not being graded in a timely manner in your first review, you will want to make sure that you make the corrections in a way that eliminates this criticism in subsequent reviews.

Now that you know more students, you can expand your relationships with them through advising and mentoring activities. Inviting students to present or write with you is a great way to move content from the classroom into the professional realm. However, Lee and Arredondo (as cited in Bradley, 2005) have found that professors of color are often called on to mentor students of color, which creates additional time demands. If there are doctoral students in your program, being open to coteaching is another way to support their development. Perhaps you have an idea for a new course that could benefit your program. Learning the steps of curriculum development and putting your own personal stamp on one aspect of your program will demonstrate your ability to contribute to the teaching mission of your program. Adding a new course could even link with presenting these concepts at a professional conference as well as lead to a pilot study on the impact of this educational experience.

Research

As soon as you finish the reappointment or midcycle review, your research agenda takes center stage. You should have manuscripts at the point of submission as well as studies in progress. In earlier studies, you may have felt honored to be asked to become a contributing author on a manuscript. Now is the time for you to take the lead as either sole or first author. A lack of publications at this point can be a source of disappointment and stress, a reflection provided by the participants in the Magnuson et al. (2006) study. Work closely with your mentor to develop a strategic plan for the next 2 years. In our college, we have a wonderful group of research professors who are willing to look at studies that have been rejected and help restructure them into more powerful documents.

One of the major additions to the tenure document is the use of outside reviewers for your research. Typically you are asked to provide a number of your research publications that will be reviewed by tenured professors in the field. These reviewers will be asked to assess both the quality of the research and its contribution to the field. You may be asked to submit the names of potential reviewers, but these reviewers cannot be former professors, coauthors, or those with whom you have had a working relationship. Chances are you may have met some qualified reviewers through professional conferences because of shared interests. Being active in professional organizations will help you identify those who have an interest in and understanding of your work.

By this point in your career, you should be able to articulate a clearly defined research agenda that has evolved over time. It will be your responsibility to convey how your research relates to the field and how your contributions help advance the knowledge base. By making strategic choices, you will find that your research informs your teaching while your teaching and service are aligned with your research interests.

Service

The service expectation for tenure concerns your sustained contributions to the community, the profession, and the institution. You will need to demonstrate continued involvement with the community and practitioners in your specialty area since the time of your reappointment or midterm review. You may have formed a partnership with a school or been appointed to the board of a local mental health facility. Your expertise will be highly valued within these organizations, but it is important to identify the impact of your contributions for your tenure document. In terms of contributions to the profession, some combination of state, regional, or national involvement will be expected. This contribution may include appointed or elected positions of leadership. Joining a task force or chairing a committee will highlight your developing leadership skills. You will want to make sure to document the accomplishments of these activities. You may also be asked to provide the names of those who can provide letters of support for the quality of your service work. Within your university, college, and program, you want to demonstrate being a good member of the community by contributing to the vision and mission of the institution. Your ability to demonstrate the integration of your teaching, research, and service will highlight the importance of the work you have accomplished as well as demonstrate your future value to the academic community.

Tenure Challenges

Perhaps the biggest challenge faced by new professors is managing all of the diverse demands of an academic position. Hill (2004) identified four themes from the literature: (a) multiple demands and time constraints, (b) professional and personal isolation, (c) unrealistic expectations, and (d) insufficient feedback and recognition. Throughout studies on the 2000 cohort of new assistant professors in counselor education, the workload was characterized as unrealistic and overwhelming (Magnuson et al., 2006, 2009). Learning to be more efficient and to set limits was essential to their ability to manage the varying demands of the position. Developing clear goals in conjunction with your administrator's support may help you determine which commitments will keep you focused on tenure. Not every activity is valuable in helping you achieve tenure.

Academia can be a lonely field given that course planning and writing can be solitary activities. You are hired into a faculty with individuals who have established professional and personal lives, so it is often up to you to build new relationships. Early in the job, you may have opportunities to go to events for new faculty, which will provide a chance to meet people in your same situation. Use these occasions to make connections with those with similar interests. I have seen wonderful friendships evolve from linking with those facing some of the same anxieties and fears as well as the excitement of the new position. Finding strong mentors both formally and informally can help foster a feeling of belonging (see Chapter 4 for more information on mentoring).

For diverse faculty members, racism may be a primary source of stress in addition to research and publishing, faculty meetings, and teaching load (Bradley & Holcomb-McCoy, 2004). Job satisfaction was found to be significantly related to perceptions of departmental racial climate (Holcomb-McCoy & Addison-Bradley, 2005). It is most important to try and get a sense of the program's climate around issues of diversity when interviewing. If the program itself does not have a diverse faculty, what connections can be made within the college or university? Support outside of your department can help provide the encouragement you need for success. Female pretenured faculty members may also benefit from understanding the program's culture for women around research demands, job satisfaction, and family responsibilities to see whether the environment is a good fit for them (Alexander-Albritton & Hill, 2015).

Many new professors are overwhelmed with what are seen as unrealistic expectations. I imagine you felt this way early in your doctoral program as well. Think about how you learned to manage all of the reading, research, writing, presentations, clinical experiences, and graduate assistantships to reach this point. With the guidance of your mentor, you can establish a work plan to meet all of the expectations. You will be hired into this position because the faculty believe you can achieve tenure, and most people who enter a tenure-track position in counselor education are able to achieve their goal. But it does take commitment to working more than a 40-hour week along with devoting time in the summer to writing. And do not forget how much you actually love this work. I can remember my first months of being a professor after working as a clinician and thinking that I was getting paid to read all of this exciting material. What a great job to have.

Hill's (2004) last point on insufficient feedback and recognition is one not often addressed in the literature. Counselor educators may not even like to admit that we need this type of acknowledgment. In some programs, faculty members have a regular sharing of accomplishments that are celebrated by all. In others, you may have to find those faculty colleagues whom you believe will be supportive of your efforts and build on those relationships. More experienced faculty members who have already built their careers may welcome the chance to nurture your development. As mentioned previously, you may find it beneficial to build a peer network with other new professors so you can support one another's efforts and accomplishments. Finally, learn to value the small appreciations that happen with your students. The student who seeks your guidance after class or who drops by your office for encouragement—this is the true reason why we are here.

An Unfavorable Tenure Decision

On those occasions when tenure is not awarded, the affected faculty member has the option of filing a grievance but would need to have permissible grounds, such as a violation of First Amendment rights; discrimination based on the faculty member's race, color, creed, sex, disability, sexual orientation, religion, age, national origin, or veteran status; or another form of discrimination prohibited under policies established by the institution or state. There are often specific time frames within which this process must be initiated. More frequently, however, the faculty member understands the rationale for the unfavorable decision because of previous feedback on research or teaching contributions. In some instances, the faculty member is allowed to continue teaching for an additional year, which provides him or her with the opportunity to pursue an alternative career path. Perhaps the type of institution was not a good match for the faculty member in terms of publication expectations. In other instances, the overwhelming nature of the first several years creates a situation in which the faculty member is always trying to catch up in terms of publications. Perhaps pursuing a different type of counselor education position would be in the faculty member's best interest. Or it may be that the individual learns that academia is not the best career option and seeks a more satisfying counseling position. It is important that a change in career path is viewed not as the end of a career but as the beginning of another satisfying pathway. During this process, working with one's mentor or even the university counseling center can help make for a smooth transition.

Conclusion

Becoming a counselor educator is the beginning of an amazing career path, as evidenced by the number of professors who spend so many years in the field. Achieving tenure, although demanding, is possible with careful planning and sustained effort. It is a process that takes individual effort, but the path does not have to be traveled alone. With the support of colleagues and mentors, you can enjoy the journey while also being focused on the outcome. Once tenured, you can enjoy watching the success of your students as they touch the lives of clients, knowing you had a part in their success. As I watch my former doctoral students who are now counselor educators, I take pride in how they are creating the next generation of practitioners. It is the ultimate sense of knowing that your work matters.

References

Alexander-Albritton, C., & Hill, N. R. (2015). Familial and institutional factors: Job satisfaction for female counselor educators. *Counselor Education and Supervision, 54,* 109–121. doi:10.1002/ceas.12008

Allen, H. L. (2000). Tenure: Why faculty, and the nation, need it. *Thought & Action, 16,* 95–110.

Bertsimas, D., Brynjolfsson, E., Reichman, S., & Silberholz, J. (2015). Tenure analytics: Models for predicting research impact. *Operations Research, 63,* 1246–1261. doi:10.1287/opre.2015.1447

Bradley, C. (2005). The career experiences of African American women faculty: Implications for counselor education programs. *College Student Journal, 39,* 518–528.

Bradley, C., & Holcomb-McCoy, C. (2004). African American counselor educators: Their experiences, challenges, and recommendations. *Counselor Education and Supervision, 43,* 258–273. doi:10.1002/j.1556-6978.2004. tb01851.x

Brown-Rice, K., & Furr, S. (2015). Gatekeeping ourselves: Counselor educators' knowledge of colleagues' problematic behaviors. *Counselor Education and Supervision, 54,* 176–188. doi:10.1002/ceas.12012

Center for Postsecondary Research. (2016). *2015 update facts and figures.* Retrieved from http://carnegieclassifications.iu.edu/downloads/CCIHE2015-FactsFigures-01Feb16.pdf

Chait, R. (2002). *The questions of tenure.* Cambridge, MA: Harvard University Press.

Council for Accreditation of Counseling and Related Educational Programs. (2015). *CACREP 2016 standards.* Alexandria, VA: Author.

Council for Accreditation of Counseling and Related Educational Programs. (2017). *CACREP annual reports: Annual report 2016.* Retrieved from www.cacrep.org/about-cacrep/publications/cacrep-annual-reports/

Elsevier. (2017). *SCOPUS site scores.* Retrieved from https://www.elsevier.com/solutions/scopus

Euben, D. R. (2004, October). *Termination and discipline.* Retrieved from https://www.aaup.org/file/Termination_Discipline_2004.pdf

Furr, S., & Brown-Rice, K. (2016). Doctoral students' knowledge of educators' problems of professional competency. *Training and Education in Professional Psychology, 10,* 223–230. doi:10.1037/tep0000131

Hill, N. R. (2004). The challenges experienced by pre-tenured faculty members in counselor education: A wellness perspective. *Counselor Education and Supervision, 44,* 135–146. doi:10.1002/j.1556-6978.2004.tb01866.x

Hirsch, J. E. (2005). An index to quantify an individual's scientific research output. *Proceedings of the National Academy of Sciences of the United States of America, 102,* 16569–16572.

Holcomb-McCoy, C., & Addison-Bradley, C. (2005). African American counselor educators' job satisfaction and perceptions of departmental racial climate. *Counselor Education and Supervision, 45,* 2–15. doi:10.1002/j.1556-6978.2005.tb00126.x

Magnuson, S. (2002). New assistant professors of counselor education: Their 1st year. *Counselor Education and Supervision, 41,* 306–320. doi:10.1002/j.1556-6978.2002.tb01293

Magnuson, S., Black, L. L., & Lahman, M. K. E. (2006). The 2000 cohort of new assistant professors of counselor education: Year 3. *Counselor Education and Supervision, 45,* 162–179. doi:10.1002/j.1556-6978.2006.tb00140.x

Magnuson, S., Norem, K., & Lonneman-Doroff, T. (2009). The 2000 cohort of new assistant professors of counselor education: Reflecting at the culmination of six years. *Counselor Education and Supervision, 49,* 54–71. doi:10.1002/j.1556-6978.2009.tb00086.x

Scheuerman, W. E. (1997). Public higher ed: Battleground for tenure wars. *Thought & Action,* 63–73. Retrieved from www.nea.org/assets/docs/HE/Tenure4Battleground.pdf

Tierney, W. G., & Lechuga, V. M. (2010). Differences in academic work at traditional and for-profit postsecondary institutions. In G. C. Hentschke, V. M. Lechuga, & W. G. Tierney (Eds.), *For-profit colleges and universities: Their markets, regulation, performance, and place in higher education* (pp. 71–90). Sterling, VA: Stylus.

Trepal, H. C., & Stinchfield, T. A. (2012). Experiences of motherhood in counselor education. *Counselor Education and Supervision, 51,* 112–126. doi:10.1002/j.1556-6978.2012.00008.x

Ziker, J. (2014). *The long, lonely job of Homo academicus.* Retrieved from https://thebluereview.org/faculty-time-allocation/

Chapter 8

Adjunct, Part-Time Faculty, and Nontenured Positions in Counselor Education

Lisa L. Schulz and Leslie D. Jones

As you walk onto campus, you feel exhilarated by the excitement of possibility: the possibility of your own personal and professional growth and development. Perhaps knowing that you want to become a counselor educator to contribute to your field in a broader, more encompassing way than clinical practice alone offers you have a transpersonal experience. Perhaps you are wondering what role as an educator will feel most gratifying. You have heard that you should want to secure that tenure-track position, churn out those publications, and take your place among the ranks of the professoriate. However, you have some questions—or even some hesitation about the tenure-track path and if what it requires is fitting or fulfilling. So perhaps a question to ponder as you read this chapter is this: What most attracts you to working in a higher education setting?

To begin this exploration of working as contingent faculty in the counselor education (CE) context, let us clarify that the professoriate has been steadily shifting away from a research-oriented tenured or tenure-track workforce. The permanent tenured and tenure-eligible workforce, those persons imagined to do the actual standing and de-livering of education and training, is essentially not who is standing in today's college and university classrooms, either in vivo or online.

In their stead are non-tenure-eligible, temporary workers who primarily function as instructors, carry out little research, tend to receive lower pay with practically no benefits, and may work in two or three institutions to make ends meet. The dramatic reduction in tenured and tenure-eligible faculty in higher education has created a new tier of faculty identified as contingent. As defined by the American Association of University Professors (AAUP, 2013b), contingent faculty may be identified as adjuncts, postdocs, teaching assistants, full-time non-tenure-track and clinical faculty, part-timers, lecturers, instructors, or nonsenate faculty. This contingent faculty now makes up more than 73% of current faculty in all higher education settings. Kezar and Maxey (2014) offered a unique perspective on the most tangible consequence of this shift in faculty:

> The emergence of the "new faculty majority" not only reveals the general lack of understanding around faculty's central role in providing a high quality education to students, but this shift also threatens to undermine one of the most important predictors of student success: frequent and high-quality interactions between faculty and their students. (p. 30)

Given more people are attending colleges and universities (Schudde & Goldrick-Rab, 2016), gaining an understanding of the role and function of contingent faculty in the CE context is essential for the prospective counselor educator. For those contemplating a career in higher education, understanding one's prospects is imperative.

This chapter outlines and clarifies the role contingent faculty have in higher education in general and in CE specifically. This chapter aims to present both the positive and negative aspects of life as a contingent faculty person. However, the current discourse in higher education is rife with controversy around and critique of the position of contingent faculty. Thus, this discussion treats the controversy and critique as central while also attending to the advantages and disadvantages of working as a non-tenure-earning part- or full-time counselor educator in various professional settings. Discussions related specifically to career outlook, professional growth and development, and promotion of the efficacy of contingent faculty are presented in stand-alone sections. Consideration of institution and program type, institutional policies and practices concerning non-tenure-earning faculty, plus consideration related to social justice are integrated throughout. You are encouraged to consider your own educational experience and your perceptions of the function of career positions such as researcher and instructor along with the values and standards espoused by the *ACA Code of Ethics* (American Counseling Association, 2014), the *ACES teaching Initiative Taskforce: Best Practices in Teaching in Counselor Education Report 2016* (Association for Counselor Education and Supervision, 2016), and the Council for Accreditation of Counseling and Related Educational Programs (CACREP) Standards (CACREP, 2015).

The Current Trend in Higher Education

Over the past 45 years, the composition of the professoriate has transformed significantly across all types of institutions. Although faculty members were once predominantly on the tenure track, currently non-tenure-track faculty (NTTF) constitute more than 73% of all faculty (AAUP, 2013b). These NTTF, otherwise known as *contingent*—a term that is inclusive of both part- and full-time faculty—hold instructional assignments, generally of one to three courses per quarter or semester, and are offered varying degrees of commitment on the part of the university. According to the AAUP (2013a), more than 50% of all faculty appointments are part time, classified as adjuncts, part-time lecturers, or graduate teaching assistants. Although reliance on NTTF is greatest at community colleges and for-profit universities, this shift to contingency is also clearly seen at public and private 4-year colleges, research universities, and liberal arts colleges (Goldstene, 2012).

Although some private institutions offer a tenure system similar to that of public institutions, growing numbers offer contracts (from 1 to 5 years depending on the length of continuous employment) in a nontenure system. These positions are designed to focus on teaching and service to the program and may be offered in a nonvertical hierarchy in which communication regarding course and service load is handled through inquiry personnel rather than chairs and deans. Regardless of whether positions are offered as part time and continuous or adjunct and on demand, compensation trends are based on market trends and institution philosophy.

Between 1976 and 2012, the number of private nonprofit institutions increased by 15% whereas the number of for-profit institutions increased from 2% to 25% of all higher education institutions (Schudde & Goldrick-Rab, 2016). Increasing student enrollment, in particular the enrollment of those representing racial minorities and low-income families, has realized both benefit and ruin in the private sector. Access to graduate-level degrees has increased along with enormous loan debt levels, resulting in saturated professional fields and potential federal and state regulation. Concerns have surfaced about the quality of education that private nonprofit and for-profit institutions offer, the amount of money they receive in scholarships and loans, the tactics they use to attract students, and the employment rates of their graduates. Evaluators of for-profit institutions argue that many schools and programs leave students with large amounts of debt, with few employable skills, and at a greater than average risk for not completing a degree at all (Goldstene, 2012; Schudde & Goldrick-Rab, 2016; Wilson, 2010). Notwithstanding these claims, counselor and CE degrees offered via online and ground-based modalities from private nonprofit and for-profit institutions do prepare students for entry into the field using the same codes and standards. Students are proffered the choice of institution based on their needs, leaving the institutions to compete for their enrollment dollars.

Considerations for NTTF from both unionized and nonunionized systems include working conditions, the ability to engage in shared governance, economic security, and academic freedom. Adjuncts and part-time lecturers are generally compensated on a per-course or hourly basis, whereas full-time NTTF receive a salary. The growth in the contingent workforce, fundamentally a result of the corporatization of higher education (McHenry & Sharkey, 2014), has resulted in a distinction being made between the tenured and tenure-track faculty and a largely itinerant, mostly part-time, and largely invisible teaching staff identified as adjuncts, lecturers, clinical faculty, and teaching fellows. According to the American Federation of Teachers (n.d.), "The growth of the contingent instructional workforce over the past four decades has tracked the ongoing cutback in the proportion of state funding to public colleges and universities"(para. 3). Loss of funding from both federal and state sources since the 1980s coupled with stagnation in student enrollment (Geiger, 2016) led to privatization and shifting priorities toward high enrollment and low expenditure (Altbach, 2016). Given the shift in faculty composition as well as the waning of the predominant rewards of the professoriate—chiefly shared governance, academic freedom, and job security for the vast majority of college- and university-level instructors—deliberate consideration when contemplating and navigating a career in higher education seems most prudent. The emergence and acceptance of this two-tier system is now the standard that both categorizes and compensates faculty across all types of institutions and allows colleges and universities to structure the system for optimal realization of the twin goals of education/training and economic upsurge. Essentially contingent faculty working in all settings experience similar considerations and concerns regarding workload, economic security, and expectations for professional fit.

The practices of many institutions have not yet evolved to allow contingent faculty to supply the teaching quality and instructional oversight that meets institutions' goals for student learning, vocational training, and graduation (Kezar & Maxey, 2014). Kezar (2013c) identified the following trends as consequences of the reversal of numbers of tenured, tenure-track, and contingent instructors: lower graduation rates for students taking more courses with NTTF, worse performance in follow-up courses among students taking courses with adjuncts compared to tenure-track faculty, and lower rates of transfer from 2-year and 4-year institutions among students taking courses from adjuncts. Furthermore, studies of NTTF instructional practice imply that "part-time faculty use less active learning and service learning and fewer student-centered teaching approaches, educational innovations, and culturally sensitive teaching approaches" (Kezar, 2013c, p. 3). Some argue that these negative trends are a result of existing policies and practices not designed to support the effectiveness and value of contingent faculty and expose disproportionate numbers of female and racially nondominant hires (Hoeller, 2014; Kezar, 2013c; Kezar & Maxey, 2014; McHenry & Sharkey, 2014). The employment of contingent faculty does not yet offset high teaching loads and service expectations via full equity in salary and benefits, the opportunity to teach courses in one's specialty, involvement in shared governance, and retirement benefits. Despite ongoing efforts by a number of organizations, including the AAUP, the American Federation of Teachers, the Coalition of Contingent Academic Labor, United Academics, and the National Education Association, to advocate for the equitable treatment of continent faculty, not all stakeholders are in agreement. Thus, many contingent faculty currently suffer from a failure on the part of stakeholders to secure the safeguards of academic due process, fitting working conditions, and appropriate compensation (Rhoades, 2013).

According to Eron (2014), the boon for administrators associated with the growth in the number of continent faculty is threefold: "flexibility, increased revenue, and the silence of the vast majority of faculty" (p. 31). Eron continued:

> When administrators can impose policy across the spectrum without having to deal with 70 percent of their faculty, the other 30 percent—many of whom, in the academic tradition, champion themselves as existing above the prosaic considerations of university politics—quickly fall in to step. Faculties pose no impediment to corporate imperatives.
>
> Today, meaningful shared governance—the guarantee that education experts, rather than administrators subject to the political and economic pressures of the marketplace, are in charge of the educational product—has all but disappeared from the higher education landscape. (p. 31)

The now heavy reliance on part- and full-time contingent faculty has consequences for all educational systems, faculty, and students. As described by Eron, a weakening of shared governance plus the nonexistence of due process for the majority of teaching faculty can only result in the inevitable erosion of quality education and training as contingent faculty struggle to maintain a professional identity and financial solvency. Often contingent faculty are not part of curricular and other academic decisions, nor are they supported by representation on or inclusion in program committees and other governance bodies (AAUP, n.d.). Lack of health-related and employment insurance benefits, lack of comparable salary for comparable work, and limited representation in program and systemic procedures inhibit the potential for allegiance, investment, and professional growth for the ranks of NTTF.

Although by now you may be wondering why anyone joins the ranks of the contingent, the prospects for those contemplating a professional path as a full- or part-time career instructor or clinically focused faculty member are not necessarily bleak. According to Herbert (2016), there has been a discernible increase in representation of the interests of contingent faculty due to the growth in collective bargaining units over the past 4 years. Herbert identified a "significant growth in unionization efforts and collective bargaining relationships in higher education" (p. 1); the largest area of growth has been with respect to NTTF. Growth is most notable at private nonprofit colleges and universities, including religiously affiliated institutions, and continued growth is noted in the number of bargaining units in the public sector among tenured and tenure-track faculty, NTTF, and graduate student organizations. The National Center for the Study of Collective Bargaining in Higher Education and the Professions (n.d.) offers, among other services and publications related to collective bargaining, a directory of faculty contracts and bargaining agents containing a compilation and a statistical analysis of full-time and part-time faculty and graduate student employee collective bargaining agreements throughout the United States broken down by state and institution. Clearly, some colleges and universities do commit to offering equitable benefits, salaries, and working conditions for contingent faculty. Therefore, it behooves the job seeker to explore the systems offering employment in terms of the relationship between administration and the labor force.

Given the current lack of research, research on the working conditions for NTTF, how NTTF experience their working conditions, and how such conditions affect student outcomes is required for educational institutions and specific programs to more completely understand the benefit and danger of hiring and working as contingent faculty. The level of institutional commitment to a stable, full-time, tenured faculty is connected to the working conditions of the contingent faculty (Rhoades, 2013). Thus, exploring institutions' priorities related to recruitment and retention, improved infrastructures, and profit-oriented ventures may offer insight into the motivation for creating and accepting an NTTF position.

Trends in CE

NTTF are represented in CE programs as adjunct, part-time, temporary and full-time lecturers; part- and full-time clinical faculty; and, in doctoral programs, graduate assistants and teaching fellows. They typically provide instruction in clinical courses, which includes the majority of clinical gatekeeping responsibilities, management of clinical facilities, and major program service components that may include coordination of field experiences such as practicums and internships plus additional typically assigned service duties such as student advisement and program maintenance. The increase in contingent faculty in CE (chiefly as full-time clinical faculty or full-time lecturers) parallels the overall increased use of contingent faculty across higher education (Isaacs & Sabella, 2013). The number of full-time contingent positions (both clinical and lecturer positions) advertised via *The Chronicle of Higher Education* and HigherEdJobs has increased markedly in the past 5 years, and the adjunct descriptions focus on hiring for specialty courses (i.e., school, group, and skills-based clinical skill development). In part the use of contingent faculty affords programs the benefit of hiring those who specialize and bring a wealth of experience to the clinical aspects of training when many tenured and tenure-track counselor educators do not practice or have clinical experience limited to their own master's and doctoral programs. According to one department chair whose program has added three full-time clinical faculty positions in the past 7 years, "The clinical positions allow for focus on teaching and service which, in turn, frees tenure-track faculty to pursue their obligation of research, publication, and external funding to ensure the survival of the program" (J. Holden, personal communication, January 17, 2017). Although each program has its specific hiring requirements based on its current faculty composition, student enrollment, and community need, the growing numbers of NTTF demonstrate a trend in CE to divert certain training responsibilities away from tenured and tenure-track faculty. Therefore, in keeping with the trend in higher education, CE programs are developing two- and multitiered compensation systems.

Of further concern when it comes to the use of the contingent workforce to meet the demands of the institution is the potential for undercompensating contingent faculty and the advent of tenurism. Although approximately 21% of all higher education systems (35% in public universities) are unionized, and thus by law comply with collective bargaining agreements, 79% do not offer faculty protections. Alongside the concern for adequate and equitable compensation come the social implications of working in the contingent tier. Hoeller (2014) characterized the term *tenurism* as a negative attitude of tenured and tenure-track faculty toward the nontenured and a prejudice that is a

> natural solution to cognitive dissonance, which holds that when people's belief systems conflict with their behavior, they will sometimes modify their beliefs in order to justify their behavior. The problem posed for tenure-track faculty is this: how can they justify why they are treated so well while so many of their non-tenure-track colleagues are treated so badly? (p. 119)

In an unpublished study exploring the use and valuing of clinical faculty in CE programs, Schulz, Jones, Wagner, and Cheatham (2012) found that most respondents who identified as tenured professors with more than 10 years of CE experience described full-time clinical faculty as invaluable and essential to the training of counselors and adjunct instructors necessary to supply the specialized education and training of counselors and counselor educators. We understand that full- and part-time contingent faculty have a valuable role and are valued in CE, yet the concerns related to economic and social equity are real and generally unaddressed.

A splintering between those who research and those who teach and train may create unintended tension between both the faculty and students. For example, I (Schulz) have encountered various microaggressions on the part of colleagues related to my contribution to the program. On one occasion, I was identified as a "service heavy hitter" because 40% to 50% of my position involved program coordination; the implication of the label was that I functioned as the program grunt and that tenure-track faculty members could focus on earning tenure without the distraction of service. In addition, we have witnessed students, particularly those at the doctoral level, decide on committee membership and mentorship based on whether they wanted to identify as career researchers or career practitioners—an unfortunate either/or perspective that limits student potential as well as deepens an already existing divide between the valuing and compensation of tenured, tenure-track, and contingent faculty. A perceived negative attitude on the part of administration and tenured and tenure-track faculty toward their contingent colleagues may be one reason for the institutionalized (and internalized) bias experienced by many contingent faculty. A pending consideration in CE is how to ensure equitable recognition for all faculty who contribute to the quality training and scholarly advancement of the field regardless of the distribution of the contribution. When faculty work at a research institution where scholarship and the garnering of endowment are prized and rewarded via tenure, delving into how contingent faculty receive due compensation may help determine that system's attitudes and corresponding policies.

The opening of non-tenure-track lines with a primary focus on teaching and service supports administrators' efforts to reduce budget expenditures for labor and benefits while meeting programmatic needs to increase enrollment, procure endowment, and secure publication. CE programs have made efforts to reduce the potential erosion of quality instruction and supervision by hiring full-time lecturers and clinical professors who are educated and trained and hold the same qualifying degrees, experience, and credentials as those hired into the tenure-track lines. Standing in contrast to the belief that such hiring practices expose an indifference to a program's academic mission when many of the basic required core courses (and grounding of professional identity) are removed from core faculty (AAUP, 2014), CE programs are charged to ensure that due process, equity, and accountability for contingent faculty and their students are heeded. The current reality, however, is NTTF overall are paid less than assistant professors, often do not receive adequate health and retirement benefits, and are not typically represented in university governance, and their academic freedom is not protected (AAUP, 2014; Coalition on the Academic Workforce, 2012).

Currently the career ladder for contingent faculty in CE programs seems uninviting if receiving a full-time position with the potential for a high salary and job security is among your professional goals. Beyond a promotion in rank (i.e., from clinical assistant to associate to full professor), contingent faculty generally will not experience an increasing sense of academic freedom, options for teaching specialized courses at either or both the master's or doctoral levels, or the ability to serve in shared governance and thus are unable to self-advocate. As suggested by Isaacs and Sabella (2013), the profession must consider how to counter the potential decline in quality in teaching and training to achieve the "economic efficiencies and resource flexibilities that a contingent workforce achieves" (p. 46). The challenge to support the mission of the institution to maintain or increase its ranking, reputation, and status to attract a capable and stable student body as well as financial sponsorship while providing the necessary attractions for faculty must be a constant consideration for both the administration and tenured and tenure-track faculty, those who are in the best positions to advocate for both academic freedom and comparable compensation.

Before closing this section on CE, we need to make clear that many faculty prefer the contingent position, as they elect not to align themselves full time with an academic institution, are not interested in pursuing scholarship, prefer instead to commit themselves to excellence in teaching and training, and may prefer greater involvement in the practice of counseling. As a way to explore your preference for working contingently or seeking a tenure-earning position, reflect on the following questions:

1. Of the three general areas identified for evaluation for continuation of employment (scholarship, teaching, service), excellence in which will feel the most fulfilling for me professionally?
2. To what degree might I feel disheartened by accepting a contingent position when internally I aspire to the lifestyle and social reward of a tenured scholar?
3. To what degree am I able to tolerate the overt and covert inequities and microaggressions I may perceive in the system in which I choose to work?

Professional Identity Development for Contingent Faculty

Recent research has shown that job insecurity in higher education harms the mental well-being of NTTF; a substantial number of NTTF report feelings of stress, anxiety, and depression associated with their position (Reevy & Deason, 2014). There is some indication that administrators are creating policies and support for NTTF (Hollenshead et al., 2007). However, there exists a paucity of research pertaining to the working conditions and professional identity development of NTTF. Shaker (2008) suggested that NTTF are heterogeneous and that their experiences are fragmented and complex, lending to the perception of disconnection from the work environment and their professional fields. Differences in experience, personal preference, personal characteristics, organizational forces, and academic conditions suggest a nonnormative experience. In addition, according to Levin and Shaker (2011),

> it has also been established that the predominant role of [full-time NTTF] is in teaching and that their instructional role is centered in the lower divisions and the lower prestige classroom assignments.... However, [full-time NTTF] are akin to tenure-track faculty in their high level of work satisfaction. (p. 1463)

By interviewing full-time NTTF to explore their academic identity, agency, positionality, and self-authoring, Levin and Shaker found that despite findings of work satisfaction, full-time NTTF "are characterized as divided between several units or fields or communities. These are discipline, program, department, and the university" (p. 1467). Participants described themselves as possessing incoherent or conflicting identities. In turn, Kezar's (2013c) effort to explore the social construction of supportive work environments revealed an amelioration of understanding of NTTF by introducing new key factors such as newness to teaching, comparison groups, life phase, credentials, and career path to identify how NTTF experience their working conditions. Thus, CE programs need to understand more explicitly the impact the high numbers of NTTF have on the field to determine who will most effectively provide foundational knowledge, skill development, and structural support for future counselors.

To date, no research focused solely on NTTF in CE programs has been published, which leaves a vacuum in understanding how programs are affected, students are influenced, and clients are served. One might extrapolate from the findings of Gibson, Dollarhide, Leach, and Moss (2015) that the professional identity development of NTTF in CE programs is quite complex and that one cannot separate the dimensions of identity nested in experience, personal preference, personal characteristics, organizational forces, and academic conditions. Perhaps, then, the existence of a two-tier system could lead to the construction of a two-tier preparation for counselor educators. Could programs create separate and distinct tracks for those who choose a research, tenure-track path and for those who choose either a part- or full-time practitioner one? Could the field envision a tenure track for career instructors, supervisors, and directors of clinics? As more NTTF positions are offered, more attention will need to be focused on their contributions along with job satisfaction and professional identity development.

Qualifications and Work Satisfaction of Contingent Faculty

With the increase in NTTF in the academic setting, the factors that contribute to work satisfaction among contingent faculty need to be explored. The increasing numbers of NTTF in higher education have led "administrators to consider how to best include, evaluate, manage, and recognize these faculty on their campuses" (Waltman, Bergom, Hollenshead, Miller, & August, 2012, p. 411). Even so, institutional response to reformulating university policies and procedures is often inconsistent and incomplete regarding NTTF members' rights, roles, and evaluation criteria (Levin & Shaker, 2011). This task is complicated by the variety of roles NTTF, including adjuncts, lecturers, and clinical faculty, assume in the academic setting and can contribute significantly to job satisfaction or dissatisfaction among NTTF. Compared to their tenured and tenure-track counterparts, NTTF face vast differences in the hiring process, evaluation of job performance, and representation in governance (Kezar, 2013b), all of which contribute to an overall work environment that affects job satisfaction. Although many factors may lead to job dissatisfaction, Levin and Shaker (2011) noted that a duality exists in overall job satisfaction among NTTF:

> On one hand [full-time non-tenure-track] faculty feel marginalized, desire respect, lack a peer networking group on campus, and are frustrated by the dearth of the role clarity; on the other hand, they find collegiality in their collaborative work and praise the benefits of being part of the academic community. (p. 1463)

One critical area that affects job satisfaction among NTTF concerns the qualifications and hiring process. Full-time tenure-track faculty are hired through rigorous national searches with clearly defined qualifications and expectations, whereas NTTF are often hired under different circumstances. NTTF are many times hired quickly by department chairs and are rarely reviewed or evaluated during the hiring process (AAUP, 2014). This creates an atmosphere in which the qualifications and experiences of NTTF can be minimized and undervalued. Specifically, for NTTF in CE programs, the minimum qualifications are often equivalent to those of their tenure-track counterparts, especially in CACREP-accredited programs. According to CACREP Standards 1.W. and 1.X., core CE faculty, whether tenure- or non-tenure-earning, have an earned doctoral degree in CE and identify with the counseling profession through professional membership and maintaining appropriate licensure or certifications (CACREP, 2015). In addition, Standard 1.Z. indicates that noncore faculty members must hold a graduate or professional degree that supports the program mission. The tendency for NTTF qualifications to be undervalued or minimized, even though NTTF meet many of the same qualifications as tenure-track faculty, may additionally contribute to job dissatisfaction. A candidate interested in a non-tenure-earning position may want to inquire respective of Standards 1.S.–1.V. to understand how the program is using NTTF to meet the indicated faculty-to-student ratios and workload distribution.

NTTF are further affected by the misperception of qualifications related to scholarly pursuits. Most often responsibilities of NTTF focus on teaching and service, despite the fact that many NTTF have the qualifications and the desire to initiate and participate in scholarly endeavors. However, teaching is the key valued behavior for NTTF, whereas research and publication are the valued behaviors for tenure-track faculty (Levin & Shaker, 2011). This creates a dynamic in which the NTTF workload is composed primarily of teaching responsibilities, which leaves little time to focus on scholarly activities that would allow NTTF to fully use their qualifications and allow for greater job satisfaction. The difference in position descriptions seems to be the expectation for research and scholarly productivity from the applicant, which leads to this postulation: Fewer resources are devoted to the hiring of contingent faculty, as their overall value to the institution is regarded as less than that of those who will bring in endowment and garner reputation based on publication output.

One of the preferred qualifications for lecturers and clinical faculty is a valid license and clinical experience beyond their master's and doctoral programs. Ray, Jayne, and Miller (2014) validated this preference by stating that "in counselor education, the delivery of content and process of learning is likely influenced by the instructor's professional counseling experiences" (p. 78). Furthermore, respondents in an unpublished study by Schulz et al. (2012) identified clinical experience as the most important qualification for clinical faculty in CE programs, followed by a doctoral degree and licensure in the field. The field experience of NTTF becomes a tremendous asset for their heavy teaching responsibilities. Specifically, in CE programs, many NTTF teach in the clinical course sequence focusing on skill development through supervision. Ray et al. reported that the clinical experience of counselor educators was most influential in supervision and working with ethical dilemmas. In addition, the clinical experience of counselor educators also influenced teaching methodologies such as lecture and facilitated class discussion, offering students a more practical experience. NTTF's ability to draw from their own clinical experience and focus increases job satisfaction by integrating professional experiences in the classroom.

Departmental Cultures

The culture of academic departments also contributes to the job satisfaction of NTTF. Factors that influence the academic culture for NTTF include salary, job security, mentoring, and overall support. Kezar (2013a) described four departmental cultures that affect NTTF: destructive, neutral, inclusive, and learning cultures. Destructive and neutral cultures have a negative impact on NTTF, whereas inclusive and learning cultures have a more positive impact. Characteristics of destructive cultures include a lack of orientation, mentoring, support, and professional resources. This leads to NTTF being disenfranchised and negatively affects their opportunity to perform and their overall job satisfaction. Neutral cultures are characterized by NTTF feeling invisible and isolated from tenure-track faculty. Lack of communication reinforces isolation and negatively impacts job satisfaction and performance.

Inclusive learning cultures increase NTTF's opportunity for increased job satisfaction and opportunity to perform. Inclusive cultures are characterized by NTTF being included in governance and curricular decisions as well as other aspects of the profession, such as professional development, autonomy in teaching, and leadership roles, being made available (Kezar, 2013a). Even in inclusive cultures, NTTF may experience inequitable pay and minimal benefits. Yet even with this discrepancy, NTTF job satisfaction increases in this type of culture. Finally, characteristics of the learning culture are similar to those of the inclusive culture, with increased mutual respect and inclusion. In this culture, NTTF experience the importance of "support for NTTF an equity issue and an issue of commitment to students and learning" (Kezar, 2013a, p. 175). This type of culture values NTTF as an integral part of the academic environment.

Other Factors

Job security and academic freedom also affect the job satisfaction of NTTF. Many NTTF are hired for 1-year appointments or for each semester or quarter, depending on departmental needs. Contingent employment terms result in NTTF feeling anxious about continuing in their employment from year to year. In addition, procedures for evaluation and promotion may be minimal or absent, which makes it difficult for NTTF to know where they stand in terms of their job performance. Terms of promotion and unclear or inconsistent titling systems create confusion for NTTF around responsibilities and advancement opportunities (Waltman et al., 2012). To increase job satisfaction, universities need to reformulate policies and practices that address the promotion, rights, and roles of NTTF. Without policies that address these issues, NTTF will continue to be outsiders excluded because of their designated workload and role in the academic setting (Levin & Shaker, 2011). On a fundamental level, the absence of tenure decreases academic freedom and the lack of appreciation demonstrated via inequitable compensation leads to job dissatisfaction for NTTF.

Although many factors may decrease NTTF job satisfaction, Waltman et al. (2012) identified factors that increased NTTF job satisfaction. Teaching and working with students, job flexibility, and decreased stress and pressure contributed to an overall sense of job satisfaction and professional fulfillment. CE programs are rife with such opportunities. Clinically focused faculty have the opportunity to both teach and supervise, which may increase their investment in exploring pedagogy and clinical development. Given that certain clinical courses require the investment of out-of-classroom time by the instructor, such courses may be ideal for part-time faculty, who may be more willing to invest in student development and possess the requisite teaching and clinical experiences doctoral students and other faculty may not have. In Waltman et al.'s study, NTTF reported that classroom teaching as well as mentoring and supporting students contributed greatly to job satisfaction. Classroom teaching in particular contributes to job satisfaction because it allows NTTF to share their expertise with students. In our experience, students thoroughly enjoy hearing about the real-world experiences of their professors as practitioners. The credibility that is earned by modeling effective and ineffective counseling skills and intentionality makes for a powerful teaching tool. Providing support for students and working with high-quality students were reported by Waltman et al. as themes for NTTF when mentoring and supporting students. NTTF feel rewarded when students develop and are energized by their students' learning process; this is increased when NTTF work with those they perceive as high-quality students. Finally, job flexibility was cited as a strong source of career satisfaction for NTTF. This flexibility relates to the personal responsibilities of living and the absence of stress associated with tenure-track responsibilities (Waltman et al., 2012). For the part-time counselor educator, this could allow time for both clinical practice and family.

Recommendations for the Professional Identity Development of Contingent Faculty

With the increasing numbers of NTTF, CE programs must address how to successfully incorporate NTTF into academia. The roles and responsibilities of NTTF in university CE programs need to be explored to better understand how NTTF contribute to program effectiveness. There are many things for programs to consider when choosing to incorporate NTTF into their programs. Decisions must be made regarding the roles and responsibilities, evaluation, and compensation of NTTF. If these areas are not clearly defined, it creates obstacles to NTTF becoming a regular and effective part of the program.

Through the lens of social justice, trends that endorse the use of contingent faculty to perform a bulk of the academic and service tasks may model tolerance of discriminatory policies and practices. Programs need to give credence to the aspects of highly effective counselor educators that grow reputations and produce quality graduates, such as clarity in theoretical orientation, a dedicated philosophy of teaching and learning, and intentional selection of course materials (Calley & Hawley, 2008). Given that counselor educators are responsible for clarifying the values of the profession and transmitting them to future counselors and counselor educators, attention must be paid to the equitable distribution of duties, the capacity for meaningful contribution, and the unintended impacts of tenurism on faculty and students. Paralleling the outcomes of a study conducted by Kezar and Holcombe (2015), we support increasing the number of full-time faculty and reducing reliance on part-time faculty, creating teaching-only tenure-track positions, ensuring some level of scholarly component in all full-time faculty roles, revising incentives and reward structures and policies to reflect position expectations and contribution to program success and institutional goals, "allowing some differentiation of roles focused on teaching and research, and developing a broader view of scholarship such as that epitomized in Boyer's *Scholarship Reconsidered*" (p. 15).

Clearly Defined Roles and Expectations

Roles and responsibilities related to teaching, supervising, and student advising are most often associated with NTTF and support the clinical development of trainees and program function. These roles are also associated with the job satisfaction of NTTF. Within a master's-only program, this could mean that NTTF serve as coordinators of off-site practicums and internships. In programs with doctoral-level training, NTTF roles could include directorships of onsite clinics. NTTF tend to teach clinical courses and courses not designated within the specialty areas of full-time faculty. For example, given my level of prior experience, I (Schulz) generally taught prepracticum and internship courses and later, as the need arose, doctoral-level courses related to clinical development and teaching. I (Jones) regularly teach master's-level courses in my specialty area (play therapy) and doctoral-level clinical courses. However, in both instances, seniority and need among tenured and tenure-earning faculty continues to be a determining factor in how courses assignments are made.

CE programs must continue to establish clearly defined roles and expectations to successfully incorporate NTTF into the overall functioning of the program. This can be accomplished by

> providing greater authority for [full-time non-tenure-track] faculty in curriculum and instruction decisions; enhanced integration into decision making in departmental business and appropriate opportunities to lead,

administer, and serve; and fewer divisions in institutional opportunities for research support and professional development as well as less status differentiation between those whose primary responsibilities are teaching and those whose primary responsibilities also include research. Divisions of labor should not mean status divisions. (Levin & Shaker, 2011, p. 1481)

The NTTF role provides an increasing opportunity for doctoral students in CE and counselor educators to explore career development and professional fulfillment. With clearly defined roles and responsibilities, candidates will be able to consider this option a viable career path. By considering the expectations of both NTTF and tenure-track positions, faculty can ascertain their level of fitness for each path and make decisions that allow them to use their unique strengths and passions in the academic environment.

When NTTF serve in administrative roles, such as clinic director or coordinator of clinical experiences, tenure-track faculty can focus on administrative demands for faculty-generated endowment and publication. These service responsibilities provide the essential foundation for programs and are vital in meeting the educational needs of students. Thus, these roles allow NTTF to serve in leadership roles within CE programs. By focusing on being more thoughtful and equitable in framing the roles of both NTTF and tenured and tenure-track faculty, programs can be begin to address the hurdles for professionalizing NTTF (Levin & Shaker, 2011).

Roles and responsibilities associated with scholarship and university service are less defined for NTTF. Some roles appropriate for NTTF include dissertation committee member, dissertation committee chair, college committee member, college committee chair, conference presenter, and publisher of scholarly work. Many academic settings still preclude NTTF from participating in faculty governance, scholarly activities, and service roles (Waltman et al., 2012). Clearly defining the roles for NTTF can facilitate a process that allows NTTF to become a regular part of CE programs while upholding the values of the profession, including socially just policies, procedures, and practices.

Once roles and responsibilities are defined, programs can address evaluation and compensation for NTTF. For NTTF to become integrated into CE programs, they must be seen as a vital and valuable part of the overall function of the program. This can be accomplished through clear evaluation guidelines related to their clinical position and compensation that is commensurate with their work, responsibilities, and qualifications (Waltman et al., 2012). Although they may focus on teaching and service, NTTF provide needed support that allows tenure-track faculty to satisfy administrative demands for faculty-generated endowment and publication and clinical expertise to students that helps safeguard the clinical development of trainees and client welfare.

A Climate of Inclusion

Another approach to increasing professional identity development for NTTF in CE programs focuses on creating a climate of inclusion. One way to create a climate of inclusion is to allow NTTF to teach in their area of expertise. According to Kezar (2013a), scheduling at the last minute and not scheduling collaboratively negatively affect NTTF. When programs assign classes to NTTF with short notice, it creates an atmosphere that ignores the expertise of NTTF and lacks autonomy and inclusivity. NTTF are often not able to offer input on textbook selection and course syllabi. The expertise of NTTF can benefit the curriculum of the department and allow NTTF to contribute knowledge they often have related to current trends in the field and their experience in the classroom. As Kezar (2013b) stated, "Given NTTF spend so much time with students in the classroom because their primary role is teaching and not research, they get a strong sense of what materials [and methods] work well with their student body" (p. 584) and thus can capitalize on their expertise and focus on clinical development and training.

Increasing the respect NTTF receive for their contributions to the academic environment can also foster a climate of inclusion. As previously stated, NTTF are often unable to participate in shared governance, receive lower wages, and lack job security in terms of the length of their contract. In systems of shared governance, allowing NTTF to participate at departmental, college, and institutional levels increases respect for NTTF and creates a more inclusive climate. Currently the level of involvement NTTF experience varies from full participation at all levels to exclusion from all meetings (Waltman et al., 2012). In settings in which NTTF are not allowed to participate in faculty governance, tenure-track faculty (who more often than not marginalize and overlook the experiences of NTTF) represent them. Overall, a climate of inclusion is created when NTTF are valued, policies and practices are put into place to support their professional development, and they are provided with the requisite knowledge to be successful in their roles as teachers and advisers (Kezar, 2013b). This includes making professional development, promotion opportunities, inclusion in program and university decision making, autonomy in teaching, and leadership roles available to NTTF.

Conclusion

The increase in NTTF is evident in higher education and CE programs. With the increase in NTTF, the field must address how to successfully incorporate NTTF into academia. For faculty in tenured and tenure-track positions, roles, responsibilities, and evaluation criteria are clearly defined. Tenure is seen as a reward for significant accomplishment and leads to higher salaries and benefits, academic freedom, and job security. NTTF do not have the same clear guidelines, which diminishes their academic freedom, financial security, career outlook, and level of job satisfaction.

According to the AAUP (n.d.), this inequity begins as early as the appointment process. The appointment process for tenure-track positions is rigorous, whereas the process for NTTF is often imprecise and uncertain. From there, the inequity continues with the definition of roles, processes of evaluation, and salary compensation. Tenured and tenure-track faculty have clearly defined roles and responsibilities in the areas of teaching, scholarship, and service. Guidelines for promotion and performance review are clearly defined, and such reviews are conducted by peers. This creates an environment of consistency and stability for tenured and tenure-track faculty that promotes academic freedom. In contrast, the roles and responsibilities related to teaching, supervising, and student advising, tasks most often associated with NTTF, in most cases do not carry specific guidelines and clearly defined expectations and outcomes. For most NTTF, the position is renewable, and they are not eligible to receive tenure.

For NTTF to become integrated into CE programs, they must be seen as an integral part of the overall function of the program. This can be accomplished through clear evaluation guidelines related to their position and compensation that is commensurate with their work, responsibilities, and qualifications. Although they may focus on teaching and service, they provide much-needed support that allows tenured and tenure-track faculty to satisfy administrative demands for faculty-generated endowment and publication. By addressing the obstacles NTTF face, CE programs can successfully create a both/and environment that can help meet the expectations of instruction, service, and scholarship by modeling socially just and unbiased policies and practices, specifically including protection of academic freedom, inclusion in shared governance, equitable pay, opportunities for career advancement and professional development, fair grievance procedures and due process, and access to resources to conduct one's work.

As you read this chapter, you have ideally been contemplating your fit in CE. Perhaps by now you have answered the three questions posed to you earlier in the chapter and feel more clarity in terms of the current status of contingent faculty in CE programs and how you may choose to both engage and advocate for contingent faculty regardless of the role you eventually take. We believe that there is a place for us all and that each place deserves to be highly valued—especially in the ways our society chooses to express its valuing!

Additional Online Resources

American Association of University Professors
    https://www.aaup.org/
American Counseling Association
    https://www.counseling.org/
American Federation of Teachers
    https://www.aft.org/
Association for Counselor Education and Supervision
    https://www.acesonline.net/
Coalition on the Academic Workforce
    www.academicworkforce.org/
Council for Accreditation of Counseling and Related Educational Programs
    www.cacrep.org/

National Center for the Study of Collective Bargaining in Higher Education and the Professions
www.hunter.cuny.edu/ncscbhep

References

Altbach, P. G. (2016). Harsh realities: The professoriate in the twenty-first century. In M. N. Bastedo, P. G. Altbach, & P. J. Gumport (Eds.), *American higher education in the 21st century: Social, political, and economic challenges* (4th ed., pp. 84–109). Baltimore, MD: Johns Hopkins University Press.

American Association of University Professors. (n.d.). *Background facts on contingent faculty.* Retrieved from https://www.aaup.org/issues/contingency/background-facts

American Association of University Professors. (2013a). *Figure 4: Instructional faculty by rank and reporting category, 2013.* Retrieved from https://www.aaup.org/sites/default/files/files/2015salarysurvey/Fig4.pdf

American Association of University Professors. (2013b). *Status of the academic labor force, 2013.* Retrieved from https://www.aaup.org/sites/default/files/Status-2013.pdf

American Association of University Professors. (2014). *Contingent appointments and the academic profession.* Retrieved from https://www.aaup.org/file/Contingent%20Appointment.pdf

American Counseling Association. (2014). *ACA code of ethics.* Alexandria, VA: Author.

American Federation of Teachers. (n.d.). *Academic staffing.* Retrieved from www.aft.org/position/academic-staffing

Association for Counselor Education and Supervision. (2016). *ACES teaching initiative taskforce: Best practices in teaching in counselor education report 2016.* Retrieved from https://www.acesonline.net/sites/default/files/ACES%20Teaching%20Initiative%20Taskforce%20Final%20Report%20Oct%2023%202016%20.pdf

Calley, N. G., & Hawley, L. D. (2008). The professional identity of counselor educators. *The Clinical Supervisor, 27,* 3–16. doi:10.1080/07325220802221454

Coalition on the Academic Workforce. (2012). *A portrait of part-time faculty members: A summary of findings on part-time faculty respondents to the Coalition on the Academic Workforce survey of contingent faculty members and instructors.* Retrieved from www.academicworkforce.org/CAW_portrait_2012.pdf

Council for Accreditation of Counseling and Related Educational Programs. (2015). *CACREP 2016 standards.* Alexandria, VA: Author.

Eron, D. (2014). The case for instructor tenure: Solving contingency and protecting academic freedom in Colorado. In K. Hoeller (Ed.), *Equality for contingent faculty: Overcoming the two-tier system* (pp. 28–64). Nashville, TN: Vanderbilt University Press.

Geiger, R. L. (2016). The ten generations of American higher education. In M. N. Bastedo, P. G. Altbach, & P. J. Gumport (Eds.), *American higher education in the 21st century: Social, political, and economic challenges* (4th ed., pp. 3–34). Baltimore, MD: Johns Hopkins University Press.

Gibson, D. M., Dollarhide, C. T., Leach, D., & Moss, J. M. (2015). Professional identity development of tenured and tenure-track counselor educators. *Journal of Counselor Leadership and Advocacy, 2,* 113–130. doi:10.1080/2326716X.2015.1042095

Goldstene, C. (2012). The politics of contingent academic labor. *Thought & Action, 28,* 7–15. Retrieved from www.nea.org/assets/docs/HE/2012-TA-Goldstene.pdf

Herbert, W. A. (2016). The winds of changes shift: An analysis of recent growth in bargaining units and representation efforts in higher education. *Journal of Collective Bargaining in the Academy, 8,* 1–24. Retrieved from http://thekeep.eiu.edu/jcba/vol8/iss1/1

Hoeller, K. (Ed.). (2014). *Equality for contingent faculty: Overcoming the two-tier system.* Nashville, TN: Vanderbilt University Press.

Hollenshead, C., Waltman, J., August, L., Miller, J., Smith, G., & Bell, A. (2007). *Making the best of both worlds: Findings from a national institutional-level survey on non-tenure track faculty.* Ann Arbor, MI: Center for the Education of Women.

Isaacs, M. L., & Sabella, R. A. (2013). Counselor educator compensation, work patterns, and career outlook. *Journal for International Counselor Education, 5,* 32–49. Retrieved from https://digitalscholarship.unlv.edu/cgi/viewcontent.cgi?article=1035&context=jice

Kezar, A. (2013a). Departmental cultures and non-tenure-track faculty: Willingness, capacity, and opportunity to perform at four-year institutions. *Journal of Higher Education, 84,* 153–188. doi:10.1353/jhe.2013.0011

Kezar, A. (2013b). Examining non-tenure track faculty perceptions of how departmental policies and practices shape their performance and ability to create student learning at four-year institutions. *Research in Higher Education, 54,* 571–598. doi:10.1007/s11162-013-9288-5

Kezar, A. (2013c). Non-tenure track faculty's social construction of a supportive work environment. *Teachers College Record, 115.*

Kezar, A., & Holcombe, E. (2015). The professoriate reconsidered. *Academe, 101,* 13–18.

Kezar, A., & Maxey, D. (2014). Faculty matter: So why doesn't everyone think so? *Thought & Action, 30,* 29–44. Retrieved from www.nea.org/assets/docs/HE/e-Kezar.pdf

Levin, J., & Shaker, G. (2011). The hybrid and dualistic identity of full-time nontenure-track faculty. *American Behavioral Scientist, 55,* 1461–1484. doi:10.1177/0002764211409382

McHenry, L., & Sharkey, P. W. (2014). Of Brahmins and Dalits in the academic caste system. *Academe, 100,* 35–38.

National Center for the Study of Collective Bargaining in Higher Education and the Professions, The. (n.d.). Available at: http://www.hunter.cuny.edu/ncscbhep

Ray, D., Jayne, K., & Miller, R. (2014). Master counselors as teachers: Clinical practices of counselor educators. *Journal of Mental Health Counseling, 36,* 78–94.

Reevy, G. M., & Deason, G. (2014). Predictors of depression, stress, and anxiety among non-tenure track faculty. *Frontiers in Psychology, 5.* Retrieved from http://journal.frontiersin.org/article/10.3389/fpsyg.2014.00701/full

Rhoades, G. (2013). Disruptive innovations for adjunct faculty: Common sense for the common good. *Thought & Action, 29,* 71–86.

Schudde, L. T., & Goldrick-Rab, S. (2016). Extending opportunity, perpetuating privilege: Institutional stratification amid educational expansion. In M. N. Bastedo, P. G. Altbach, & P. J. Gumport (Eds.), *American higher education in the 21st century: Social, political, and economic challenges* (4th ed., pp. 345–374). Baltimore, MD: Johns Hopkins University Press.

Schulz, L. L., Jones, L. D., Wagner, T., & Cheatham, K. (2012). *Clinical faculty in counselor education: A both/and proposition.* Unpublished study, University of North Texas, Denton.

Shaker, G. (2008). *Off the track: The full-time NTTF experience in English* (Unpublished doctoral dissertation). Indiana University, Bloomington.

Waltman, J., Bergom, I., Hollenshead, C., Miller, J., & August, L. (2012). Factors contributing to job satisfaction and dissatisfaction among non-tenure-track faculty. *Journal of Higher Education, 83,* 411–434.

Wilson, R. (2010). For-profit colleges change higher education's landscape. Retrieved from *The Chronicle of Higher Education* website: www.chronicle.com/article/For-Profit-Colleges-Change/64012/

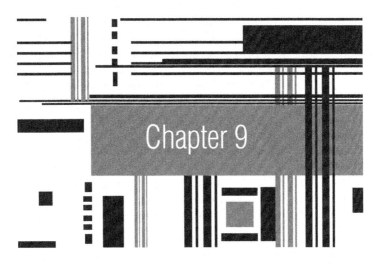

Chapter 9

Administration (Program Coordinator, Department Chair, Associate Dean, or Dean) in Counselor Education

Danica G. Hays

Counselor educators often land in administrative positions for multiple reasons, often unexpectedly, and they may be initially ambivalent to the idea of serving in a leadership role. It may be their turn, particularly for roles such as program coordinator or department chair. Some counselor educators decide to enter administration because they want to make a difference or leave their mark on a unit, whether that unit is a counselor education program, larger department, or college. Other counselor educators may enter administration for career advancement or financial gain. Still others may enter administration as a defensive strategy to prevent others from serving who are perceived to be harmful to a unit.

No matter the reason for entering administration or the number of academic leadership positions held, counselor educators are well suited from a skills perspective to serve in these roles. Specifically, counseling skills such as empathy, unconditional positive regard, active listening, and genuineness can create an invaluable toolbox for those in leadership roles. In addition, counselor educators often have extensive experience in community engagement, interacting with school districts, agencies, community colleges, and the surrounding community. Counselor educators also tend to be well versed in accreditation processes with bodies such as the Council for Accreditation of Counseling and Related Educational Programs (CACREP), which primes them for understanding and responding to accreditation and program review needs within and across units. Furthermore, counseling and social justice are inextricably linked, and counselor educators value advocacy in their work. Collectively the skill set and array of experiences prime counselor educators who lead in the academic setting well to make positive changes for students, personnel, and academic programs and beyond.

In summary, serving in administration relates to the sphere of influence within a program, department, or college or across colleges. That is, depending on the level of the leadership appointment, counselor educators can help shape colleagues and students within and across various units. I begin this chapter with a couple of sections to orient you to the characteristics of the administration pipeline and specific administrative positions. Another section follows that addresses key intrapersonal and interpersonal challenges of serving as an administrator. Then I include a major section on the essential operational and strategic ingredients for being an effective administrator. The chapter concludes with sections on working effectively with administrators and training recommendations for counselor education programs.

The Administration Pipeline

Understanding the administration pipeline is an important first step in understanding the context of counselor educators entering academic leadership positions. Given the increasing need to select and prepare diverse counselor educators to meet the challenges and opportunities of academic institutions today, diversifying and expanding those who constitute the administration pipeline is especially imperative. The administration pipeline represents eligible individuals in the queue to serve in academic leadership positions. To have a successful pipeline, the queue should be composed of individuals with diverse leadership experiences and diverse cultural backgrounds in general. For instance, beginning in doctoral training programs, individuals should receive adequate training in leadership skills, be exposed to administrative tasks that further their professional development, and be encouraged to partake of leadership opportunities that foster their personal and professional growth while allowing them to facilitate growth in others and units as a whole. Throughout their careers, counselor educators incrementally take on new opportunities (e.g., field placement coordinator, program coordinator) to bolster the queue and perhaps engage in more advanced leadership opportunities (e.g., department chair, dean) in the future.

Even with an emphasis on diversity to ensure an adequate administration pipeline, securing gender and racial/ethnic diversity can be particularly challenging. With respect to gender, what has historically been valued in terms of leadership traits and leadership models is often characterized as more masculine (e.g., assertiveness, stoicism) and thus may limit women's aspirations for leadership (Dunn, Gerlach, & Hyle, 2014). Data certainly indicate—particularly at upper levels of academic administration—that women are underrepresented as university presidents (22%), chief academic officers (40%), and other senior-level administrators (43%); these percentages are even lower at research-intensive universities (Almanac of Higher Education, 2013).

If one considers that the administration pipeline requires individuals to graduate from college and graduate school, then progress successfully through the ranks of a counselor education academic position, and then aspire to varying administrative positions, the playing field for women and people of color is far from level compared to White men. The Institute of Education Sciences, a division of the U.S. Department of Education, highlighted in a report, *Status and Trends in the Education of Racial and Ethnic Groups 2016,* obstructions in the pipeline related to college graduation (National Center for Education Statistics, 2016b). Six-year college graduation rates averaged about 59% overall in 2013, yet rates for Black/African American and American Indian/Alaska Native students were 41% each (compared to a rate of 71% for Asians and Asian Americans). Furthermore, the percentage of adults age 25 and older who obtained a bachelor's degree in 2013 varied considerably: Asians/Asian Americans (52%), Whites (33%), multiracial individuals (32%), Blacks/African Americans (19%), American Indians/Alaska Natives (15%), and Latinos/Hispanics (14%). Thus, if individuals of racially and ethnically diverse backgrounds have disproportionate graduation rates at these levels, they will not be represented proportionately in more advanced degrees and thus will not engage in even the lower rungs of the administration pipeline.

Demographics of those in academia support this clog in the administration pipeline: Data from 2011 indicate that only about 18.7% of faculty members and 19.9% of college administrators (at all levels) identified as a racial/ethnic minority (Almanac of Higher Education, 2014). Disaggregated by gender, percentages of full-time faculty (across all ranks) were 43% White men, 35% White women, 6% Asian/Pacific Islander men, 4% Asian/Pacific Islander women, 3% Black men, 3% Black women, 2% Hispanic men, and 2% Hispanic women; and less than 1% constituted American Indian/Alaska Native men and women. The proportion of professors and associate professors showed even greater disproportionality, which is troubling given that faculty members at these ranks hold the majority of administrative positions in higher education. Specifically, White men made up the majority of professors (58%), followed by White women (26%); Asian/Pacific Islander men (7%); Black men, Hispanic men, and Asian/Pacific Islander women (2% each); and then Black women and Hispanic women (less than 2% each). For the associate professor rank, percentages were as follows: White men (44%), White women (34%), Asian/Pacific Islander men (7%), Asian/Pacific Islander women (4%), Black men and women (3% each), and Hispanic men and women (2% each; National Center for Education Statistics, 2016a).

The intention of sharing the nature of the administration pipeline today is to emphasize the importance of mentoring potential future leaders early in their training and/or counselor education careers, with a focus on women and those with culturally diverse backgrounds. Counselor educators entering administration—particularly women and/or those who may endorse more feminine leadership characteristics—have an opportunity to develop new ways of leading, particularly during times of great financial and sociopolitical challenges within institutions today (Dunn et al., 2014). That is, the landscape of higher education institutions is changing—particularly within colleges of education, where counselor education programs are typically housed. Students and faculty are increasingly more culturally diverse, and the academic and psychosocial needs and expectations of the average traditionally aged student—as well as the number and type of nontraditional students entering education-related programs—are much different from previous generations. These demographic shifts create demands for how units prepare students for the workforce, requiring flexibility in academic leadership and thus more diversity today (Buller, 2015; Wolverton & Gmelch, 2002).

As future academic leaders from counselor education backgrounds are mentored to lead in dynamic and changing institutions, it is also important to explore ways in which a current unit's structure may be discouraging eligible leaders—intentionally or not—from transitioning into academic administrative positions. For example, counselor educators may need to educate deans and others within an institution about the unique expertise that counselor educators possess and thus can contribute to department and college-level administrative positions.

Types of Academic Administrative Positions

Counselor educators have opportunities to engage in multiple administrative positions throughout their careers; opportunities to enter the positions described in this section tend to become available in a fairly sequential manner (i.e., program coordinator, then department chair, then associate dean, then dean). At times, counselor educators may enter administration and then return to an academic faculty position after an administrative term has ended.

These position descriptions are designed to represent typical examples of the positions; how any administrator leads, however, is a function of what he or she brings to the position as an individual as well as an agent of the institution in which that position is housed. Thus, the ways in which positions are actually expressed will vary from person to person and context to context. Furthermore, administrators respond to and are responsible to multiple stakeholders; some of these stakeholder groups may have opposing needs or agendas, and administrators often have to serve as conduits among those groups. Stakeholder groups include students, staff, adjunct faculty, tenured and nontenured faculty, department chairs, deans, central university administrators, alumni, advisory and regulatory boards, potential students, employers, donors, competing programs, colleges and institutions, professional associations, community partners, and so on. Throughout the position descriptions in the following section, I present sample activities for these categories, although some of these activities may be delegated to others depending on the size and complexity of the program. In areas in which different administrative positions share activities, the lower rank position serves as the earlier point of contact to try and address any issues or concerns within that category.

Program Coordinator

A program coordinator is an individual who oversees operational and strategic activities associated with a counselor education program. No counselor education program composition is quite alike, as some programs include a combination of certificate, undergraduate, master's, education specialist, or doctoral-level options. Furthermore, the course modalities offered (e.g., traditional, online, hybrid), number and type of faculty, and level of involvement with the surrounding community will influence the type of work a program coordinator might do. In some instances, there may be program coordinators who oversee each degree option as well as another individual who serves exclusively as a field placement or practicum and internship coordinator. In some programs with fewer resources, a program coordinator may oversee and direct several degree program options along with field placement activities for the counselor education program.

One of the common tasks of program coordinators is scheduling courses in partnership with a department chair or another administrator. Program coordinators are tasked with developing course schedules that meet students' enrollment needs in a way that progresses them through a program efficiently in modalities that maximize learning, developing and advocating for curricular offerings that help to market to prospective students or meet the changing needs of a discipline, and avoiding scheduling courses in a manner that competes with other popular courses or fails to use the available scheduling periods well.

In addition to course scheduling, program coordinators—often in partnership with department chairs—oversee enrollment management (i.e., recruitment, admissions, enrollment, progression, and completion of students), advisement activities (e.g., curricular advisement, thesis and dissertation support), mentorship activities (e.g., teaching support for graduate assistants or junior faculty, career networking, professional development, diversity recruitment and retention), and resource advocacy and support (e.g., graduate research and teaching assistantships and fellowships, faculty and student travel awards and scholarships). Many of these activities carry high stakes for those counselor education programs that offer doctoral degrees and that seek high national rankings through outfits such as *U.S. News & World Report*.

Course scheduling and enrollment management are key activities for this position, but there are many others. Program coordinators also perform the following: (a) mediating conflict between students and/or between students and unit faculty members; (b) supporting student organizations and other methods to foster students' professional development; (c) serving as a point of contact for hiring adjunct faculty members; (d) mentoring faculty; (e) facilitating program-level meetings with faculty; (f) representing program needs at department meetings; (g) developing and maintaining program handbooks and program-related initiatives; (h) advocating for adequate personnel and other resources for the program; (i) monitoring student and program-level records; (j) ensuring that policies and procedures at the program level are followed; (k) developing a strategic plan, goals, objectives, and indicators for the program; (l) building program culture, attending specifically to diversity and advocacy; (m) managing conflict and crises as well as the daily life of the program; and (n) establishing program advisory councils and boards to support general program quality.

Furthermore, program coordinators in CACREP-accredited programs often serve as the primary point of contact for accreditation procedures. In their role, they are to see that the academic unit maintains the appropriate student-to-faculty ratio along with reasonable teaching and advising loads, recruits and retains diverse students and faculty, and infuses CACREP (2015) curricular objectives into relevant instructional and supervision experiences. Also, the program coordinator leads faculty in developing and maintaining systematic evaluation systems as well as establishing clear and fair policies and procedures for student onboarding, advisement, retention, remediation, and dismissal (CACREP, 2015). Aligned with these accreditation requirements, program coordinators are expected to advocate for their students, faculty, and program to ensure adequate personnel and fiscal resources.

Department Chair

Department chairs are the gatekeepers for curriculum changes, budget decisions, and promotion and tenure processes. Department chairs tend to have significant interactions with program faculty, program coordinators, and college-level administrators. Depending on the size of the department, their experiences can be quite different (Buller, 2006). In smaller departments, department chairs may receive little to no release time from teaching and may share administrative staff resources with other departments. In some small departments, department chairs may not be the primary individuals who evaluate faculty and staff within their department, advocate for salary increases, or make course scheduling decisions. Nevertheless, a smaller department may yield more intimate, collegial interactions between a department chair and his or her faculty.

In larger departments, department chairs may have minimal to no teaching duties. They may have a more indirect responsibility concerning course scheduling, assigning student workers and assistants to various duties, and other common activities. With this setup, department chairs, having integral roles in merit, promotion, and tenure decision conversations, usually have line authority over faculty members within their department.

Depending on the institution, the department chair's role can vary tremendously. Other typical activities are as follows: (a) mediating conflict between students and/or between students and faculty members; (b) engaging in the community on the behalf of departmental programs or the college; (c) advocating with deans for graduate assistantship and fellowship allocations; (d) mentoring faculty, staff, students, and program coordinators; (e) supporting faculty scholarship and teaching; (f) recommending new hires for programs and the department; (g) fostering workload and salary equity for faculty and staff; (h) serving as a communications link between the department and others; (i) representing the department at the college level and beyond; (j) managing the flow of information within the department; (k) developing and maintaining the departmental budget, including budgeting requisitions from faculty and programs; (l) evaluating faculty, staff, graduate assistants, and student workers; (m) recommending faculty for promotion, tenure, and merit pay; (n) recruiting faculty, staff, and students; (o) generating reports about departmental operations for internal and external audiences; (p) ensuring that policies and procedures are followed at the department level and working with program coordinators on program-level considerations; (q) leading departmental implementation of the college mission; (r) mobilizing departmental resources; (s) stimulating the curriculum; (t) building department culture, attending specifically to diversity and advocacy; (u) managing conflict and crises as well as the daily life of the department; and (v) fostering alumni relations.

Assistant, Associate, or Executive Associate Dean

Assistant, associate, and executive associate dean positions are considered midlevel college positions, often entered into by those with program coordinator or department chair experience but who are not ready or interested in a deanship or other upper administrative role. Individuals in these positions have an interest in knowing broadly the positions and programs within and across colleges, creating a network across campus.

Defining these three types of associate dean positions can be complicated. The difference between an assistant dean and associate dean will depend on the institution. In some cases, the associate dean may have more seniority or advanced skills than an assistant dean. Or an assistant dean may lack a terminal degree, faculty classification, and/or tenure status. In other cases, the distinction between the positions may be related to the amount of administrative service the individual is completing in the context of his or her total academic workload. In still other cases, there may be very little difference if any at all. As Buller (2015) noted, "The simplest way to view this distinction ... is whatever your institution says it is" (p. 270).

Some colleges have the position *executive associate dean*, a term that can be used interchangeably with the term *vice dean*. Executive associate deans have substantial responsibility for internal college activities (e.g., faculty affairs, student affairs, facilities management, communications) and may supervise or oversee in some way the work of assistant or associate deans.

Assistant, associate, and executive associate deans work on the dean's behalf and are usually responsible for high-level tasks without having great authority to complete those tasks. They tend to specialize in a single administrative area, such as assessment, research and sponsored projects, undergraduate programs, graduate programs, diversity, or faculty development. They are typically selected because they complement the dean's strengths and counterbalance any weaknesses. Thus, they are often the front line for many internal activities of the college, addressing operational and strategic initiatives related to focused areas and working in consultation with the dean.

Dean

The dean serves as the advocate for a collection of programs and initiatives that hold a common historical purpose in local, regional, national, and international communities. Deans have an array of responsibilities that help to set direction for the college, departments, and programs; empower others in the college; and build a sense of community internal and external to the college (Buller, 2015; Wolverton & Gmelch, 2002). Specifically, they tend to have the responsibilities of (a) generating and apportioning external funds and development dollars for the college; (b) meeting with external partners in the local community and within the legislature to help advocate for the needs of the college and inform policy decisions; (c) overseeing hiring decisions and protocols related to faculty and staff; (d) guiding promotion and tenure procedures and mentoring faculty throughout the process; (e) managing multiple day-to-day operational details; (f) promoting and marketing college-level initiatives; (g) engaging in diversity initiatives that help to recruit and retain faculty, staff, and students; (h) allocating funds to students (e.g., graduate assistantships, fellowships, scholarships) and programs (e.g., research centers, community projects); (i) developing a cohesive vision and set of goals that continue to motivate other college personnel; and (j) establishing, encouraging, and evaluating curricula that both benefit students and also generate revenue, to name a few activities. In addition to the aforementioned activities, deans ensure that department chairs, program coordinators, and other leaders within the college are doing an effective job as well as provide support as needed to them to be effective. Furthermore, deans continually engage with students, staff, and faculty within the college as well as those in upper administration (e.g., the provost, the president).

Challenges of Administration

With a foundational understanding of the four common department and college-level administration categories described in the previous section, it is important to highlight several key challenges of administration. Counselor educators should be prepared for these common challenges as they enter administration and find continual support to address them. These challenges—work–life balance, tensions regarding professional identity, interpersonal challenges with unit colleagues, and competition with other units—often relate to larger themes of balance and competition.

One key challenge is maintaining a work–life balance. The nature of some administrative work requires counselor educators to attend events or respond to emails and telephone calls outside of the typical workday and workweek. Although academic leadership positions tend to be reserved for tenured faculty, junior faculty may be tasked with leadership responsibilities in smaller units or smaller institutions. Thus, junior faculty can face challenges of work–life balance from both the demands of an administrative position as well as the demands associated with seeking promotion and tenure. Furthermore, demands on time and loss of time to pursue personal interests can be particularly challenging when one is caring for young children or aging parents. In fact, the overwhelming nature of the work—in the context of the depletion of time resources—has been viewed as a major barrier to entering and remaining in administration (DeZure, Shaw, & Rojewski, 2014).

Another common challenge involves tensions regarding professional identity. This refers to the tension between identifying as a counselor educator (affiliated with professional associations and discipline values respective to that profession) and identifying as an administrator (aligned with or at least engaging at a deeper level in professional associations and values associated with that role). As counselor educators advance in administration, having a greater sphere of influence to change systems creates more of a tug of war between identities. This tension extends beyond simply affiliating with multiple roles: With increased administrative demands, counselor educators face challenges of decreased attention to their scholarly work and thus less connection to the content of their specialty area. In a qualitative study conducted with 19 administrators and 16 faculty identified as "emerging leaders" (DeZure et al., 2014), one participant described this challenge as "tak[ing] faculty from the things they most love about academic life: research, teaching, and students" (p. 7).

As counselor educators move into department or college-level administrative positions, they will certainly encounter interpersonal challenges with their colleagues. For example, counseling program faculty and those training to be counselor educators are likely familiar with the phrase "going to the dark side," used to describe the transition from faculty to administrative positions. Even with their best efforts to maintain trust and connection—and advocate for their programs at a broader level—going to the dark side can represent the notion that counselor educators are choosing the priorities of others over their programs. DeZure et al. (2014) noted that there is often a cultural divide between administrators and faculty members, resulting in a lack of trust as well as a distancing within relationships. In DeZure et al.'s research, participants described this phenomenon as "us against them," "joining forces with the devil," and "making decisions without faculty input." They reported that those who go beyond serving as department chair would not be "faculty anymore … a traitor to [their] discipline" (p. 10). Furthermore, depending on the level of the position, counselor educators in administrative roles are expected to make decisions that may not benefit their discipline. A major implication of these interpersonal challenges is that administrators are often faced with loneliness within their respective units and must seek out support networks, typically outside of their units.

In addition to potentially not being trusted by colleagues, counselor educators face interpersonal challenges within their units just by the nature of wearing many hats as an administrator (e.g., colleague, supervisor, manager, supervisee). For example, administrators are constantly challenged to advocate for their subordinates while supervising them—while being supervised by someone else (Buller, 2015). Depending on the size, complexity, and available resources of the unit, it may also be difficult to motivate colleagues to take ownership and complete necessary tasks when there are no incentives to offer.

Administration involves competition among units, which is another key challenge. The reality of persistent budget cuts and limited grant funding and development dollars in colleges and universities can create high levels of competition for resources. To leverage resources, counselor educators as administrators are required to develop a unit culture that is distinct from that of surrounding units, with unique needs yet clear examples of unit viability. Thus, counselor educators have to be adept at advocating for unit needs while promoting potential and actual unit successes to access or retain resources. An additional downside of this required competition is that, to deal with other challenges, administrators often need to develop support networks with individuals they are ultimately competing with in some manner for resources.

Essential Ingredients for Being an Effective Administrator

Although the aforementioned challenges can seem substantial, counselor educators with essential leadership components and ongoing support can mitigate these challenges to maximize success for their students, staff, faculty, and units as a whole. Counselor educators serving as effective administrators require a balance of administrative talent and an extensive understanding of academics as well as a blend of task orientation and interpersonal skills. The essential ingredients for being an effective administrator can involve operational or strategic skills, and effective administrators constantly weave between these two skill categories.

Some of these skill areas can be learned on the job; the important piece is that prospective and current administrators understand who they are, taking stock of their personal and professional strengths and weaknesses. With knowledge of their strengths and weaknesses, administrators can compose a team that counterbalances any challenge areas. Furthermore, administrators, no matter their type, should have a clear sense of their role, what they are trying to accomplish in that role, and who they are in terms of long-term career goals. No administrator implements these principles and skills in the same way: There is no specific prototype for what an administrator should look like, and skill sets necessary to be a successful academic leader vary depending on the institution or even the timing of the position.

Embedded within effective leadership principles and skills is the notion of promoting diversity. Administrators should constantly encourage and sustain increased participation from culturally diverse students, staff, and faculty within their respective units. Examples of promoting diversity include having culturally affirmative student recruitment and faculty and staff hiring practices, developing culturally appropriate and culturally sensitive policies and procedures, offering curricular and extracurricular activities that cater to a broad range of individuals, and building infrastructure that supports specific challenges of underrepresented groups. Administrators should develop a diversity plan for their unit, communicating the value of diversity in various formats to relevant stakeholders.

Operational Ingredients

Operational ingredients are the requisite knowledge and skills that help a person to conduct the day-to-day business of a particular administrative position (Berdrow, 2010; Buller, 2006, 2015). The depth and breadth of these operational knowledge and skills will vary depending on the administrative position.

Exploring Leadership Style

One of the foundational operational ingredients is having a solid understanding of one's leadership style—administrators cannot engage in their work without one. It is important to know one's leadership style and the strengths and challenges of that style. In addition, at the department and college levels, administrators should be aware of the leadership styles of those making up any leadership teams in the department or college.

An effective leadership style embodies what scholars identify as common characteristics of successful academic leaders. For example, Wolverton Bower, and Hyle (2009) noted several common characteristics of successful leaders in higher education: self-confidence, passion and commitment to make a difference, and self-awareness of how one's own various dispositions may be beneficial and difficult in a position. Furthermore, Dunn et al. (2014) noted that selflessness—that is, facilitating success in others and being flexible and bending the rules to facilitate others' successes—is an important indicator for success. This notion of getting out of the spotlight to shine it on others has been associated with a facilitative leadership style, which is common among women administrators in educational settings (Porat, 1991).

Understanding Students, Staff, Faculty, and Programs

Administrators working within a respective unit need to be knowledgeable about their students, staff, and faculty and the work they do and why. For example, they should know the curriculum offered within their unit and changes that have occurred in the curriculum during the course of a particular academic program. Thus, they should understand course and degree offerings, how those offerings benefit students and the strategic vision of the unit and the university as a whole, and what technological resources are available to promote teaching and learning. In addition, administrators should understand curricular trends and benefits and challenges for students and faculty members. Furthermore, they should be aware of any accreditation requirements and ensure that those standards or protocols are met in the curriculum or unit experiences. In fact, administrators have a good working knowledge in general of program-level and region-level accreditation requirements relevant to the college, as these requirements affect multiple units in different ways.

Administrators should also be aware of faculty areas of expertise and relevant projects and initiatives. This knowledge can be useful for forming alliances with peers, promoting colleagues externally, and identifying colleagues with particular skills and interests to achieve more in the unit. Furthermore, administrators should know what current and prospective students need for their academic success, the extent to which students are learning and how satisfied they are with their learning experiences, and a general assessment of the learning environment climate in terms of curricular and extracurricular activities as well as how well diversity needs are met.

Knowing Relevant Policies and Procedures

To fulfill the operational needs of a unit, administrators need a solid understanding of policies and procedures affecting that unit. In addition, they need to understand how past decisions were made, how new decisions are made, and procedures for challenging policies and procedures—or when exceptions can and should be made to those policies and procedures. Policies and procedures can be related to recruitment, hiring, evaluating, firing, rewards and merit, grievance, and program and curricular changes, to name a few. Related to this, Buller (2015) noted that "decision-making is best done at the lowest possible level of any institution" (p. 173). Thus, administrators in more advanced positions (e.g., associate deans, deans) should empower those at other levels to develop and follow policies and procedures—and address any violations before stepping in and governing for other administrators.

Furthermore, Buller (2015) asserted that policies and procedures should exist to make individuals' work easier and safer, not harder. If a policy or procedure is too burdensome, it can impede productivity and also wear down the relationship between faculty members and administrators. Part of understanding policies and procedures is acknowledging when they no longer work but are sticking around because that's the way things have always been done. Thus, administrators need to be willing to make adjustments as needed to foster unit productivity, efficiency, and satisfaction. When developing new policies and procedures, it is important to make sure that they are absolutely needed, not reactive to solve a new problem prematurely, and are clearly written, communicated, and vetted.

Communicating Effectively With Personnel

Counselor educators in administrative roles also need strong communication skills. Communication skills have several facets: having interpersonal or people skills; gathering information, interpreting it, and providing it to multiple groups; holding continual formal and informal meetings with individuals, small groups, and large groups; being able to consider multiple perspectives as one engages with others; and listening, speaking, and writing effectively to others within and across units as well as to external stakeholders. Administrators communicate all the time, including when they are not intending to communicate. It is important to express clear expectations within the unit and convey new information in a timely manner to maintain trustworthiness and transparency within and across units. Clarifying one's role as an administrator versus as a counselor education faculty member may be an important part of communication.

Managing Time, People, and Tasks

Administrators must possess several types of management skills, including the ability to manage time, people, and tasks. Management skills involve being effective and efficient and resource oriented: The best managers are hard working, high energy, efficient, and timely. With respect to time management, having daily to-do lists with tasks prioritized and ranked is important. In addition, counselor educators need to set aside time for scholarship and teaching activities as applicable as well as personal leisure time to help manage stress. Furthermore, managing people and tasks are also essential skills that can get expressed in several ways: locating personnel strengths and minimizing the impact of any weaknesses on the unit; managing conflicts; motivating and influencing others; and planning, coordinating, and delegating tasks.

Supervising and Evaluating Personnel

Related to managing people is possessing supervisory and evaluation skills. Supervision entails supervising the day-to-day operations of personnel as well as conducting authentic, comprehensive, interactive, and on-time evaluations that include concrete goals and expected outcomes of those goals. Department chairs and deans are typically the two types of administrators involved in faculty and staff evaluations, although input from program coordinators and departmental faculty may be sought as part of procedures. Evaluation of faculty usually involves assessment in the areas of teaching, research, and service; the weight of each of these areas will vary depending on the type of institution. Evaluations should be clearly tied to job responsibilities, and the process of evaluation itself can offer an opportunity to revise unclear or inappropriate job tasks. Additional advisement and dissertation service may be expected of faculty involved with doctoral programs. Administrators in their supervisory roles should convey that any formative and summative evaluations conducted present an opportunity for professional growth as well as a time to reflect on individual strengths and contributions to the unit. Furthermore, evaluations should serve as a tool for coconstructing goals that lead to long-term success at the institution.

Budgeting

The final key operational ingredient to effective administration involves budget and financial management skills; these include understanding how budgets work, including planning, managing, and supervising funding sources. Specifically, administrators are faced with budgetary decisions because of resource cuts as well as ongoing pressure to generate revenue and use allocated resources effectively. With each higher level administrative position, budgets get larger; however, most skills are similar across positions. Administrators at more advanced levels will have greater control and influence over a budget, although a dean may be limited in what he or she can apportion to departments and other levels. Three primary types of budgeting exist (Buller, 2015): (a) zero-based budgeting, in which budgets reset to zero with each new budget period and are then developed from scratch; (b) historical budgeting, or the use of a past record of income and expenditures to guide future budgets; and (c) performance-based funding, in which budgets are allocated based on what predetermined targets were met by a unit. No matter your administrative level, it is important that you be aware of the type(s) of budgeting that other units in your institution use.

Strategic Ingredients

Strategic ingredients are those skills that allow administrators to set a long-term agenda that promotes the viability of their respective units. In addition to the aforementioned operational ingredients, possession of the following strategic ingredients requires that administrators grasp the broader university context. Thus, administrators need to understand how various pertinent organizational structures function individually and interdependently, what offices to contact across an institution to resolve issues, and whom to contact at those offices.

Establishing a Vision

Setting a vision is a core strategic skill for administrators. It is important to coconstruct a vision with relevant personnel within a respective unit. Administrators need to clarify their mission as a unit, often in the context of an institution's larger strategic vision. To begin thinking about a shared vision, administrators can process with faculty and other relevant staff what the shared values within the unit are, what makes the unit better than other similar units, what individuals are deeply passionate about (i.e., values), and whether those values help move the unit in a positive and innovative direction.

Developing a vision is important to promote the growth and advancement of the unit and may be accomplished through a series of steps. First counselor educators should consider how their program, department, or college is distinct (i.e., what its unique attributes are). Then they should work with others to build on and improve those unique attributes, basing that vision in innovative teaching, scholarship, or service priorities that can also gain national or international recognition as relevant. Often it is useful to connect the unit's vision to other higher level vision statements for cohesion and to illustrate a larger commitment to the institution (Buller, 2015). Cashwell and Barrio Minton (2012) noted that one way in which counselor educators can establish a vision—and program mission—is to conduct a strengths, weaknesses, opportunities, and threats analysis (see Hill & Westbrook, 1997). Results of a strengths, weaknesses, opportunities, and threats analysis can be shared with multiple stakeholder groups as the vision is established and refined at various administrative levels. Once a vision is developed, administrators should be consistent yet flexible in its messaging and implementation, creating buy-in along the way. Furthermore, they are to acknowledge, often publicly, how various individuals are contributing to the unit and vision.

Setting Goals

Related to establishing a vision is the strategic skill of goal setting. Buller (2006) used the analogy of taking a road trip to discuss goal setting. To illustrate the importance of goal setting as a strategic ingredient of leadership, imagine not having direction on a road trip: The driver may not have a starting place or destination in mind, may be unaware of what resources he or she has and needs along the way, and is likely unable to communicate to passengers the logistics of the trip. Similar to a driver beginning a road trip, it is important for administrators to know where they are now, who they are, where they would like to go, what they will need along the way, the various routes available and the pros and cons of each path, who will be a part of the journey, and when they will arrive at their goals. Administrators, depending on the level of their role, are tasked with aligning and rewarding individual and unit-based goals with larger strategic plans.

Recruiting and Hiring

Making good recruitment and hiring decisions—or at least advocating for good recruitment and hiring decisions—is another essential strategic area for administrators, no matter their level of authority. Hiring is more than replacing individuals who leave the university; counselor educators must use a hiring opportunity to not only align more closely with a unit's strategic plan but also recruit individuals who can potentially serve across programs and departments so that more faculty and students benefit. That is, hiring should seek to recruit someone who has a skill set that can both address content area gaps as well as fulfill larger unit needs (e.g., advising, grant activity, program development, community engagement, interdisciplinary teaching).

The recruitment and hiring process is an investment in a long-term colleague that will maximize your unit's success. Hires for a particular unit should represent a balance of ways of thinking and working, tied together by allegiance to the unit's mission and strategic vision. Furthermore, hiring requires flexibility in terms of cultural considerations. For example, if a dean wants to hire a department chair or assistant or associate dean, he or she may be naturally inclined to search for a full professor with specific experiences; however, data presented earlier suggest that there is a disproportionate number of White men in higher academic ranks. Thus, the diversity of an initial recruitment pool may be limited by having too stringent criteria. Furthermore, when hiring personnel with families, administrators need to consider the possibility of offering options such as flexible work schedules, child care incentives, or dual-career hiring.

In addition to recruiting and hiring faculty and staff, administrators also need to attend to recruiting high-quality and culturally diverse students. An effective recruitment process is founded on a solid enrollment management plan and the promotion of cultural diversity within the student body. Effective administrators of various levels pay close attention to trends in student recruitment and regularly solicit feedback from students on their perceptions of the learning environment.

Building Strong Networks

Effective administrators also build strong networks with students, parents, advisory boards, other administrators at both higher and lower places on the organizational chart, upper administrators, media outlets, outside community members, and politicians, to name a few. Depending on the administrative role, a strong network can be useful for accreditation functions, fundraising, alumni relations, community engagement, and policy making. Building support networks within and outside the university is an indicator of successful leadership (Dunn et al., 2014). It is important to remember that it may be difficult for female administrators to build large networks given the disproportionate number of women in academic leadership.

Valuing Innovation

Given changes in institutions today, administrators should be innovative. Being innovative often involves making changes to operationalize a strategic vision, and innovation can be proactive or remedial. However, innovation should not be taken on for the simple exercise of making changes. Thus, although leaders are naturally change oriented, administrators need to be sure that specific changes should be made in the first place. To consider how to integrate innovation into the unit, counselor educators should reflect with other personnel on what critical challenges or specific problems the unit needs to address or solve and what the costs (e.g., opportunity, time, personnel, financial) of making those changes are. Administrators should realize that change is slow and should expect that less change will occur than was initially less welcomed by those within the unit. Furthermore, they need to communicate openly about what changes are being made and why, get input throughout the change process, and provide incentives when possible to implement the change (Buller, 2015).

Embracing Data

Institutional and community data can be very useful to administrators because they can be used to help promote a unit to external audiences, showing how it is distinct and an asset to the community and nation. Data can also help inform fundraising and scholarship initiatives. In addition, understanding and communicating data about student, staff, and faculty successes are useful for supporting the unit climate as well as promoting the unit. Having knowledge of what data are out there, and how they can be mined and communicated and for what purposes, will allow administrators to showcase their leadership efforts even further.

Building the Administration Pipeline

Effective administrators think strategically about future leaders, particularly how counselor educators from culturally diverse backgrounds can be cultivated for administration. Thus, one of the essential ingredients of administration is having culturally diverse administrators within and across units in terms of gender, race/ethnicity, sexual orientation, ability status, and age. Diversity helps to bring innovative ideas to grow units as well as invaluable perspectives on academic and institutional concerns that plague the academy. Moreover, cultural diversity is an essential ingredient in academic leadership, and administrators can model this opportunity to others who may have viewed administration as out of their reach. Administrators who identify with majority cultural groups (i.e., Whites, males, heterosexuals, the able-bodied) are to ensure that they are mentoring and advocating for individuals of minority statuses to engage in leadership opportunities. However, as DeZure et al. (2014) cautioned, this engagement should be in activities that enhance versus undermine their careers.

In addition to making good hiring decisions, administrators are to identify which faculty members within their unit(s) at different ranks seem to value multiple perspectives, care about the general welfare of the unit, solve problems, and in general exhibit the actual or potential for other skills mentioned in this section of the chapter. Administrators can also encourage potential leaders by pointing out their potential and actual leadership strengths, demystifying specific administrative roles by explaining what the roles entail and what skills are involved, and conversing periodically with them about their future plans and interest regarding leadership and leadership development (DeZure et al., 2014). Once they identify potential leaders, administrators can, as DeZure et al. (2014) suggested, assign them tasks of varying levels and see how well they do and/or develop opportunities for job shadowing. Delegation of tasks or job shadowing not only help to solidify a pipeline but also help to create trust between faculty members and administrators while getting rid of some of the stereotypical views of what administration is or what administrators are like.

Working Effectively With Administrators

I hope that counselor educators working with administrators at the department, college, and even university level can use the information in this chapter to better understand the life of an administrator. This knowledge of administration can be used to better leverage individual and program needs in light of competing priorities administrators have. For example, a counselor education program may advocate with a department chair for additional graduate assistants and in exchange offer to serve as an advocate for a department-led initiative (e.g., a pilot technology program). Or a counselor educator could approach a dean because he or she is concerned about the lack of diversity representation in the program. That counselor educator may agree to assist the dean with a specific recruitment campaign for the college.

CACREP accreditation can also provide a platform for working well with administrators, including offering specific standards related to training doctoral students in leadership and advocacy (Standard 6.B.5.; CACREP, 2015). More explicitly, counselor educators serving in leadership roles at the program, department, or college level are to ensure that institutions for which they work support an optimal learning environment, such as that outlined by the CACREP (2015) Standards. Specifically, Standards 1.A.–1.I. note that the institution in which a counselor education program is housed should clearly describe and represent the program to internal and external constituents as well as provide financial, scholarly, technological, professional development, and physical and virtual instructional space resources to program faculty and students. Thus, adhering to CACREP Standards can provide counselor educators with a forum for working more effectively with administrators while getting their program needs met at multiple levels.

I conclude this section with what is likely an intuitive statement: Administrators are simply human beings. Even the most effective administrators are prone to make mistakes, and they often welcome support from their colleagues. They want to interact with colleagues beyond the instances when those colleagues need a favor or want to voice a complaint. Thus, it is important for counselor educators to consider how they can give back to their colleagues who happen to also be administrators. The likely return in investment will be more collegial relationships as well as a united front to address concerns that multiple units face.

Training Best Practices for Counselor Education Programs

Given the context of the administration pipeline today, counselor educators play a frontline role in strengthening that pipeline as they prepare counselor trainees. Counselor educators should intentionally encourage trainees, particularly those of more marginalized statuses, to consider academic leadership. Whether they enter administrative positions themselves, counselor educators have an obligation to equip future counselor educators entering academic faculty positions with information about leadership positions.

There are several ways in which counselor educators can encourage their trainees to consider a potential administrative path, such as facilitating self-awareness of leadership skills and imparting knowledge about leadership in general and leadership as a counselor educator more specifically. More specifically, counselor educators could provide the following opportunities to counselor trainees: (a) instruction on available leadership models and theories, with a critical lens on diversity and challenges within the administration pipeline and why those challenges exist; (b) self-awareness activities for trainees to assess their leadership strengths and challenges through multiple opportunities (e.g., formal course work, class discussions, assessments); (c) research opportunities to investigate leadership in counselor education, particularly related to diversity; (d) informational interviewing assignments so that trainees are able to observe and speak with counselor educators about leadership effectiveness and challenges; (e) mentoring networks between trainees and faculty and administrators at their institution and beyond; (f) opportunities for doctoral students to participate in program- and department-level meetings to gain knowledge of how administrative processes work; (g) development of a chapter of Chi Sigma Iota International if one is not available; (h) encouragement and incentives for trainees to participate in professional associations, such as the Association for Counselor Education and Supervision and the American Counseling Association, to begin building leadership skills and experiences that can later serve them well in administrative positions; and (i) scholarship resources so that trainees stay abreast of the profession's literature related to leadership. This is by no means a comprehensive list of ways in which counselor educators can facilitate trainees' interest in academic leadership positions. As counselor educators engage in these activities, they are to emphasize to trainees the benefits of counselor educators becoming involved in administration in general.

Conclusion

I hope that this chapter has served as a primer for counselor educators and trainees interested or potentially interested in entering into administration at the department and college levels. What should be evident in a discussion of administration is that counselor educators in administrative roles are not effective when they prioritize their own interests and need for power. Buller (2015) succinctly clarified that "leadership isn't synonymous with power. Power is the ability to get what you want. Leadership is the act of helping others achieve what they need" (p. 14). Thus, success in academic leadership centers on working on behalf of others and bringing people and groups together for a common goal. Counselor educators, by the nature of the work they do in counseling, are well suited for success in academic leadership.

I close with a poignant quote that has helped me in my administrative roles when the work seems too challenging or change is not happening fast enough for the common good. The quote reminds me why I entered and have stayed in administration, and I hope it is helpful to you:

[Administrators] are needed to move our institutions forward and to make the case for higher education. The work that we do—and the vital teaching, research, and outreach that it facilitates—transforms lives, organizations, industries, communities, and nations. We could not ask for a more compelling contribution. Colleges and universities are in the business of creating the future every day. As academic leaders, we can help that happen when we bring deep insight into the dynamics of our institutions and the requirements to lead them, confidence in ourselves, clarity about our vocation, and commitment to purpose. That is a worthy and sacred legacy and an emblem of a life well spent. (Bolman & Gallos, 2011, p. 221)

Additional Online Resources

American Academic Leadership Institute, Programs
   https://americanali.org/aali-programs/
American Council on Education, Leadership
   www.acenet.edu/leadership
The Chair Academy, Academy Programs
   www.chairacademy.com/index_acad.html
Higher Education Resource Services
   https://hersnet.org/

References

Almanac of Higher Education. (2013). *Distribution of presidents and senior administrators at 4-year institutions, by age, gender, race and ethnicity.* Washington, DC: Chronicle of Higher Education.

Almanac of Higher Education. (2014). *Race and ethnicity of college administrators, faculty, and staff, fall 2011.* Washington, DC: Chronicle of Higher Education.

Berdrow, I. (2010). King among kings: Understanding the role and responsibilities of the department chair in higher education. *Educational Management Administration & Leadership, 38,* 499–514. doi:10.1177/1741143210368146

Bolman, L. G., & Gallos, J. V. (2011). *Reframing academic leadership.* San Francisco, CA: Jossey-Bass.

Buller, J. L. (2006). *The essential department chair: A practical guide to college administration.* Bolton, MA: Anker.

Buller, J. L. (2015). *The essential academic dean or provost: A comprehensive desk reference* (2nd ed.). San Francisco, CA: Jossey-Bass.

Cashwell, C. S., & Barrio Minton, C. A. (2012). Leadership and advocacy in counselor education programs. In C. Y. Chang, C. A. Barrio Minton, A. L. Dixon, J. E. Myers, & T. J. Sweeney (Eds.), *Professional counseling excellence through leadership and advocacy* (pp. 165–183). New York, NY: Routledge.

Council for Accreditation of Counseling and Related Educational Programs. (2015). *CACREP 2016 standards.* Alexandria, VA: Author.

DeZure, D., Shaw, A., & Rojewski, J. (2014, January/February). Cultivating the next generation of academic leaders: Implications for administrators and faculty. *Change, 46,* 7–12. doi:10.1080/00091383.2013.842102

Dunn, D., Gerlach, J. M., & Hyle, A. E. (2014). Gender and leadership: Reflections of women in higher education administration. *International Journal of Leadership and Change, 2,* 9–18. Retrieved from https://digitalcommons.wku.edu/ijlc/vol2/iss1/2/

Hill, T., & Westbrook, R. (1997). SWOT analysis: It's time for a product recall. *Long Range Planning, 30,* 46–52. doi:10.1016/S0024-6301(96)00095-7

National Center for Education Statistics. (2016a). *The condition of education 2016* (NCES 2016-144). Retrieved from https://nces.ed.gov/pubs2016/2016144.pdf

National Center for Education Statistics. (2016b). *Status and trends in the education of racial and ethnic groups 2016* (NCES 2016-007). Retrieved from nces.ed.gov/pubs2016/2016007.pdf

Porat, K. L. (1991). Women in administration: The difference is positive. *Clearing House, 64,* 412–415.

Wolverton, M., Bower, B., & Hyle, A. E. (Eds.). (2009). *Leading ladies: Presidents and policy makers in higher education.* Sterling, VA: Stylus.

Wolverton, M., & Gmelch, W. H. (2002). *College deans: Leading from within.* Westport, CT: American Council on Education/Oryx Press.

Chapter 10

Professional Leadership at the State, Regional, National, and International Levels

Nicole R. Hill and Erin N. Friedman

The values and beliefs of counselor educators are strongly aligned with the qualities and competencies associated with effective leaders (Lewis, 2012; McKibben, Umstead, & Borders, 2017; Paradise, Ceballos, & Hall, 2010). Individuals who are becoming counselor educators believe in the dignity and well-being of each person, in the possibility of change and transformation, and in the criticality of positively contributing to the growth and development of others. All of these values are integrated into the definition of leadership in counselor education that we espouse: the ability, through vision, engagement, and embodiment, to evoke a shared mission toward action and change. Leadership then becomes a central role that counselor educators evince through their dedication to serving as catalysts for growth and development and as advocates at the micro-, macro-, and mesolevels (Myers, 2012). Counselor educators in the higher education setting engage in varied types of leadership, including association leadership at the state, regional, national, and international levels.

Leadership is a construct that is discussed pervasively in today's society, with ongoing deconstruction of leaders' styles, identities, and impact as well as their competence. Although there is a substantial body of literature regarding leadership, the theoretical exposition and scholarly exploration of leadership within counselor education is still at a neophyte stage of development. The literature on leadership within counseling is very limited, and the literature on leadership for counselor educators specifically is even rarer. In a content analysis of the literature on leadership in professional counseling, McKibben et al. (2017) identified 11 empirical articles, nine conceptual manuscripts, and 13 profiles of leaders from 1974 to 2014. Across 40 years of professional counseling discourse, only 33 manuscripts focused on leadership in counseling. Leadership in counseling, let alone counselor education, has been largely overlooked in our discipline's scholarship, yet most of us as beginning and experienced counselor educators will be invited to and/or will pursue leadership positions at state, regional, national, and international levels during our careers.

Being prepared as a counselor educator to navigate the different levels of professional association leadership while balancing the demands of academia is a critical area of competence for emerging counselor educators. Serving as leaders in professional associations provides counselor educators with an opportunity to evidence the service expectation articulated in tenure and promotion guidelines across institutions. Higher education settings require faculty members to engage in three primary roles, namely, teaching, scholarship, and service. Association leadership provides a compelling opportunity for counselor educators to meet faculty demands while contributing to the larger profession. Many institutions of higher education expect counselor educators to articulate their scope of influence in the service domain, and professional association leadership can provide a benchmark for how the individual counselor educator is affecting the profession of counselor education at the state, regional, national, and/or international levels.

In this chapter, stand-alone sections describe leadership practice and competence, the core components of being a counselor educator-leader, benefits and challenges of being a leader in a professional association, professional leadership within the context of higher education, program accreditation and professional leadership, diversity and social justice issues in leadership practice, the trajectory of leadership practice in counselor education, recommendations for facilitating counselor educator-leaders in graduate programs, and finally a case example of both of our evolution as leaders. Discussions of the influence of program type, Carnegie classification, nonprofit/for-profit status, and public/private status are embedded in the chapter. Given counselor education's overlap with the counseling profession as a whole, some literature on leadership in counseling is referenced to contextualize our understanding of leadership in higher education settings. Our training as counselor educators encompasses the skill and professional socialization we experienced as counselors, so there is an integration of our identities as professional counselors as we assume the role of counselor educators. Our development of leadership as counselor educators is built on the foundation of our competence and values as counselors.

Counselor educators have varied opportunities to serve the profession through association leadership. You can become involved in the Association for Counselor Education and Supervision (ACES), the American Counseling Association (ACA), Chi Sigma Iota (CSI), the National Board for Certified Counselors (NBCC), or a variety of divisions associated with ACA and other affiliates (such as the American School Counselor Association). In addition, you can serve as a reviewer of self-studies submitted by programs for accreditation review by the Council for Accreditation of Counseling and Related Educational Programs (CACREP). You can also elect to serve as a team member who participates in site visits for counselor education programs undergoing accreditation review. Another professional organization that can be an excellent opportunity for service is NBCC. CSI also provides many committee-level and elected positions for those who have been inducted. As you consider your future as a counselor educator, we would encourage you to identify an association or two that resonates with you and your professional goals. You can then decide at what level to interact with the association. For example, you can become involved with ACES at the state level by serving on the branch division, or you can serve on a committee at the regional or national level. My (Hill) first association leadership role with ACES was serving as president of the Idaho branch of ACES. This experience shaped my trajectory because later I served as regional and national president of the organization in addition to having other committee roles within ACES. The complexity of opportunity allows you to identify areas and roles that fit your personal and professional goals.

Leadership Practice and Competence

Most of the scholarship and theory on leadership concludes that leadership competence can be developed and honed across time and that a propensity for leadership is not something that one has to be born with. A complex interplay of factors ranging from interpersonal qualities to systemic opportunities influence one's leadership development. Figure 10.1 provides an overview of different factors affecting leadership development for counselor educators. Counselor educators who assume roles as professional association leaders within the counseling profession need to be cognizant of the intrinsic and extrinsic factors contributing to their personal leadership competence.

One model of leadership practice, the five practices of exemplary leadership model (Kouzes & Posner, 2011), has been integrated into school counseling practice and research (Shillingford & Lambie, 2010). The guiding principles of this leadership model are (a) model the way, (b) inspire a shared vision, (c) challenge the process, (d) enable others to act, and (e) encourage the heart. These are important leadership practices for counselor educators and graduate students to actively integrate into their professional behaviors. A counselor educator's experiences, such as level of mentorship, access to role models, trainings, and access to professional opportunities, are correlated with his or her ability to enact the five practices of exemplary leadership. In higher education settings, much attention is

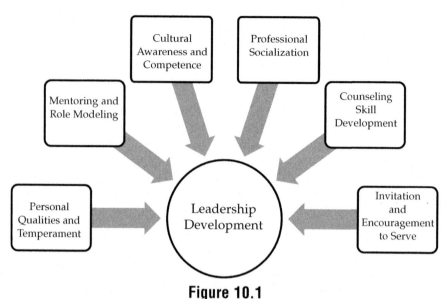

Figure 10.1

Factors Influencing Leadership Development

paid to how effective mentoring can position counselor educators to be successful across roles, including fulfilling service expectations.

Mentoring is identified consistently in the literature on leadership, within and beyond counselor education, as a positive factor influencing leadership engagement and competence. For example, Lockard, Laux, Ritchie, Piazza, and Haefner (2014) surveyed 228 counselor education doctoral students about their leadership development. When asked to identify what experiences they felt were the most critical to their leadership development, 90% of students identified observational learning and 70% identified mentorship as important to their development as leaders (Lockard et al., 2014). Having access to role models and receiving mentoring significantly shaped doctoral students as they were developing their identities as leaders in the counseling profession.

As Figure 10.1 highlights, the successful development of leadership competence is contingent on a robust and comprehensive interaction with the profession of counselor education and the individuals who currently serve in the profession. To steward the next generation of leaders, our counselor education profession needs to endorse a servant leadership paradigm in which service and contribution to others is the primary motivator. Servant leadership prioritizes the needs of others and service to the larger system over the individual leader's priorities (Greenleaf, 1977).

Models of Leadership in Counselor Education

Servant leadership is a framework of leadership that resonates with the values of counselor education, such as promoting the well-being of others and training competent counselors who will *serve* the communities in which they work (Lewis, 2012). When professionals mentor, encourage, and provide opportunities to new counselor educators, such an orientation enhances the systemic factors captured in Figure 10.1. Greenleaf (1977), who developed the theory of servant leadership, posed foundational questions to all who choose to lead: "Do those served grow as persons? Do they, while being served, become healthier, wiser, freer, more autonomous, more likely themselves to become servants? And, what is the effect on the least privileged in society?" (p. 22). Greenleaf's servant leadership focus is on developing people, a construct consistent with counselor education's emphasis on promoting the growth and development of all people (Parris & Peachey, 2013). It can serve as a framework for new counselor educators and graduate students as they embark on professional association service and as they work to navigate the multiple demands inherent in those leadership roles.

Shifting from a theoretical model to practice, West, Bubenzer, Osborn, Paez, and Desmond (2006) proposed a three-phase model of counseling leadership practice that is highly applicable to counselor educators and is grounded in findings from a Q sort of experienced counseling leaders. West et al.'s findings capture the developmental process of a leadership effort that begins with the creation of a vision, then continues with an implementation of such vision, and finally culminates in a celebration of success and reflection on what worked and did not work. Figure 10.2 highlights the different leadership practices across the three phases of the leadership endeavor—beginning, middle, and ending phases.

The emphasis on vision as a leadership practice transcends through all of the phases, with counselor education leaders developing, then collaboratively situating and ultimately working to ensure, the continuity of the vision. New counselor educators and doctoral students can identify important behaviors that they can implement as leaders from the actions captured in the West et al. (2006) study. To effectively serve as profes-

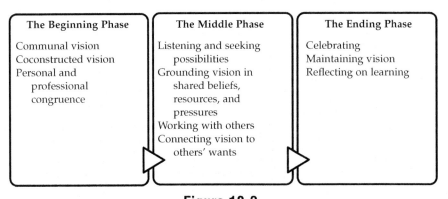

Figure 10.2
West et al.'s (2006) Phases of Leadership Practice

sional association leaders, you are expected to showcase the leadership practices exemplified across the three phases of leadership efforts. For example, serving as a membership committee chair of a professional association will require that in collaboration with members of the executive board, you create a vision, grounded in the needs of potential and current members, of how to be responsive to members and to recruit members (beginning phase). As you work to implement the identified strategies and ideas, the membership committee chair will need to continue to listen, galvanize the efforts of others, and explicitly tie goals with the members' needs (middle phase). As outcomes are evaluated, recognizing accomplishments and maintaining commitment to member benefits will be important (ending phase).

Leadership Development in Counselor Education

Approximately a decade after West et al.'s (2006) work related to counselor leadership practice, McKibben et al. (2017) conducted a content analysis of counseling leadership–related scholarly articles to parcel out key themes on dynamics within counseling leadership. McKibben et al. conducted a literature search on articles within counseling journals that specifically targeted leadership within counseling and identified 13 leadership profiles, 11 empirical articles, nine conceptual articles, and one article that focused on school counseling leadership but that was not published in a counseling journal. Using an inductive coding approach, the authors identified 24 themes related to leadership dynamics present within the counseling profession, many of which apply directly to counselor education. These themes were then collapsed into three broader categories: leadership values and qualities, personal and interpersonal qualities, and interpersonal skills. As we develop as counselor educators, we integrate the training we receive on counseling leadership while simultaneously informing leadership in counselor training. Because we are serving as leaders in professional associations, we are generating the applied practice data and reflection on identity development that is articulated in our existing scholarly works.

McKibben et al. (2017) described the leadership values and qualities category as including the role or purpose of the leader and the values and qualities of leaders according to the reviewed literature. They identified 13 themes within this category: professional identity, advocacy, vision, modeling, mentorship, service, dealing with difficulty and setbacks, leadership-specific cognitive complexity, high standards for self and others, passion, sense of humor, creativity/innovation, and wellness. New counselor educators can build on their existing identities as professional counselors to resonate with the values and qualities showcased in the professional literature, such as those identified by McKibben et al., on leadership in counseling.

McKibben et al.'s (2017) personal and interpersonal qualities category describes the dispositional qualities leaders possess: intrinsic motivation, authenticity, humility, intentionality, dependability, openness, principles, and leadership development catalysts. The dispositional qualities of leaders identified by McKibben et al. are consistent with many of the dispositional qualities educators try to foster in counselors-in-training and counselor-educators-in-training. To be an effective professional association leader, counselor educators must reflect on their own dispositions and actively cultivate those that will allow the association to be successful. The last category, interpersonal skills, describes how leaders within the profession have enacted their leadership in their work with others. The themes identified include interpersonal influence, assertiveness, and role competence. McKibben et al.'s work highlights the fact that leadership encompasses several interactive components, including considering the objective of the leader, the qualities leaders within the profession possess, and how leaders enact their leadership in their work with others to achieve goals.

In their conclusion, McKibben et al. (2017) highlighted the qualities that are inherent in professional counselors and their transferability to leadership competence. Because counselor educators are trained as counselors before transitioning into the role of faculty member, they also benefit from the transferability of skills. Specifically, they asserted, "The counselor who shares power with (rather than over) the client, assists in defining and redefining presenting concerns, and helps the client set goals and work toward wellness can be viewed as a leader" (p. 200). As new counselor educators transition into the professoriate, they can ground themselves in their skills as counselors to inform their developing identities and competencies as counselor educator-leaders. Engaging in professional association service becomes an important pathway for new counselor educators and doctoral students to build their professional networks, expand their knowledge of professional counseling issues and concerns, and positively enact their commitment to advocacy and change.

The Counselor Educator-Leader: Engagement in Professional Association Service

This section explores the role of counselor educators in professional associations at local, state, national, and international levels. Leadership within professional associations is a critical role that counselor educators can assume to positively affect the advancement of the profession. Given their historical legacy of leaders shaping the development and establishment of professional counseling, and given their philosophical values of social justice, advocacy, well-being, and growth, counselor educators and doctoral students can develop as counselor educator-leaders, which is an identity focused on cultivating one's leadership synergistically with one's counselor personhood. The counselor educator-leader values most highly the welfare of clients and communities and places this at the heart of his or her leadership practice (McKibben et al., 2017). Social justice and advocacy are two other professional commitments that inform the counselor educator-leader in professional association leadership. The counselor educator-leader finds renewal, balance, wellness, challenge, inspiration, and motivation through role models and through the people who surround him or her with support (Meany-Walen, Carnes-Holt, Barrio Minton, Purswell, & Pronchenko-Jain, 2013). Principles of ethical values and practices guide the counselor educator in the role of counselor educator-leader in professional association leadership.

Leadership Principles in Counselor Education

For counselor educators, being a leader requires vision, professional identity, collaboration, and tenacity. In their qualitative study of six non-tenured assistant professors serving as presidents(-elect) of divisions of ACA, Gibson, Dollarhide, and McCallum (2010) recognized how leadership development is shaped by "professional role models in counseling, seized opportunities, professional passion, identity, and affiliation" (p. 285). The benefits that emerge from these opportunities can transform one's career and sense of fulfillment. The synergy of passion, identity, and opportunity can help build resiliency as leaders encounter challenges.

An overview of the CSI *Principles and Practices of Leadership Excellence* (CSI Academy of Leaders, 1999) provides practical guide points for counselor educators and doctoral students who are serving in professional association leadership positions. In 1999, CSI's Academy of Leaders developed and formally endorsed 10 *Principles and Practices of Leadership Excellence* that provide burgeoning counselor educators with guidance as they begin their leadership experiences in the profession. These principles are the most developed framework of leadership ethics that exists within the counselor education profession, and they provide a framework to articulate expectations for the counselor educator-leader to follow during professional association leadership (Myers, 2012). Other models that inform counselor educator-leaders are the phases identified by West et al. (2006) and the synthesis of qualities and competences identified by McKibben et al. (2017). The first CSI principle grounds professional association leadership in service to others and the profession. Hallmarks of this principle include the prioritization of what is best for the profession over a focus on personal gain and a commitment to collaborative and consultative decision making. The second principle emphasizes a commitment to mission in which the counselor educator-leader is continually aware of and responsive to an association's mission and vision. Strategic decisions and the allocation of resources are connected back to the association's mission and vision. The third principle prioritizes a protection of association history as a guiding principle. Leaders need to value the history of an association and consider that as a foundation for future growth and development. Counselor educators and doctoral students preparing to serve in professional association leadership positions are responsible for grounding themselves in the history of a professional association and acquainting themselves with archival materials and recent decisions and directions.

The fourth principle in the CSI *Principles and Practices of Leadership Excellence* (CSI Academy of Leaders, 1999) includes a commitment to how vision can build on the rich history of an association while guiding it into future strategic growth and development. The fifth principle encourages counselor educator-leaders to have a perspective that is long term and expansive. Service to a professional association extends beyond the specific parameters of one's office or committee role. Counselor educators and doctoral students must consider both the short-term and long-term ramifications of their decisions. The sixth principle requires counselor educators and doctoral students to be stewards of the association's resources, both material and personal. Leaders assume a fiduciary responsibility in their roles that can be overlooked or minimized. The consideration of resources connects to the seventh principle, which is to respect the membership of the professional association. This requires counselor educators in leadership positions to actively engage with members and to honor their professional interests in the decision-making process.

The last three principles espoused in the CSI *Principles and Practices of Leadership Excellence* (CSI Academy of Leaders, 1999) focus on mentorship, celebration of others, and commitment to reflexive practice. The final principle emphasizes how effective leaders are consistently reflecting on themselves as leaders and integrating feedback from others about their leadership competence. Participating in professional association leadership requires an ongoing commitment to self-awareness and self-interrogation. Such reflexivity not only positively affects the individual by strengthening his or her leadership identity and skill development but also positively shapes the profession by ensuring that future leaders are advancing the profession in meaningful and effective ways.

Counselor educators serving in leadership roles in professional counseling associations have a responsibility to provide evidence of all behaviors present in the CSI *Principles and Practices of Leadership Excellence* (CSI Academy of Leaders, 1999). They are called on to steward the financial and personal resources of the organization, set an agenda for action that is reflective of the association's history and current membership, and ensure a level of integrity between their actions as leaders and the mission of the association. New counselor educators can become involved at multiple levels of professional association leadership ranging from state and regional to national and international. Examples of state leadership include becoming involved in the appropriate branch of ACA that is connected to your community, serving on a state licensing board, and serving on a committee of one of the branch divisions. As a doctoral student, I (Hill) became involved in state-level division leadership for the Ohio Association for Spiritual, Ethical, and Religious Values in Counseling and the Southeast Ohio Counseling Association, a regional chapter of the Ohio Counseling Association. These initial state-level leadership opportunities helped me learn about how professional associations within the counseling field are structured and helped me build professional networks that proved invaluable for providing future opportunities. As a doctoral student or new counselor educator, you can actively seek out state-level opportunities and begin to gain experience in association leadership.

Examples of regional-level professional association service include serving as part of one of ACA's or ACES's regional structures or as a regional chapter facilitator for CSI. ACA has four regional structures that are managed through regional chairs. Serving as an ACA regional chair is one potential pathway for ultimately serving in the role of ACA president if that is someone's long-term professional leadership goal. Being an ACA regional chair was an opportunity that I (Hill) was not aware of during my time as a graduate student, so it is important to highlight how this regional structure of ACA provides another opportunity to become involved and meet professionals from a larger area of the country. Unlike ACA, ACES has an additional regional structure with five areas of the country represented by the Western, Southern, Rocky Mountain, North Atlantic, and North Central regions. All of these regional ACES structures have designated roles for graduate students, and there are multiple opportunities for chairing or serving on committees and boards. Each of these regional ACES associations also sponsors emerging leader workshops every year that provide graduate students and new professionals with opportunities to learn about the association, expand their professional networks, and develop leadership competence.

At the national level, graduate students and new counselor educators can serve on journal editorial boards as well as committees and executive councils for professional counseling associations. ACA and its 20 chartered divisions have a network of committee responsibilities as well as elected leadership opportunities. In some division elections, only one nominee is put forward on the slate, which means that there are multiple opportunities to pursue elected positions as a new counselor educator. Serving at the national level requires a systems perspective, as the scope of service tends to be more comprehensive.

At the international level, interested counselor educators and doctoral students can become involved in CSI, the International Association for Counselling, or the NBCC International's Mental Health Facilitator program. Some pretenured counselor educators are actively involved in international professional leadership based on their passion to engage in global efforts related to professional counseling. Immersing oneself in the existing scholarship and reaching out to leaders who are championing internationalization in counseling would be helpful pathways for those interested in focusing on professional association service at the international level. Figure 10.3 provides an overview of the different levels of professional association service with some examples of how to enact such service.

Benefits and Challenges of Professional Association Leadership

The benefits of professional association leadership are numerous in that counselor educators build important professional networks through such leadership opportunities and experience a high level of fulfillment

International Leadership	National Leadership
• CSI Leadership • International Association for Counselling • NBCC International's Mental Health Facilitator Program	• Professional Counseling Associations • Journal Editorial Boards • Nonprofit and Foundation Boards

Counselor Educator-Leader
Personal Leadership Identity and Action Planning

Regional Leadership	State Leadership
• ACA Regional Chairs • Regional ACES Boards • Regional Chapter Facilitators for CSI	• Branches of ACA and Divisions • Licensure Boards • Community-Based Service

Figure 10.3
Levels of Professional Association Leadership

Note. CSI = Chi Sigma Iota; NBCC = National Board for Certified Counselors; ACA = American Counseling Association; ACES = Association for Counselor Education and Supervision.

regarding contributing to a profession that fosters human growth and development. Professional association service provides many counselor educators and doctoral students with a concrete way to enact their values as counselors and educators and to manifest their identities as counselor educator-leaders. Another benefit of professional association leadership is that the experience can help to clarify one's professional trajectory by highlighting roles that are meaningful, opening up new possibilities, and expanding one's professional connections. The level of reflexivity that is required of effective association leaders also helps to solidify one's professional identity, professional values, and professional goals. Because professional association leadership demands collective engagement by working collaboratively with boards and committees, counselor educators benefit from a diversity of perspectives and generative ideas. Similarly, they are afforded the opportunity to gain support and mentoring from others. Actively engaging in professional association leadership can profoundly shape how a counselor educator understands the complexity of the profession and how impactful one person can be in influencing services to clients and communities.

Professional association leadership is also influenced by challenges that range from a lack of resources to a lack of opportunity. For many graduate students and counselor educators, professional association service begins as an invitation from one's faculty members, a current ACA leader, or an encouraging mentor. For some new professionals, such pathways and personal connections are not as present or available, which means that they may lack the opportunity to gain access to professional association service. As leaders share how impactful mentors and others were to the beginning of their journeys, it is critical to remember that such access is not universally available to all doctoral students and new faculty. Similar to lack of access, another challenge is a lack of programmatic and/ or institutional valuing of such leadership. Given the time commitments inherent in professional association service, it is advantageous to be in a system that recognizes the contributions and efforts being made by a leader. For many, however, their university or program does not value professional association service, which means that resources and supports are not readily provided to those engaged in leadership.

In the content analysis conducted by McKibben et al. (2017), several challenges emerged that affect counselor education leaders. Specifically,

> in counselor education, some leaders faced adversity from other faculty, particularly related to race/ethnicity, sex, and religion. Counseling leaders were aware of the systems stacked against them (e.g., racism), as well as gaps in their experience of self, role, responsibility, personal expectation, credibility, professional relationships, and preparation for leadership. (p. 195)

The cultural complexity of individual leaders operating within dominant systems of influence such as counseling and counselor education programs and professional associations can generate macrolevel challenges that require advocacy toward systemic change. An additional challenge that some counselor educators may encounter is a lack of knowledge and preparation for the political dynamics present in professional associations. Misinterpreting or misunderstanding the political landscape in a professional association can hinder leaders from making active progress toward their vision and the association's mission. Understanding the types of challenges that can be experienced in professional association leadership prepares a new leader to develop strategies for navigating challenges and for creating supports throughout the leadership process.

Professional Leadership in the Context of Institution Type and Program Focus

As you pursue faculty opportunities, it is critical that you recognize how the type of institution will affect your opportunity to engage in professional association leadership as well as the degree of recognition you receive for such service. As higher education has evolved to be more driven by accountability and outcomes, more and more institutions have quantified the distribution of faculty workload across the three primary domains of the professoriate: teaching, service, and research. Workload distributions can vary widely, and because of that we want to describe a few examples. At research-intensive universities, the service expectation will be much lower than at those attributed to scholarship and teaching. Some promotion and tenure policies specifically articulate that service is weighted less than the other two domains. At teaching-intensive institutions, the workload distribution will place more value and weight on teaching and perhaps equal or less weight on service, with research being least important. In these institutions, although service may be differentially valued, a high-quality portfolio of service will not counteract an absence of effective and quality teaching. Many higher education institutions provide weighted percentages across the three domains to frame expectations of faculty workload. The promotion and tenure policies at one institution that I (Hill) was at described the distribution as 40% teaching, 40% scholarship, and 20% service. If counselor educators are working in non-tenure-track positions, the emphasis may be more on clinical and teaching domains than scholarship, and the service expectations can vary considerably and can be weighted substantially less than the teaching domain. Therefore, across the academic spectrum, service can be valued variably, but it will not be the primary determinant for promotion and tenure.

It is critical that you are well informed of how valued your professional association leadership is in the evaluation structure of your institution. Asking for such detail across multiple levels is also important as your department chair or program director may value professional association service because of factors such as increased program visibility and exemplification of accreditation standards related to professional identity. This departmental and program-level valuing can exist even if the institution overall does not weight service as highly. Understanding differentiated expectations as well as the evaluation structure for promotion and tenure will help you make informed decisions about how your engagement in professional association leadership will contribute to your professional portfolio and advancement.

Research from the early 2000s examined how professional leadership and service was reflected in the professorial work of counselor educators. For example, Magnuson spearheaded two studies that examined the 2000 cohort of new counselor educators across 3 years (Magnuson, Black, & Lahman, 2006; Magnuson, Shaw, Tubin, & Norem, 2004). Within the context of those studies, professional association leadership was notably absent in how the new counselor educators contextualized their trajectories toward promotion and tenure. Davis, Levitt, McGlothlin, and Hill (2006) surveyed CACREP liaisons, and their results showed equal weighting across teaching, service, and scholarship for counselor educators. These results were not disaggregated based on academic rank or type of service, which complicates the interpretation of how counselor educators meaningfully engage in professional association leadership.

More recently, Gibson et al. (2010) conducted a phenomenological study with six nontenured counselor educators who were serving in national leadership positions within professional associations. The six participants' faculty positions were across universities with different research classifications ranging from Research 1 to Comprehensive in the Carnegie system. The researchers identified seven themes after completing a round of interviews and an email follow-up. One of the themes highlighted how all of the participants had experienced mentorship and modeling by counselor educators when they were doctoral students. Service and leadership was embedded into the culture of the programs and was continually modeled by program faculty. Leadership then is integrated into the emergent identities of counselor educators as they acquire the knowledge and skills required of them during the doctoral program. Another theme expanded the sphere of influence from program faculty to leaders within ACA. Having an adviser, mentor, and/or current national leader recognize leadership potential and encourage professional association leadership was transformative for the participants in the study conducted by Gibson et al.

The participants in Gibson et al.'s (2010) study discussed the tension between professional leadership and the promotion and tenure system. One participant concluded that teaching and research are the primary factors correlated with promotion and tenure, and this nontenured assistant professor also envisioned professional leadership as contributing meaningfully to a career by expanding professional networks and establishing an area of specialization. Professional leadership is perceived by many institutions as valuable, but it does not tend to drive decision making in the promotion and tenure process.

As a counselor educator progresses through the academic ranks, there is an expectation of increased national and international professional association service. Being regarded as a national and international scholar and professional can be linked to one's service portfolio as well as one's research agenda. Having chaired the Promotion and Tenure Committee at a research-intensive institution, I (Hill) experienced a reward system that privileges the scholarly productivity and teaching effectiveness of candidates over their service portfolios. Yet the most compelling promotion and tenure cases presented at the research-intensive institution were those that evidenced a high level of synergy among research, teaching, and service. It is recommended that counselor educators working in research-intensive universities pursue professional association service as a complement to meeting other tenure and promotion expectations, not with the expectation that high levels of service will offset a dearth of published research. Finding ways in which professional association leadership can inform one's scholarship will create a high level of resonance and integration that will minimize some of the challenges of meeting all scholarly expectations while carrying a high service load. At institutions with more emphasis on teaching, professional association service should be interwoven into a narrative that frames how it synergistically informs one's teaching and/or research. Because there is variance across the academic spectrum in terms of how much such service is valued by institutions, it is imperative that new counselor educators actively seek feedback about how workload is actually interpreted in the promotion and tenure process and which metrics of accomplishment are weighted more substantially.

Program Accreditation and Professional Leadership

CACREP articulates standards related to professional leadership and engagement in professional service. The 2016 CACREP Standards (CACREP, 2015), address professional leadership in terms of faculty role and expectations, institutional support, curriculum, and student engagement. Core counselor education faculty and students are not only expected to identify with the counseling profession through membership in professional associations but also required to evidence sustained engagement through service and leadership roles.

Regarding institutional and faculty expectations, CACREP expects institutions to provide support for counseling program faculty to engage in service to the profession (Standard 1.E.; CACREP, 2015). Professional service and advocacy is one of the specified roles that core counselor education program faculty need to evince to fulfill Standard 1.X. on faculty counselor identity. Such explicit language regarding professional association leadership from the primary accrediting body highlights how critical professional service and leadership is for counselor educators. In preparation for assuming a faculty position at accredited institutions, doctoral students and recent graduates need to understand how professional leadership will be a required facet of their professional dossier regardless of institution type and program focus. Because the accrediting body does not specify the level at which leadership must be enacted, counselor educators are expected to develop their own trajectories regarding leadership and service. Leadership at the state, regional, national, and international levels can all be recognized as fulfilling the accreditation requirement for active engagement and service. As counselor educators develop their own leadership action plans, they can enact leadership at any of the levels represented in Figure 10.3.

Leadership and professional service are interwoven explicitly into the 2016 CACREP Standards (CACREP, 2015). Standard 2.C. asserts that all counseling students "actively identify with the counseling profession by participating in professional counseling organizations" (p. 9), and Standard A.2. of the doctoral standards expands that expectation to include preparation to serve in "positions of leadership in the profession and/or [the student's] area(s) of specialization" (p. 34). Accreditation standards strongly emphasize membership and leadership in professional associations. New counselor educators can frame their promotion and tenure narratives in a way that captures this important reason for valuing association leadership service.

Professional Leadership Across the Profession of Counseling

Across all academic specialties within counselor education opportunities to engage in leadership during one's graduate studies are abundant. Be they within state or national counseling associations, university and/or student organizations, or counseling honor societies, there are many opportunities for counselors-in-training and counselor-educators-in-training to develop their leadership skills while in school. For many counselors-in-training and counselor-educators-in-training, opportunities within local chapters of CSI serve as their first foray into professional leadership. Luke and Goodrich (2010) found that engagement with CSI contributed positively to students' engagement in future leadership opportunities.

A study by Meany-Walen et al. (2013) examined 58 current leaders within the field (i.e., in ACA and ACA's divisions and/or CSI during 2010), the majority of whom were counselor educators, and the progression of their leadership experiences over the course of their careers. The authors found that 38% of those sampled were leaders within state counseling associations during their time as graduate students. An additional 34% of participants were members of their state counseling associations. Some of the most common themes around why participants got involved were professional development, personal relationships (such as having a mentor), and past leadership opportunities before graduate school in counseling that made continued involvement in leadership opportunities a natural progression. When current leaders were asked to give advice to graduate students about developing their leadership experience, the overwhelming majority encouraged students to take initiative: "Getting involved in anything, regardless the size of the task, was deemed as important and instrumental in moving up the proverbial leadership ladder" (p. 212).

Diversity and Social Justice Issues in Leadership Practice

Multicultural leadership competence is required for new counselor educators to be ethical and competent in their leadership roles within professional associations. Such competence is a complex synergy between skills, awareness, and systemic support. Amatea and West-Olatunji (2007) highlighted how professional counselors are trained in multicultural counseling, are aware of how privilege and oppression operate within society, and can use empathy to engage in the taking of multiple perspectives. Counselor educators, as students and professionals, are expected to continue their development of cultural competence and their training in multiculturalism beyond the master's-level preparation. Accreditation standards include advanced social and cultural diversity competencies at the doctoral level (CACREP, 2015). This uniquely positions counselor educators to be leaders on diversity and social justice issues in the context of their professional practice. In their interviews with five past-presidents of the Association for Multicultural Counseling and Development (AMCD), Smith and Roysircar (2010) concluded that African American men who served as professional association leaders were motivated to lead within dominant cultures while honoring their and others' culturally diverse narratives. Such effective multicultural leadership required a high level of awareness of diversity, racism, oppression, and discrimination. These findings were consistent with those of Storlie, Parker-Wright, and Woo (2015), who conducted a phenomenological study with eight counselor education doctoral students who served as emerging leaders for ACES. For the participants in Storlie et al.'s study, multicultural leadership development was related to one's own awareness of cultural identity. Similar to the cohort of African American male AMCD past-presidents interviewed by Smith and Roysircar, the participants in Storlie et al.'s study emphasized how their own awareness served as a catalyst for enhancing multicultural leadership in the profession. Understanding their own cultural identity as well as continually striving to develop multicultural cognitive complexity and consciousness will position new counselor educators to address the diversity and social justice issues present in professional association leadership.

Despite the positive development of multicultural leadership for many counselor educators, there continues to be an ongoing need to focus on diversity and social justice issues in counseling and counselor education preparation, practice, theory, and research. The doctoral students in Storlie et al.'s (2015) qualitative study reported that their doctoral programs were not sufficiently prioritizing or addressing multicultural leadership in the training of master's or doctoral students. Counselor education programs need to continually examine how well they are training their students to be multiculturally competent counselors and to be effective leaders in a diverse society with complex social justice issues. In addition, McKibben et al. (2017) noted a lack of representation of cultural diversity in the existing counseling research, especially in leadership profiles. Given the dearth of culturally diverse perspectives in the counseling leadership literature, McKibben et al. encouraged the development of research on leadership across culturally diverse counselors.

What's Next? The Trajectory of Leadership Practice in Counselor Education

With increased attention to leadership skills and competencies in the accreditation standards of counselor education doctoral programs (CACREP, 2015), the next developmental phase for leadership practice in counselor education is to advance understanding of leadership practice and how training programs can effectively contribute to student learning outcomes in leadership. As a profession, we need to establish a set of leadership competencies that can guide our development of effective leaders. We also need to embrace the construct of counselor educator-leader, which situates our role as counselor educators as intricately tied to our role as leaders. Building the identities of emerging counselors to emphasize leadership is an ongoing component of our profession.

With many graduate students and beginning counselor educators assuming roles in professional associations, especially at the state and national levels (Gibson et al., 2010; Meany-Walen et al., 2013), the counselor education profession needs to ensure that it is adequately encouraging, mentoring, and supporting new leaders who assume important professional association leadership roles. The assumption that professional association leadership is being enacted by more advanced and experienced counselor educators after they have achieved tenure is outdated, as demographics have evolved, and from my (Hill) perspective, a vacuum in leadership has emerged. New counselor educators bring passion, energy, and inclusive ideas to the leadership context, and the field will need to develop ongoing strategies to support them in translating their values and ideas into realized leadership impact.

Recommendations for Fostering the Counselor Educator-Leader: Counselor Preparation and Practice

Counselor education program faculty play a critical role in socializing doctoral students and beginning counselor educators into the roles of the professoriate. Because of this, counselor educators are uniquely positioned to role model a culture of service (Gibson et al., 2010) that greatly influences the leadership identity development of new counselor educators. Counselor educators can nurture new leaders through recognition and by modeling their own involvement in professional association leadership (Gibson et al., 2010). Although there have been assertions by counseling scholars that the skills of counseling are transferable to leadership competence, continued attention needs to be focused on ensuring that the identity development of new counselors and counselor educators expands to claim the ideal of counselor educator-leader. Because the success of leadership is coupled with self-efficacy and perceived competence (Dollarhide, Gibson, & Saginak, 2008), focusing on identity development begins the framework for developing self-efficacy and professional esteem (Mason & McMahon, 2009).

Considering both curricular and cocurricular opportunities can shift the leadership development in counselor education from on-the-job training to an intentional and robust professional preparation process (Paradise et al., 2010). At the curricular level, structured assignments can be implemented that focus on developing a personal mission and vision statements regarding leadership. This will help develop clear goals that are tied to successful leadership outcomes (Dollarhide et al., 2008). In addition, students could be asked to develop individualized action plans regarding their own leadership development. Other recommendations include creating structured opportunities in training to build leadership skills (Amatea & West-Olatunji, 2007) and establishing leadership courses (Paradise et al., 2010; Young, Dollarhide, & Baughman, 2016) and professional conferences (Young et al., 2016).

Although the majority of the 228 counselor education doctoral students in Lockard et al.'s (2014) study agreed or strongly agreed that they felt that they were being prepared in each of nine different areas of leadership (clinical counseling, research, teaching, supervision, writing and

publishing, professional advocacy, leading others, leading an organization, and motivating others), there were identified areas for growth for
counselor education training programs to help develop leadership skills
in other domains relevant to the profession. For example, 18% of students
identified as neutral—and more alarming 10% disagreed—when asked
whether they felt prepared to engage in leadership within the domain of
professional advocacy. In addition, in the domain of feeling prepared to
lead an organization, 26% of students felt unprepared and an additional
25% were neutral about their ability to lead within this capacity. These
findings provide direction to counselor education doctoral programs
about domains in which students would benefit from having additional
attention on how they could enact leadership.

For the participants in the study by Gibson et al. (2010), an evolving
approach to professional leadership was recommended in which state and
committee service serve as prerequisites to regional, national, and international service and to executive board leadership. Participants shared how
valuable it was to be a committee chair within a division before assuming
the presidency. Getting involved and engaging in service was also a recommendation that emerged from the study by Meany-Walen et al. (2013).

An additional recommendation for individual doctoral students and
new counselor educators is to actively seek out mentors. Mentoring and
consultation (Dollarhide et al., 2008; Storlie et al., 2015; Young et al., 2016)
opens up possibilities when encountering difficult situations and provides
support and encouragement. Many doctoral programs are not providing the level of mentorship that is needed through the advising process
(Storlie et al., 2015); therefore, considerable attention needs to be paid to
ensure that doctoral students and new counselor educators are receiving
the "depth of mentorship" (p. 161) necessary to support them as they
develop multicultural leadership competence. New counselor educators
and doctoral students can be intentional in cultivating mentors, outside
of their current program if needed, to ensure that they are receiving the
benefits associated with such supports.

Finally, counselor educators and doctoral students can dedicate themselves to being reflexive and inclusive leaders. Self-reflection helps to
bolster leader effectiveness in times of resistance, self-doubt, and lack of
resources (Dollarhide et al., 2008). Cultivating an inclusive stance that
advocates for all in the community privileges the voices of others who
tend to be marginalized or silenced (Storlie et al., 2015). New counselor
educators and doctoral students can focus on establishing collaborative
and collective perspectives and intentionally seeking out diverse viewpoints. Such leadership practices will enhance leadership competence and
effective outcomes in professional association work.

In reflecting on her own leadership trajectory, Jane Myers concluded
that she "found [her] passion … [while] doing [what] was captured by
Gardner (1990): 'living by example to motivate others to take action
for the greater good of all'" (Myers, Chang, Dixon, Barrio Minton, &
Sweeney, 2012, p. 70). We encourage you, as a new counselor educator

or doctoral student who is engaged in leadership practice already and is envisioning ongoing, and perhaps increased, engagement in professional association leadership, to be inspired and guided by these notions of role modeling, collaborative engagement, and servant leadership. Situating these values in an area of professional passion will optimize the benefits you experience from professional association leadership and foster resiliency as you encounter the challenges inherent in professional association leadership.

Leadership Profile of a Current Doctoral Student, Erin N. Friedman

As you've read in this chapter, there are a number of ways to meaningfully engage in leadership. In fact, in my experience, I have found that sometimes the sheer enormity of opportunities leads me to feel paralyzed, unsure of which opportunities to pursue. If the literature demonstrates anything, it is that taking the step to get involved is most important; there is no single right way to get involved. Be it gaining experience at a local level, or beginning your experiences at a national level, what matters is being actively engaged and working toward a cause you believe in. I was fortunate that my mentors offered me opportunities to get involved; this has now allowed me to advocate for leadership opportunities. Opportunities sometimes stem from who you know. However, I've learned that I can have some degree of control over who I get to know and the networks I become involved in. I could choose to diversify my experiences.

My leadership experiences began with my local CSI chapter. I was an active member my first year of graduate school and was elected co-president for my second year. This allowed me to get more connected with other graduate students, form deeper relationships with faculty, and form collaborations with other CSI chapters and eventually with our state counseling association. I transitioned from my work with CSI as copresident to collaborating with another graduate student and former instructor to cofound an interest group (which is in the process of becoming a full-fledged division) of the Illinois Counseling Association called the Illinois Association for Supporting First Responders. Through engaging in one of my instructor's passion projects, I developed my own passion for this population. I learned about developing division/interest group bylaws and other protocols as well as discovering ways I could be a leader as I progressed through my degree in counselor education. One of my passions that grew from this experience was my interest in community–university and community–professional partnerships, which can be a great way to develop leadership skills, especially for those with strong clinical interests. Although my leadership experiences and areas of clinical practice were diverse, what mattered the most to the people who interviewed me (for various opportunities) was that I was able to talk meaningfully about them and connect those experiences to my larger professional goals.

Leadership Profile of a Tenured Professor of Counselor Education, Dr. Nicole R. Hill

Since I was young, I have believed that each of us has the opportunity and ability to positively influence others and to change the world. I volunteered at various community organizations as a young woman and started to develop a professional trajectory of service as an undergraduate student. My double major of sociology and psychology at Hanover College positioned me to integrate both individual and contextual understandings of issues and experiences. As a master's student at Ohio University, I began to be involved in professional counseling association leadership when I joined the Alpha chapter of CSI and served as a student chapter leader. From that moment, I was socialized to believe in collective actualization as a profession. I believe that we can optimize our potentialities and strive most fervently toward our success if we are collaborative and committed to the group's growth. This commitment to collective actualization has been threaded through my experiences from the local chapter level of CSI to the national level. Since my time as a chapter leader as a graduate student, I have served on the CSI Executive Council as secretary, as a regional chapter facilitator, as a chapter faculty adviser for 10 years, and on committees focused on chapter development and student members. I am now president-elect of CSI, and I believe that this one example of my path of service in CSI exemplifies the recommendations provided in our research about how we grow into ourselves as leaders.

One of the most meaningful facets of my experiences being a leader in professional associations is finding the opportunities that resonate with my own values and beliefs. A high level of congruence between myself and the mission and momentum of a professional association engenders a level of resiliency when challenges are encountered or unexpected demands unfold. Leadership in professional associations does require us to navigate challenges, and the level of resonance between my own values and professional goals has helped me in those times of urgency. For example, CSI embodies the principles of celebrating excellence, promoting a strong sense of counselor identity, fostering a legacy of leadership, and cultivating an emphasis on wellness and development. One of the things I most appreciate about CSI is that we, as a collective, couple values and words with action. We not only celebrate excellence but create excellence.

My path as a leader has been shaped by mentors and colleagues who inspired me to be my best self and be involved. I began my professional association leadership in ACA and ACES as a doctoral student. One of my doctoral peers was enthusiastically involved in regional and divisional branch leadership in Ohio. Her personal invitation, her continual encouragement, and the shared experience of being involved helped me take risks and pursue opportunities for leadership. Having faculty members who asserted that professional association leadership was an expectation of our counselor education profession helped me to see myself as an emergent leader at the state level and to build on that foundation as my career expanded into the regional and national realms. Because of this, I encourage doctoral students and new counselor educators to build their community of mentors and catalysts for their own growth as leaders. If you are not able to identify a mentor in your current professional community, please reach out to others or to professional association leaders and ask for support and opportunity. My own journey has been propelled forward by opportunities and access, and I realize that not everyone has the same context from which to start. As a community of mentors and exemplars is a necessary facet of effective professional association leadership, I encourage you to fervently pursue opportunities and take risks. Your vision, energy, and commitment are needed to shape our future and to ensure that we as counselor educators continue to transform our communities and empower others to realize their potential.

Conclusion

The counseling profession is beginning to explore leadership competence in a more intentional and robust manner, with increased scholarship, accreditation focus, and practice standards emerging since the early 2000s. The field must continue to shift from an on-the-job training paradigm (Paradise et al., 2010) to one of comprehensive and deliberate preparation. Graduate students and new counselor educators must be invited to engage in professional association leadership and must be socialized into a culture of service (Gibson et al., 2010). The professional esteem of counselor educators to be leaders can be enhanced by explicitly connecting the counseling skill set to those required of leaders.

A review of the literature regarding professional association leadership reveals three fundamental conclusions. First, new counselor educators and graduate students should cultivate their passions and lead through a service mentality. Second, mentors and consultants should be fervently pursued to provide critical socialization, feedback, support, and opportunity. And third, individuals should "get involved in anything" (Meany-Walen et al., 2013, p. 212), as the experience itself will be transformative.

Additional Online Resources

American College Counseling Association Graduate Students and New Professionals Leadership Opportunities
    www.collegecounseling.org/Graduate-Students-&-New-Professionals
American Counseling Association Institute for Leadership Training
    https://www.counseling.org/conference/institute
American Counseling Association Leadership
    https://www.counseling.org/about-us/leadership
American Mental Health Counselors Association Annual Leadership Summit
    www.amhca.org/conference/leadership

American Mental Health Counselors Association State and Chartered Chapters
  www.amhca.org/membership/chapters
American School Counselor Association Professional Interest Networks
  https://www.schoolcounselor.org/school-counselors-members/about-asca-(1)/professional-interest-networks
American School Counselor Association State Associations
  https://www.schoolcounselor.org/school-counselors-members/about-asca-(1)/state-associations
Association for Counselor Education and Supervision Interest Networks
  https://www.acesonline.net/forums/interest-networks
Chi Sigma Iota Global Counseling Associations
  https://www.csi-net.org/?page=Global_Associations
Chi Sigma Iota Leadership Opportunities
  https://www.csi-net.org/?page=Volunteer_Leadership
National Board for Certified Counselors Fellowships
  www.nbccf.org/programs/fellows

References

Amatea, E., & West-Olatunji, C. (2007). Joining the conversation about educating our poorest children: Emerging leadership roles for school counselors in high-poverty schools. *Professional School Counseling, 11,* 81–89. doi:10.5330/PSC.n.2010-11.81

Chi Sigma Iota Academy of Leaders. (1999). *Principles and practices of leadership excellence.* Retrieved from www.csi-net.org/page/Leadership_Practices

Council for Accreditation of Counseling and Related Educational Programs. (2015). *CACREP 2016 standards.* Alexandria, VA: Author.

Davis, T., Levitt, D., McGlothlin, J., & Hill, N. (2006). Perceived expectations related to promotion and tenure: A national survey of CACREP program liaisons. *Counselor Education and Supervision, 46,* 146–156. doi:10.1002/j.1556-6978.2006.tb00019.x

Dollarhide, C. T., Gibson, D. M., & Saginak, K. A. (2008). New counselors' leadership efforts in school counseling: Themes from a year-long qualitative study. *Professional School Counseling, 11,* 262–271. doi:10.5330/PSC.n.2010-11.262

Gibson, D. M., Dollarhide, C. T., & McCallum, L. J. (2010). Nontenured assistant professors as American Counseling Association division presidents: The new look of leadership in counseling. *Journal of Counseling & Development, 88,* 285–292. doi:10.1002/j.1556-6978.2010.tb00024.x

Greenleaf, R. K. (1977). *Servant leadership: A journey into the nature of legitimate power and greatness.* New York, NY: Paulist Press.

Kouzes, J. M., & Posner, B. Z. (2011). *The five practices of exemplary leadership* (2nd ed.). San Francisco, CA: The Leadership Challenge.

Lewis, T. F. (2012). Foundations of leadership: Theory, philosophy, and research. In C. Y. Chang, C. A. Barrio Minton, A. L. Dixon, J. E. Myers, & T. J. Sweeney (Eds.), *Professional counseling excellence through leadership and advocacy* (pp. 21–40). New York, NY: Routledge.

Lockard, F. W., Laux, J. M., Ritchie, M., Piazza, N., & Haefner, J. (2014). Perceived leadership preparation in counselor education doctoral students who are members of the American Counseling Association in CACREP-accredited programs. *The Clinical Supervisor, 33,* 228–242. doi:10.1080/07325223.2014.992270

Luke, M., & Goodrich, K. M. (2010). Chi Sigma Iota chapter leadership and professional identity development in early career counselors. *Counselor Education and Supervision, 50,* 56–78. doi:10.1002/j.1556-6978.2010.tb00108.x

Magnuson, S., Black, L. L., & Lahman, M. K. E. (2006). The 2000 cohort of new assistant professors of counselor education: Year 3. *Counselor Education and Supervision, 45,* 162–179. doi:10.1002/j.1556-6978.2006.tb00140.x

Magnuson, S., Shaw, H., Tubin, B., & Norem, K. (2004). Assistant professors of counselor education: First and second year experiences. *Journal of Professional Counseling: Practice, Theory, and Research, 32,* 3–18.

Mason, E. C. M., & McMahon, H. G. (2009). Leadership practice of school counselors. *Professional School Counseling, 13,* 107–115. doi:10.5330/PSC.n.2010-13.107

McKibben, W. B., Umstead, L. K., & Borders, L. D. (2017). Identifying dynamics of counseling leadership: A content analysis study. *Journal of Counseling & Development, 95,* 192–202. doi:10.1002/jcad.12131

Meany-Walen, K. K., Carnes-Holt, K., Barrio Minton, C. A., Purswell, K., & Pronchenko-Jain, Y. (2013). An exploration of counselors' professional leadership development. *Journal of Counseling & Development, 91,* 206–215. doi:10.1002/j.1556-6676.2013.00087.x

Myers, J. E. (2012). Professional leadership, leading well: Characteristics, principles, and ethics of effective counseling leaders. In C. Y. Chang, C. A. Barrio Minton, A. L. Dixon, J. E. Myers, & T. J. Sweeney (Eds.), *Professional counseling excellence through leadership and advocacy* (pp. 41–61). Philadelphia, PA: Taylor & Francis.

Myers, J. E., Chang, C. Y., Dixon, A. L., Barrio Minton, C. A. , & Sweeney, T. J. (2012). On becoming a leader: A journey. In C. Y. Chang, C. A. Barrio Minton, A. L. Dixon, J. E. Myers, & T. J. Sweeney (Eds.), *Professional counseling excellence through leadership and advocacy* (pp. 63–77). Philadelphia, PA: Taylor & Francis.

Paradise, L. V., Ceballos, P. T., & Hall, S. (2010). Leadership and leader behavior in counseling: Neglected skills. *International Journal for the Advancement of Counselling, 32,* 46–55. doi:10.1007/s10447-009-9088-y

Parris, D. L., & Peachey, J. W. (2013). A systematic literature review of servant leadership theory in organizational contexts. *Journal of Business Ethics, 113,* 377–393. doi:10.1007/s10551-012-1322-6

Shillingford, M. A., & Lambie, G. W. (2010). Contribution of professional school counselors' values and leadership practices to their programmatic service delivery. *Professional School Counseling, 13,* 208–217. doi:10.5330/PSC.n.2010-13.208

Smith, M. L., & Roysircar, G. (2010). African American male leaders in counseling: Interviews with five AMCD past presidents. *Journal of Multicultural Counseling and Development, 38,* 242–255. doi:10.1002/j.2161-1912.2010.tb00134.x

Storlie, C. A., Parker-Wright, M., & Woo, H. (2015). Multicultural leadership development: A qualitative analysis of emerging leaders in counselor education. *Journal of Counselor Leadership and Advocacy, 2,* 154–169. doi:10.1080/2326716X.2015.1054078

West, J. D., Bubenzer, D. L., Osborn, C. J., Paez, S. B., & Desmond, K. J. (2006). Leadership and the profession of counseling: Beliefs and practices. *Counselor Education and Supervision, 46,* 2–16.

Young, A., Dollarhide, C. T., & Baughman, A. (2016). The voices of school counselors: Essential characteristics of school counselor leaders. *Professional School Counseling, 19,* 36–45. doi:10.5330/1096-2409-19.1.36

considering taking on any service activity, faculty need to reflect on the other competing forces that can influence their life and inhibit future success (e.g., finances, family, unanticipated crises) along with supportive resources that can assist in appropriate decision making (Bracken et al., 2006; Frasier Chabot & Milinder, 2005). Time spent in faculty service can erode time spent on faculty scholarship, a necessary part of the promotion and tenure process, as well as take time and energy away from other important aspects of a faculty member's life (e.g., focus on teaching, student advising, family responsibilities, other responsibilities a person holds in his or her work–life balance). In the sections that follow, issues that influence service requirements in different contexts are explored, as are different ways for counselor educators to think about how they may allocate their time to be successful and productive university citizens.

Institutional Culture and Service

Institutional culture varies across contexts with regard to organizational values and how faculty service functions within the larger institutional mission (Kuh, 1993). Service might look and feel qualitatively different across institutional settings (e.g., online, hybrid, face-to-face settings) and types of institutions (e.g., research intensive, teaching intensive). Current thought is that faculty at research-intensive institutions are asked to focus more on scholarship, with less of a focus on teaching and service. Teaching institutions, in contrast, are typically thought to place greater demands on faculty in the areas of teaching and service, with research being viewed as a secondary goal.

Faculty members should not make assumptions regarding service expectations based on program level (e.g., master's-only institutions vs. institutions that have master's and doctoral programs), as many counselor education programs may have a different history and culture related more to their institutional history or state-level requirements (e.g., some states, such as Indiana and Idaho, only allow one program in the state to offer certain degrees because of state laws on duplication). Thus, some institutions ranked as R1: Doctoral Universities—highest research activity (Indiana University Center for Postsecondary Research, n.d.) may only have a master's program because there are other doctorate-granting programs in the state or in the region or because the institution did not desire to have a doctoral program in counseling but wished to uphold the same high standards for its faculty regardless of the program graduate level. Although the rule of thumb is typically that master's-only programs may have lower scholarship and higher service requirements, it could be that some master's-level programs may still have a stringent requirement for faculty scholarship and different expectations for faculty service compared to other master's-level programs based on the institutional culture as well as faculty history with the program (e.g., Wake Forest University, the University of Vermont). Finally, faculty service may also be divided up depending on the size of the program: Smaller programs may require faculty members to take on more tasks than larger programs, just because of the sheer number of persons available to complete certain tasks. In this way, both program size and institution type affect how service is seen and assigned to faculty.

Institutions have agreed-upon or historical values, and thus different requirements may be seen as necessary components for faculty service (Kuh, 1993). For example, some state institutions are classified as land-grant institutions; these institutions were founded to be focused on more applied disciplines (such as agriculture) and serve to be more connected to their community. However, over time many land-grant institutions have expanded their services more broadly in the education that they provide while still viewing direct service to the community as an integral part of their institutional focus (Altbach, 2016). Thus, community-engaged scholarship or applied service to the community might be seen as more typical in some of these types of institutions, which may or may not connect with current faculty scholarship (e.g., the Magnify Program at Purdue University; Purdue University, n.d.). This may be seen within counselor education programs as a reflected mission to serve underserved populations in counseling, such as students or faculty providing pro bono services to clients on campus, as well as required hours for clinical supervision of these students beyond one's typical teaching load. An example of community-engaged service might be faculty serving on advisory committees or working with public or nonprofit groups (such as a drug abuse task force or sexual health campaign) to address stigma or issues related to mental health within the community. In this way, the faculty member is relying on his or her knowledge to represent the university in the local community to serve the community's needs.

Similarly, some universities see the role of faculty engagement as integral to the mission of the institution and believe that scholarship and service should be forever combined and collaborative with institutional partners from across the local or state community (for an example, see Ward, 2003). This has brought about the movement of service learning, which focuses on how service to the larger community may be tied to teaching through the use of intentional service activities to support students in learning the concepts explored in the classroom. Scholars have taken this a step further to document a scholarship of service learning, which combines all three elements of faculty promotion and tenure requirements: researching the experience of service learning and how it ties to the curriculum or later student outcomes (e.g., Orr & Hulse-Killacky, 2006). One example is the Magnify Program at Purdue University, which uses graduate students in its school counseling program to facilitate groups with at-risk K–12 students that address issues of socioemotional health, college and career readiness, and academic achievement (Purdue University, n.d.). A faculty member from the program is required to serve as program administrator as well as the graduate students' supervisor as part of his or her faculty service requirement. This is used as a form of service learning so that graduate school counseling students can understand the roles and responsibilities of school counselors while being actively engaged with their local community.

Knowing institutional history and culture then becomes very important for determining exactly what may be required for faculty service, with regard to both expectation and type. For land-grant colleges, there may be a need to directly tie faculty service to the local community, perhaps in more applied ways. For other institutions, service learning and the ideals of community service may be important. These are things that faculty should explore when developing their faculty workload plans around service with their faculty mentors and department chairs.

Across all institutions and across time, however, the academy has valued shared faculty governance (Altbach, 2016). That is, faculty members are seen as key members of the institutional infrastructure in terms of providing appropriate self-governance to their program and university. As such, faculty have responsibility for overseeing their discipline and program requirements, are accountable for their students' learning, and participate in a shared vision and mission within their university. Thus, coordinating accreditation procedures (such as those of the Council for Accreditation of Counseling and Related Educational Programs [CACREP]), serving as program or counseling track (e.g., clinical mental health, substance abuse, school counseling) coordinators, or serving on a student admissions committee becomes important work in carrying the profession forward, but not in typical ways one thinks of in teaching and research. In this way, faculty serve both the discipline of counseling as well as the university for which they work.

Furthermore, faculty members may be asked to take on roles as department chairs, associate deans, deans, provosts, or other leaders within a college or university; these tasks are not typically framed as faculty service per se but instead viewed as different administrative roles. There can be some overlaps between the domains of administration and service, as some administration is service and some administration is part of an administrative appointment, separate from what is thought of as a traditional faculty role. (Administration is addressed further in Chapter 9.) However, it is important to note that regardless of position, faculty members have important roles as leaders in the self-governance process to ensure that institutions uphold their academic missions. These are also paramount service positions that faculty members take on regardless of university size or type. For this reason, it is disappointing to know that because of ongoing changes in higher education structure and finances, surveys of faculty morale have typically found that faculty describe their experiences on campus as fair or poor and that the majority of faculty report having negative feelings about their sense of community on campus (Altbach, 2016). Thus, it might be important for faculty to make measured decisions with careful advice from others about the types and amount of service projects they take on, as it would benefit faculty members most to hold on to responsibilities that might hold meaning for them and further their sense of investment in the academic mission.

Factors That Contribute to Similarities and Differences in the Practice of Service

Different factors influence how service is instituted or required across different colleges and universities. As noted before, program type (master's vs. doctorate granting), university focus (research intensive vs. teaching intensive), the number of program faculty, institution type (public vs. private), and institutional culture all play a role in how service is assigned. Teaching in an online or hybrid program may also affect a faculty member's service workload breakdown, as programs might expect more from faculty members who are not teaching in person. New faculty should inquire about the service requirements at their institution and how service factors into the larger faculty workload formula. For example, at my home institution, which is a public, research-intensive university, a clear faculty workload formula was established by the provost's office and university faculty senate (i.e., Faculty Senate Policy C100; University of New Mexico, 2012). This workload formula specifically defines the faculty workload breakdown to be 40–40–20, which can be translated as a requirement for faculty to spend 40% of their time on research, 40% on teaching, and the final 20% on service. Faculty can negotiate these workload breakdowns with their department chair and/or dean based on their skills and expertise as well as the needs of their program; however, for most faculty on campus this is the typical workload requirement.

Although it is very abstract in its description, there are many ways in which one can better understand this workload requirement. If one assumes a typical 5-day workweek, a faculty member could break down the 40–40–20 requirement to mean that 2 days of every week should be focused on research, 2 days focused on teaching, and a single day directed toward service. As there is no perfect workweek in which a faculty member can focus independently on one aspect of his or her job, another way to understand this is that in an assumed 40-hour workweek, a faculty member should direct about 16 hours of the week (40%) to his or her research agenda, 16 hours (40%) to teaching or teaching-related activities (e.g., course preparations, grading, student advisement), and the remaining 8 hours (20%) to service. This does, of course, assume that every week in a semester is typical, which is almost never the case; in higher education, different weeks hold different demands (e.g., midterms and finals, manuscripts being returned for revisions by journals, involvement in professional conferences or advocacy activities). It further assumes that faculty members only work 40 hours per week; this is unlikely because of the creeping demands that universities often hold along with the perception of faculty members' flexible schedules. However, this breakdown of hours serves to provide a quick blueprint that new faculty could use to structure their academic time.

As the demands between weeks of the semester can often change, one final alternative blueprint that faculty might use in considering their workload expectations is to multiply the number of hours per week that they may spend on a task (e.g., 8 hours for service) by the number of weeks in a semester (16 at my institution) to understand the typical number of hours of service expected by the university for that semester (in this case, 128 hours). This provides a faculty member with fuller figures for how to allocate their faculty service hours in relation to their other work and life demands. The idea of calculating faculty service in this way may seem obscene; however, it can be a useful guidepost for faculty in tracking the number of service commitments they are taking on from semester to semester. If the numbers are far greater than what might be expected in a 40–40–20 split (or whatever your university's requirements may be), it may be time to pare down your service commitments and learn the challenging task of saying no to others.

It should be noted that saying no can sometimes be easier said than done. Faculty from marginalized groups (e.g., women; racial/ethnic minorities; lesbian, gay, bisexual, transgender, queer, and intersex) may be the only ones of a group in their program or department and may feel the burden of mentoring all students who share their background or serving as the voice for that group as part of a committee or group to ensure that diverse perspectives are heard and validated. The nature of counseling and clinical supervision can also impose other demands, as crisis events cannot be predicted. At times faculty need to provide extra time and space to students they teach and supervise, as the client's concerns demand this of them and sometimes it cannot wait until the next week or next semester. This does, however, warrant that faculty make deliberate decisions about how and when they can say no to some potential service items and prepare themselves for the unexpected. In the field of counselor education, it is very easy to become overwhelmed with emergent and pressing demands (as there will always be emergent and pressing demands in the field of counselor education), so knowing one's boundaries and the cycle of service at an institution is important for making decisions about future service obligations.

As noted, different types of programs and institutions have differing requirements of their faculty members, and so at the job interview or after the faculty contract is issued, faculty members should know the typical expectations for service in their given academic program. Some institutions may have more explicit policies or guidelines around service requirements and other tasks, whereas others are less clear. Lack of clarity can be intentional for some universities, as it provides administrators leeway in the decision-making process for tenure and promotion of faculty based around faculty members' fit in the program or potential for long-term success at that university. Explicit policies or guidelines may be provided at some universities to protect faculty members from potentially punitive tenure and promotion decisions as well as for long-term stability of faculty academic freedom and governance. For example, at my current institution, a public institution overseen by a governor-appointed board of regents, explicit policies and guidelines were provided for faculty workload (including service activities) at a time when the state government was less friendly to higher education. Where faculty policies did not exist, the board of regents often exerted its authority and created policies or guidelines, often having negative effects on faculty members. The faculty workload policy was created in collaboration between the university's provost's office and the elected faculty senate to ensure that faculty members' time on campus would be protected and to ensure that the regular and typical tasks taken on by faculty members would be recognized when decisions of faculty member tenure, promotion, or merit pay were made.

Faculty members are tasked with understanding the policies and guidelines at their given institutions, and it is not a bad idea for them to become friends with their faculty senate (or governance representative) to ensure that they know their rights and responsibilities as faculty members. For those faculty members who come from unionized campuses, there is also value in being familiar with the institution's collective bargaining agreement and its stipulations on service. This also speaks to the role of social justice and advocacy, which itself may be service, to ensure that faculty and professors in clinical fields such as counselor education are provided credit for the various roles they are required to serve on campus (e.g., clinical supervision, program accreditation).

How Can Program Type Influence Service Responsibilities?

As noted earlier, faculty service can often be dictated by institution type (research or teaching intensive) or by the number of faculty. However, other issues play a role in the nature and type of service that faculty may be called on to complete within their institution. For example, accountability has become a key requirement in higher education (Altbach, 2016). Universities have been called on by external stakeholders to ensure that responsible actions are being taken to train students. Thus, faculty members need to be accountable to their students, and students need to demonstrate appropriate student learning outcomes before completing their program to demonstrate the program's academic success. In addition, beyond assessing students' learning outcomes, faculty are also called on to serve as gatekeepers for the field, assessing students' professional dispositions and their appropriateness to enter the field. Although accreditation varies across disciplines, within the field of counselor education, CACREP is the leading accrediting body. CACREP publishes accreditation standards on a regular basis, and the 2016 Standards are the most recent (CACREP, 2015).

Service regarding program accreditation can be quite vast and can include aggregating and analyzing student data; ensuring that student supervision is documented and occurring in appropriate ways; writing program reports; ensuring that appropriate program curriculum and program structures are in place; and serving as a liaison between the program, the university, and the accrediting body to ensure that faculty, students, and staff have the appropriate resources to meet the demands of the accreditation standards. Program accreditation is typically a multiyear process that includes writing preliminary draft reports (self-studies), submitting evidence, writing supplemental or follow-up reports from initial accreditor questions, working with a site visit team, and writing a final report following site team recommendations and the accreditation board's decision. It is typically outside of novice faculty members' purview to take on the full task of spearheading an accreditation process by themselves, but providing support and assistance to senior faculty in different parts of the process can be a wonderful learning experience and further connect faculty members to their own professional identity.

Similarly, faculty are often also called on to serve in other areas of program accountability for their department, college, or university. Most institutions are part of regional university accrediting bodies through the Higher Learning Commission, which also requires that programs, departments, and colleges collect student learning outcome data as well as prepare university-wide assessment and annual reports. Colleges may require their faculty to conduct regular graduate program reviews, and at times some state public education (or higher education) departments may require that programs map course requirements to state licensure requirements (for licensed clinical mental health or school counselors) or conduct alumni surveys to demonstrate program excellence and job placement. All of these are other forms of service that faculty might be called on to complete.

Beyond involvement with the CACREP Standards (CACREP, 2015) and other forms of accreditation, faculty members are also called on to mentor and advise students as well as, in the case of doctoral faculty, publish and present with students. Faculty can also use their service allotment to promote professional identity within their students. Scholars such as Lee, Nu, and Pedbani (2013) and Luke and Goodrich (2010) have discussed how membership in professional associations and the promotion of cocurricular activities, such as involvement in a Chi Sigma Iota International chapter, can promote student learning and translate the curriculum into authentic learning experiences outside of the classroom. Through advisement and leadership in student groups such as Chi Sigma Iota, students can be exposed to the field of counselor education at many levels as well as receive practical suggestions for how their professional identity can translate into real-world actions on behalf of or for clients through different advocacy and counselor–community engagement activities. Faculty might also use their links between the American Counseling Association and its 20 different divisions, along with state chapters and branches, to further ingrain student life with activities of the counseling profession. Taking on the role of a student group adviser can be time consuming and can lead to some boundary confusion with students based on how one represents oneself in that role or what is learned about students outside the classroom (Goodrich, 2008), so it may be important to set clear goals and boundaries between students and faculty when considering these roles to ensure the safety and welfare of all parties involved.

It is important to note that inherent within counselor education training are a host of complexities that need to be addressed and considered when navigating relationships. As counselor education requires students to take part in experiential activities through many different training models (e.g., participation in an experiential group as part of group counseling training, participation in clinical supervision that may at times address personalization concerns on the part of the counselor, course activities that require student journaling; Goodrich, 2008; Goodrich & Luke, 2012), counselor educators may learn things about students that they would not typically know in other disciplines. This can lead to multiple relationships with students. On the negative side, this challenges counselor educators' ethics related to how they can evaluate and assess students' readiness to work in the field of counseling; on the positive side, counselor educators can form additional connections and relationships with students who have similar experiences or perceptions as them. Counselor educators need to be familiar with current scholarship in the field about how to address this academically and in the form of clinical supervision (e.g., Goodrich, 2008; Goodrich & Luke, 2012); additional considerations should also be made for other service activities. When advising a Chi Sigma Iota chapter, for example, counselor educators should consider how much time to spend with students in social student group activities as well as how much to share of their own lives in these settings.

When supervising a student who is also a member of an organization, counselor educators should consider boundaries with that student, such as how much of the student's life they allow themselves to know as partners or friends and what it means if the student presents one way in supervision and another in social settings (or if the student states one thing about his or her life or internship experience in supervision and a different thing when in social group settings). Complexities embedded in fair play can be raised in academic and supervisory settings as opposed to social settings. Although there are opportunities for counselor educators to model professional behavior in social settings and discuss ways to appropriately discuss internships or one's work life with others without violating confidentiality or the policies of an organization, there can also be risks. Counselor educators need to be cautious about what they say in front of a student or about a student in front of others, as in counseling, because students may reveal personalization concerns in supervision that are not meant to be shared with others in their lives. Therefore, counselor educators need to be aware of the inherent complexities that can exist in counselor training programs and how seemingly innocuous events that may be related to different forms of faculty service can have real implications for faculty and their students.

Finally, although faculty demographics should not lead to differential service roles, the gender and race of a given faculty member have been shown to be connected to how service is considered (Bracken et al., 2006; Luke & Goodrich, 2010). Faculty members of color and women have often discussed the differing demands they perceive compared to their White and male colleagues to either serve as advisers to students from marginalized backgrounds or participate in certain committees or programs to ensure appropriate gender/race representation or because they were the only one who could actually provide a service for a given group (e.g., Bracken et al., 2006; Luke & Goodrich, 2010; Ward, 2003). Scholars have discussed the perceived sense of obligation and demands to join certain groups, lead certain committees, or volunteer with specific gender or cultural centers based on the identity of the faculty member. This may be congruent or incongruent with a faculty member's goals or aspirations, but faculty members have reported in the past pushback or judgment if they did not play the roles they were anticipated to play on campus. This does not appear to best represent the ideals of multiculturalism and social justice espoused by the field of counselor education. Prospective faculty members from certain marginalized groups (e.g., groups marginalized because of their gender, race/ethnicity, affectual orientation) may wish to consider how their identity may interact with service obligations or demands. They should also see whether they can work with their program, department, and college faculty to ensure that appropriate balances can be made to prevent their service load from jeopardizing other aspects of their academic life as well as to ensure that they do not feel targeted to take on certain tasks because of a common attribute or variable shared with others.

The Evolution of Service in the 21st Century

Service is ubiquitous and essential in a faculty member's life at a college or university. As the education accountability movement grows stronger in graduate education, a focus around student learning outcomes, marketability, and career prospects will become ever more present in faculty members' lives. Increasing demands for faculty members to play a role in accountability efforts will pull more faculty time away from other potential projects and resources.

In addition, a rising number of counselor education programs use electronic or distance-based means within their programs, through either online or hybrid education. As the field becomes more digital, and education and supervision use greater technology (Rousmaniere & Renfro-Michel, 2016), faculty service demands may not be in the face-to-face environments of a traditional university but could be in a faculty member's home office space. Committee work might take place via videoconferencing or phone calls, and faculty members may have colleagues whom they only see a few times a year at residencies in cities other than where they live. Expectations for student supervision, the creation and maintenance of program policies, the meeting of student learning objectives, and appropriate oversight of academic programs by faculty will remain, but the vehicle through which they are met may be more virtual than grounded. One issue that may remain the same, however, is that as faculty members serve longer in their roles, they may be expected to provide increasing levels of service to the university, ensuring that they can protect early-career faculty members and use the strength of their time and experience with the university to best meet the needs of all of the academic program's stakeholders.

Best Practices for Training and Practice in Counselor Education

To ensure success, I provide the following checklist of recommendations for new faculty members to consider when beginning their new position:

- Know your workload policy, if you have one, and what the expectations are for faculty scholarship, teaching, and service.
- Calculate the amount of time you should be spending on different tasks when you are new in your position. Do this every semester. If you find that the time you are spending on service is greater than the percentage of time you should be spending, work to renegotiate your service commitments with other colleagues in your program, department, or college.
- Have frank and honest conversations with your faculty mentor (if you have one) and your department chair. Know what your expectations are in terms of service and how to achieve them. See service as one necessary thread that will help you to achieve promotion and tenure, but know that this is only one leg of the stool.
- Understand that a faculty member's service is like a student's scaffolded learning experience: Big projects do not just happen at once! Faculty service is progressive; it builds over time. Earlier on in your career, take on smaller, more manageable tasks; with time your projects can increase in complexity and size. First-year faculty should not take on program accreditation as their service task, but analyzing aggregate student data from one course or a set of courses and writing a program report regarding the findings would be a fine first step. Service needs to be logical and intentional.
- Find ways to connect service to your teaching and scholarship, if possible. If you are interested in professional identity, serving as a Chi Sigma Iota International chapter faculty adviser would be a service goal. If you are interested in multicultural issues, connecting with diversity committees, student groups, and outside campus advocacy groups might make logical sense both for service and to connect with future potential research subjects or consultants. Any of these opportunities could serve for outside class speakers or connection to service groups for service learning experiences in classes. It is possible to have research inform service and service inform research.
- Make time for yourself. No one needs a hero, and no one knows how to look out for you like you. Service can be a daunting, overwhelming requirement at any university. Taking on too many tasks or overly large tasks can lead to burnout. Or other aspects of your life (e.g., scholarship, teaching, family, free time) may suffer. It is as important for faculty to remain balanced and cared for as it is for

a counselor to take steps to avoid burnout. Use the skills you have learned as a professional counselor to practice and manage self-care so that you can have a long and successful career.

Conclusion

Service is viewed as one of the three legs of the stool that make up academic life alongside scholarly/creative work and teaching. Although service may not be given as much attention in one's academic training program as the other two legs of the stool, it is both important for the mission of the academic program and university as well as a time-consuming activity that requires intentional decision making and deliberation. When considering the next steps of their academic career, counselor educators need to thoughtfully and intentionally consider the contributions they can and are willing to make to their program and university, both when moving through the job search process and when developing in their academic career. Service workload and requirements will vary by institution type, program size, method of instruction used (e.g., online, hybrid, face to face), and where one is in one's career development. It is typically assumed that junior faculty will have lower service requirements and that service load requirements will increase as one advances in rank. Regardless of institutional or program differences, individuals are called on to consider their strengths and weaknesses as well as the contributions they wish to make to their program and students before they agree to different service requirements. Service is anticipated to take at least 20% of a faculty member's time. That time is best spent allowing oneself to make meaningful and fulfilling contributions, as much as one is able, because anything less just becomes work that can be both time consuming and wearing.

References

Altbach, P. G. (2016). Harsh realities: The professoriate in the twenty-first century. In M. N. Bastedo, P. G. Altbach, & P. J. Gumport (Eds.), *American higher education in the 21st century: Social, political, and economic challenges* (4th ed., pp. 84–109). Baltimore, MD: Johns Hopkins University Press.

Bracken, S. J., Allen, J. K., & Dean, D. R. (2006). *The balancing act: Gendered perspectives in faculty roles and work lives.* Sterling, VA: Stylus.

Council for Accreditation of Counseling and Related Educational Programs. (2015). *CACREP 2016 standards.* Alexandria, VA: Author.

Frasier Chabot, H., & Milinder, L. (2005). Balancing multiple responsibilities. In S. L. Tice, N. Jackson, L. M. Lambert, & P. Englot (Eds.), *University teaching: A reference guide for graduate students and faculty* (2nd ed., pp. 248–260). Syracuse, NY: Syracuse University Press.

Geiger, R. L. (2016). The ten generations of American higher education. In M. N. Bastedo, P. G. Altbach, & P. J. Gumport (Eds.), *American higher education in the 21st century: Social, political, and economic challenges* (4th ed., pp. 3–34). Baltimore, MD: Johns Hopkins University Press.

Goodrich, K. M. (2008). Dual relationships in group training. *Journal for Specialists in Group Work, 33,* 221–235. doi:10.1080/01933920802204981

Goodrich, K. M., & Luke, M. (2012). Problematic student in the experiential group: Professional and ethical challenges for counselor educators. *Journal for Specialists in Group Work, 37,* 326–346. doi:10.1080/0193392 2.2012.690834

Indiana University Center for Postsecondary Research. (n.d.). *Basic classification description.* Retrieved from http://carnegieclassifications. iu.edu/classification_descriptions/basic.php

Kuh, G. D. (Ed.). (1993). *Cultural perspectives in student affairs work.* Lanham, MD: American College Personnel Association.

Lee, C. C., Nu, G., & Pedbani, R. N. (2013). Teaching to encourage professional development. In J. D. West, D. L. Bubenzer, J. A. Cox, & J. M. McGlothlin (Eds.), *Teaching in counselor education: Engaging students in learning* (pp. 115–124). Alexandria, VA: Association for Counselor Education and Supervision.

Luke, M., & Goodrich, K. M. (2010). Chi Sigma Iota chapter leadership and professional identity development in early career counselors. *Counselor Education and Supervision, 50,* 56–78. doi:10.1002/j.1556-6978.2010. tb00108.x

Orr, J. J., & Hulse-Killacky, D. (2006). Using voice, meaning, mutual construction of knowledge, and transfer of learning to apply an ecological perspective to group work training. *Journal for Specialists in Group Work, 31,* 189–200. doi:10.1080/01933920600777824

Purdue University. (n.d.). *Magnify program.* Retrieved from https://www. education.purdue.edu/academics/graduate-students/degrees-and-programs/graduate-programs/school-counseling/magnify/

Rousmaniere, T., & Renfro-Michel, E. (2016). *Using technology to enhance clinical supervision.* Alexandria, VA: American Counseling Association.

University of New Mexico. (2012). *C100: Academic load.* Retrieved from http://handbook.unm.edu/policies/section-c/employment-appointment/c100.html

Ward, K. (2003). *Faculty service roles and the scholarship of engagement* (ASHE-ERIC Higher Education Report, Vol. 29, No. 5). Hoboken, NJ: Wiley.

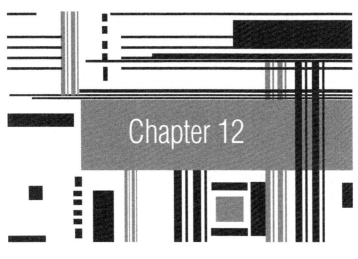

Collegiality and Wellness

Heather C. Trepal

Counselor education is a multifaceted discipline, and counselor educators wear many hats. They are teachers, researchers, supervisors, advisers, mentors, colleagues, and more. In the midst of all of these roles, counselor educators also function as members of countless teams. Given all of their job responsibilities, counselor educators must also balance the interpersonal and intrapersonal aspects of being a faculty member. Both interpersonal (relationships between students, faculty, and peers) and intrapersonal (how a faculty member is managing his or her physical and emotional well-being) aspects can influence work environments. This chapter specifically focuses on two aspects of being a faculty member: collegiality and wellness. *Collegiality* can be thought of as the quality of departmental citizenship and relational climate and is an important external interpersonal aspect of work. In contrast, *wellness* has been defined as a lifestyle combining the domains of spirit, mind, and body (Myers, Sweeney, & Witmer, 2000) and is considered an internal, intrapersonal aspect. These two aspects can affect each other. The chapter provides additional information regarding how faculty and work relationships, student interactions, and personal ways of being can affect job satisfaction, collegiality, and wellness in counselor education and supervision. This chapter also outlines issues of collegiality and wellness as they apply across the settings in which counselor educators work and are affected by and affect professional identity, accreditation status, and social justice and diversity. The chapter concludes with recommendations for cultivating collegiality and wellness in counselor education.

Collegiality in Higher Education and Counselor Education

Collegiality is so important in higher education that it has been hall-marked as "the fourth pillar" of evaluation along with teaching, research, and service (Hatfield, 2006, p. 11). In fact, it has been cited as one of the most important contributors to faculty job satisfaction and is thus very important to consider regarding faculty retention (Ambrose, Huston, & Norman, 2005). However, one cannot provide a score or reference a publication on a curriculum vita to provide evidence of collegiality. The term *collegiality* emerged in higher education when it was cited in a 1981 legal case as a reason why a university could deny tenure (Hatfield, 2006). The American Association of University Professors (2016) has taken a strong stance that collegiality in and of itself should not be considered a sole evaluation criterion for employment, promotion, tenure, or termination decisions. Unfortunately, Baporikar (2015) indicated that collegiality can also be "a code word signifying potential action against someone who does not quite 'fit in'" (p. 60).

As it is a potential criterion for faculty evaluation, it is critical to define collegiality in the context of higher education and provide concrete examples. Collegiality has been conceptualized to include dimensions of social behavior (e.g., relational contributions to organizational culture), conflict management (e.g., working to resolve concerns that naturally arise when people work closely together, honoring a diversity of opposite viewpoints), and citizenship (e.g., pulling one's weight as a citizen of the department; Hatfield, 2006). When these behaviors and attitudes are absent the following can result in each dimension: harassment and isolation (social behavior), lack of compromising and lack of shared input (conflict management), and lack of respect and unequal and unreliable engagement in work responsibilities (citizenship; Hatfield, 2006).

It is important to note that researchers have also distinguished collegiality from congeniality in that one can be congenial (e.g., be pleasant, say hello and goodbye) but not collegial (e.g., work as a team). Faculty often work closely with one another, with administrators, with academic peers, and with students, so there are a lot of opportunities for collegial—and not so collegial—interactions to occur. However, faculty can and will be evaluated on collegiality along with their achievements in teaching, research, and service. Thus, some faculty who are going up for review may be negatively evaluated on their collegiality and not successful in their bid for tenure or promotion.

New faculty members and doctoral students may wonder, "What does collegiality look like?" When I was a junior faculty member, our department chair sent out an email titled "Collegiality and Visibility." Upon reading just the title of this email, I was scared. The body of the email instructed all faculty members in the department to "increase their visibility." Although we were a seemingly productive faculty, it seemed as though some were working at home or behind closed office doors more often than was desirable for our institution. This is an example of unwritten curriculum—those institutional mores that are often all that exist to define collegiality. For our department, being seen both on campus and in one's office was important. A good question to ask a department chair is how much time and how many days faculty are expected to be on campus at the institution. In this way, new faculty can clarify any unwritten expectations about this aspect of collegiality.

Another example of collegiality is teamwork. Although faculty members are expected to teach and conduct research, departments rely and run on service work. It takes committee work to make things happen. One example is the Council for Accreditation of Counseling and Related Educational Programs (CACREP) accreditation process. In some departments, one faculty member is identified as *the* CACREP liaison. This person is expected to author the self-study (or coordinate the process) and lead accreditation efforts (e.g., the site visit, midcycle reviews). In my department, we decided that we would develop an accreditation committee. We would have committee cochairs; however, we wanted to make sure that everyone in the department contributed to our reaccreditation efforts. Over the course of two semesters we met monthly and then weekly as an entire faculty. These diverse efforts promoted increased communication and teamwork in addition to more lunches and social time together. Our efforts were successful, and our department chair gave us a celebration recognizing everyone's teamwork and investment in the process. These acknowledgments included our department staff and students who worked on reaccreditation efforts. Despite the importance of collegiality as one of the evaluation criteria for promotion and tenure, little is known about how this important concept manifests in counselor education programs.

Wellness in Higher Education and Counselor Education

There are many models of wellness. According to Goss, Cuddihy, and Michaud-Tomson (2010), "Wellness has been described as the active process through which the individual becomes aware of all aspects of the self and makes choices toward a more healthy existence through balance and integration across multiple life dimensions" (p. 30). Wellness has been researched in higher education to include various aspects that contribute to or hinder academics' vitality, or their ability to thrive in the higher education climate. A mix of individual and institutional factors contribute to personal satisfaction, job satisfaction, and well-being (Huston, Norman, & Ambrose, 2007).

Institutional factors related to wellness may include such things as location, cost of living, institutional or departmental reputation, collegiality, compensation, administration, and the promotion and tenure process. Individual factors may include things like family and relationship variables, the state of one's physical and mental health, or the ability to find meaning and satisfaction in one's work.

Personal characteristics such as those that contribute to overall wellness are vital to being able to help others (Roach & Young, 2007). In fact, it has been said that well counselors produce well clients; that mantra has been taken a step further to indicate that well counselor educators produce well counseling students (Hill, 2004). So how is wellness in counseling defined? Roach and Young (2007) defined *counselor wellness* as a journey to maximal functioning of mind, body, and spirit. Wellness also has components of both personal awareness and professional development. In fact, wellness is a core component of a professional counseling identity. Counselor wellness can be linked to career-sustaining behaviors and can serve as a buffer against burnout or impairment (Roach & Young, 2007). Conversely, stress related to one's occupation can result in decreased well-being (Myers et al., 2000). Work is a major life task requiring sustained energy and effort, so understanding the relationship between work and wellness is important (Myers et al., 2000).

Research on counselor educator wellness is beginning to emerge. Leinbaugh, Hazler, Bradley, and Hill (2003) explored the factors that contribute to the level of well-being experienced by counselor educators who work in CACREP-accredited programs. The majority of the faculty in their study reported a great sense of well-being when they had more control over the courses they taught and the topics they included in their research agendas.

Wester, Trepal, and Myers (2009) also explored the wellness of counselor educators. They surveyed 180 counselor educators across academic ranks (e.g., assistant, associate, and full professors) and found that their self-reported levels of wellness were generally high. However, there were some within-group differences. Assistant professors reported feeling realistic beliefs, perhaps related to their newness in the faculty role and lack of adjustment to academic culture. Although marital status contributed to higher wellness, perceived stress and a higher number of children were reported to equate to lower wellness levels. Myers, Trepal, Ivers, and Wester (2016) expanded this earlier study to phenomenologically examine 11 counselor educators' experiences of wellness. Analysis of the interviews resulted in three themes: time, congruence, and professional supports. Particularly important to the participants in the study was the support of their department chair, family members, and mentors.

Clearly, work and family/personal responsibilities affect counselor educators' wellness. Although the general topic of counselor educator wellness has been given some attention in professional research (Leinbaugh et al., 2003; Myers et al., 2016; Wester et al., 2009), other researchers have begun to examine more specifically wellness in various intersections of counselor education faculty (e.g., pretenured faculty, female faculty, members of underrepresented groups).

Pretenured Faculty

The early years in academia can be particularly challenging as new faculty members struggle to navigate complex work environments, prep courses for the first time, establish research agendas, develop professional networks, and strive for promotion and tenure. In fact, Hill (2004) maintained that this is a time for faculty members' growth and adaptation as they struggle with role overload in their new work setting. Magnuson (2002) explored the experiences of first-year counselor educators and their ability to adjust in an academic environment with respect to satisfaction, stress and anxiety, and feelings of connectedness. She found that responses varied across three distinct categories: consistently positive comments and elevated ratings of satisfaction, generally positive comments qualified by difficult circumstances and supported with numeric ratings, and consistently negative comments and diminished ratings of satisfaction. Many factors contributed to this variation in response, including connectedness, inclusion, adaptation to a new identity, program culture, and faculty. The vast majority of participants alluded to the impact of support from fellow senior faculty members. Program faculty can either increase feelings of connection and provide support or increase feelings of loneliness and create anxiety-provoking environments for first-year professors. Teaching and supervision were identified as areas that provided job satisfaction for many, whereas the academic environment acted as a source of satisfaction for some. Several factors (student interactions, programmatic difficulties, job requirements for tenure or promotion) were identified as sources of contention for new counselor educators, and several special circumstances (such as gender or minority status) directly affected the experiences of first-year faculty. Magnuson concluded that support, particularly from senior faculty members, and instruction on department and university policies and procedures are necessary to prevent attrition of first-year counselor educators.

Female Faculty Members

Although counseling can be considered a female-dominated profession, challenges still exist for female counselor educators related to their wellness experiences in academia. In one of the first studies on the topic specific to counselor education, Hill, Leinbaugh, Bradley, and Hazler (2005) examined encouraging and discouraging factors among 115 female counselor educators. They found that the social climate of the department and relationships were important to their participants. Of note is that supportive, growth-enhancing relationships with both students and other faculty were seen as especially encouraging. Maintaining a sense of autonomy at work and contributing to the profession were also encouraging factors. Discouraging factors included negative relationships in the department and being overcontrolled by others (Hill et al., 2005). The results from this study have implications for both collegiality and wellness in that supportive relationships enhanced female counselor educators' job satisfaction and negative interactions detracted from it. In addition, the autonomy and flexibility afforded by a faculty position was also important to the job satisfaction of the female counselor educators in the study.

One area that has received considerable attention as a factor that contributes to differences and/or similarities in experiences of female counselor educator wellness is motherhood. It has been observed that balancing academia and parenting can present significant challenges to women's physical and emotional well-being. Stinchfield and Trepal (2010) and Trepal and Stinchfield (2012) examined what counselor educators who were also mothers experienced in the profession. These female counselor educators reported greater responsibility for caregiving roles than their partners (Stinchfield & Trepal, 2010). The mothers in their study perceived the flexibility of an academic schedule as an additional stressor and also experienced overt and covert discrimination related to their parenting status (Trepal & Stinchfield, 2012). However, the women in their study achieved a greater level of balance between work and family later in their careers (e.g., as senior faculty; Stinchfield & Trepal, 2010).

Recently, Haskins et al. (2016) studied the intersectionality of African American mothers in counselor education. They found that although the participants in their study experienced racial marginalization (e.g., their scholarship was devalued; they experienced tokenism, isolation, and exclusion) they also used strategies such as internalizing their success (e.g., feeling pride in their accomplishments) and relying on support systems to thrive in academia. The authors noted the triple identity status of the counselor educators in their study (women, African Americans, mothers) and advised senior faculty and administrators to acknowledge the impact of intersectionality and the realities of racial marginalization with faculty members (Haskins et al., 2016). They also supported inclusion in the counselor education curriculum of the topic of intersectionality and its role in maintaining both oppression and opportunity and of practices to support students and faculty who are parents (Haskins et al., 2016).

As this line of inquiry evolves, researchers will continue to learn more about the experiences of parents at the intersection of identities (e.g., gay and lesbian parents, single parents, parents of differing racial and ethnic groups, parents of adopted children, fathers). As a single parent, I can definitely say that without support from my colleagues, my work–life balance (which is already questionable on most days) would be completely out of sync. Seemingly small things, like not scheduling important faculty meetings on school holidays or making considerations for course scheduling, go a long way toward recognizing that parents have extenuating responsibilities. Thus, aspects of both wellness and collegiality are affected by a department's response to parenting concerns. I hope researchers will also elucidate a counternarrative and provide information on counselor educators who are childfree so that the field can better understand their experiences as well.

Counselor Educators Who Are Members of Underrepresented Groups

Despite a mandate from CACREP calling for attention to hiring practices that promote the inclusion of diverse faculty members, and although programs vary, there is a noted lack of diversity among counselor education faculty in the overall profession (Holcomb-McCoy & Addison-Bradley, 2005). Some contend that there is a lack of recruitment of faculty who are members of underrepresented groups (Brooks & Steen, 2010).

According to research, faculty of color and those from underrepresented groups (e.g., faculty who identify as lesbian, gay, bisexual, or transgender) experience the work environment differently than their counterparts. For example, Shillingford, Trice-Black, and Butler (2013) interviewed eight ethnic minority female counseling educators and identified four categories of challenges they face within counselor education: "challenges with students, overwhelming workloads, high expectations, and feelings of alienation and lack of support" (p. 259). Holcomb-McCoy and Addison-Bradley (2005) surveyed African American faculty in counselor education programs and found that although job satisfaction was generally high, it was tempered by their perception of the department's racial climate (i.e., spoken and unspoken messages around race). Salazar, Herring, Cameron, and Nihlen (2004) also interviewed counselor educators of color and described the idea of "multicultural selfhood" (p. 46). This theme was used to capture the identities that participants constructed over their careers. Participants reported using their multicultural selfhood to navigate both challenges and opportunities in academia.

In another study, Brooks and Steen (2010) interviewed African American male counselor educators about their perceptions of their faculty position. The counselor educators in their study reported that they were satisfied with their faculty positions but they were also extremely isolated and concerned about the recruitment and retention of African American men in both counseling and counselor education. According to one of their participants, "You cannot pursue something that you are not in" (p. 148). The lack of visual representation in both classrooms and faculty offices was noted. The authors concluded with the recommendation that a pipeline be established for African American male representation in the counseling profession.

Furthermore, Constantine, Smith, Redington, and Owens (2008) studied Black faculty in counselor education and counseling psychology programs and their experiences of racial microaggressions. They discovered that their participants felt both very visible (e.g., experienced tokenism and increased mentoring requirements for underrepresented students) and invisible (e.g., were isolated, had their credentials questioned). The participants in their study also had difficulty determining whether the microaggressions were based on race or gender. They coped with the microaggressions in a number of ways using personal and professional supports, although they reported a lack of adequate mentoring.

Thus, it appears that some research has been conducted on the experiences of counselor educators who are members of underrepresented groups, particularly African American faculty (Brooks & Steen, 2010; Constantine et al., 2008; Holcomb-McCoy & Addison-Bradley, 2005; Shillingford et al., 2013). Their experiences with collegiality are affected by the racial climate, isolation, and microaggressions. In turn, these experiences also affect their wellness and how they respond to their colleagues, students, and work settings. Given the diversity of faculty members in counselor education, more research needs to be done to shed light on the experiences of others from underrepresented groups (e.g., international faculty; those who identify as lesbian, gay, bisexual, or transgender; faculty from other racial and ethnic groups).

Consider the case of Miranda, who has recently graduated with her doctorate in counselor education and supervision and is set to begin a faculty position as an assistant professor at Western American University. Miranda is married, has a 2-year-old daughter, and is moving across the country for her new position. There are 13 faculty in the Department of Counseling, and Miranda will be the only junior faculty member. What types of things might Miranda be concerned about related to collegiality? What factors may influence her colleagues' perceptions of Miranda's collegiality? What factors might support or hinder Miranda's wellness in her new position?

Additional Challenges to Faculty Collegiality and Wellness

Although attention has been paid to general counselor educator wellness and to specific populations such as women and those who are members of underrepresented groups, additional challenges may affect faculty collegiality and wellness. These include faculty burnout, challenges to competence, workplace bullying, and faculty–student interactions.

Faculty Burnout and Challenges to Competence

Moate, Gnilka, West, and Bruns (2016) noted that counselor education is a complex discipline in which faculty often face the risk of rejection (e.g., of manuscripts submitted for publication and grant applications) and intense scrutiny (e.g., course evaluations) despite their good intentions regarding aspects of their work that they must perform for tenure and promotion. These intense demands and pressures may lead to unhealthy coping mechanisms, burnout, and challenges to competence.

Sangganjanavanich and Balkin (2013) explored burnout with respect to counselor educators and the distinct environment of higher education. The authors were expressly concerned with the relationship between burnout and job satisfaction in this population. A total of 220 participants completed an online survey. As expected, the authors found that there was a significant relationship between emotional exhaustion (a major contributor to burnout) and job satisfaction: Higher levels of emotional exhaustion led to decreased job satisfaction. The study did not replicate the findings of earlier studies regarding the impact of race/ethnicity and faculty status; however, the limited variation among participants may have affected those findings. The authors suggested that all faculty receive professional development on balancing personal and professional demands and pay attention to their own wellness (Sangganjanavanich & Balkin, 2013).

The issue of student competence, including assessment and remediation, has become increasingly important in counselor education. In fact, Magnuson (2002) reported that dealing with student competence concerns is a major source of stress for new faculty. The importance of this issue has also been underscored by a number of recent legal cases on student remediation and dismissal decisions. However, little has been done to investigate counselor educators' issues with their own competence. To remedy this gap, Brown-Rice and Furr (2015) asked counselor educators about their experiences with colleagues who may have problems with professional competence. It is interesting that they found that 76% of those they surveyed indicated that they had observed a colleague with a problem with professional competence, and the majority indicated that these issues manifested in negative ways with students and other faculty in the department. Problematic issues observed ranged from an inability to control emotions, to emotional disorders, to substance abuse. What is striking is that the majority of respondents wanted more information on how to address these concerns with colleagues. It seems as though even though the profession has become increasingly focused on students' problematic behaviors, work remains to be done in this area regarding counselor education faculty.

Workplace Bullying

Workplace bullying is common, and the work environment of academia is not exempt from these behaviors (Keashly & Neuman, 2010). In fact, Keashly and Neuman (2013) found that 25% of faculty have personally experienced workplace bullying. In an environment with many inherent power differentials (e.g., junior/senior faculty, administrators/staff) and long-standing work relationships due to tenure, there exists the potential for bullying. Some of the most common types of academic workplace bullying include targeting a person's professional reputation, isolating a colleague, and limiting access to resources (Keashly & Neuman, 2010).

Keashly and Wajngurt (2016) cited peer review as a precipitating factor for academic workplace bullying. According to these authors, academic freedom gives space for all ideas to be heard. Even those ideas that are controversial must be challenged by peer review. Peer review is necessary for promotion and tenure and thus protects the system of academic freedom that is inherent in academic culture. They asserted, "Peer review as the mechanism for access to a successful academic career, is an inherently subjective process that can be subverted in undue influence in promotion, tenure, and merit review" (p. 82). Along with peer review, ambiguous tenure and promotion guidelines and the increasing scarcity of resources (e.g., travel funding, graduate assistants) may prove to be additional sources of stress and frustration, leading to a toxic work environment and the increased potential for bullying to occur (Keashly & Neuman, 2010).

The effects of academic bullying can be costly to the individual being targeted. Bullying and a negative workplace culture can affect faculty's overall health and well-being. The effects can also extend to the department, students, and the institution as a whole. For example, some faculty who are bullied may choose to simply disengage. These faculty self-protect by continuing to work on their own scholarship while disengaging from student activities, departmental decision making, and working with other colleagues via mentoring and collaboration (Ambrose et al., 2005). Thus, it can easily be seen how workplace bullying in higher education negatively affects both collegiality and wellness.

Faculty–Student Interactions

According to Dollarhide and Granello (2012), relationships between counseling students and faculty are "paramount," which means of the utmost importance to learning (p. 290). However, little is known about exactly what it is about these relationships and interactions that contributes to collegiality and wellness among faculty and students in the profession. Komarraju, Musulkin, and Bhattacharya (2010) explored the content of faculty interactions with undergraduate students. When students perceived faculty as approachable and respectful, they became more engaged in the academic experience. The students in their study also benefitted from out-of-class interactions and interactions in which faculty contributed to their career exploration and development. Although this study was completed with undergraduate students, it suggests that interpersonal dimensions of faculty–student interactions may also be important to graduate students and their learning experiences.

Although this topic has received little attention in counselor education, recently Ray, Huffman, Christian, and Wilson (2016) explored male counselor educators' experiences of being male in their professional relationships. Because most of the students in counseling programs are women (around 75% according to studies; e.g., Healey & Hays, 2012), male counselor educators may need to negotiate their faculty–student interactions in a "female-prevalent field as a person in a position of power" (Ray et al., 2016, p. 108). The male counselor educators in Ray et al.'s study experienced differences in their academic environments and worried about professional isolation and potential legal and ethical challenges of perceived misconduct. Accordingly, they engaged in strategies to avoid "the perception of impropriety" with male and female students and to create a safe educational climate (p. 118). These strategies included not meeting with students behind closed doors and favoring group interactions, among others. The importance of faculty–student interactions cannot be underestimated. However, recent research (Ray et al., 2016) suggests that the profession may need to focus attention on this area.

Experiences of Collegiality and Wellness Across the Academic Spectrum

Lechuga (2008) maintained that the traditional idea of faculty culture involves full-time tenured or tenure-track faculty who have input into faculty governance and academic freedom. These faculty members also participate in the work of nonprofit institutions of higher education through varying degrees of teaching, research, and service responsibilities. According to Lechuga, for-profit institutes of higher education operate from a corporate business model and thus defy traditional faculty norms in the areas of faculty governance, teaching schedules, the tenure system, and research and service expectations. Moreover, they are "not constrained by the traditional academic calendar" (p. 289). They offer their product (i.e., education) rather than the opportunity to simply earn a degree. Thus, faculty experiences of both collegiality and wellness may be affected by the nontraditional nature of a for-profit work environment. For example, teaching schedules may look different (e.g., a certain percentage of course work conducted online, travel to brief in-person residencies in different cities, abbreviated course schedules different from a traditional brick-and-mortar institution's semester), and this may affect child care and other life responsibilities. Also, having colleagues in cyberspace may or may not lead to increased opportunities for collegiality and professional relationships.

It has been suggested that teaching in an online environment calls on faculty to master different competencies from those required for traditional brick-and-mortar programs. For example, Alvarez, Guasch, and Espasa (2009) suggested that online faculty need to have competencies not only in technology and course design and planning but also in a social role. This social role encompasses facilitating relationships and managing interactions between students and the faculty member as well as among the students and one another in cyberspace. Thus, additional complexities may be involved with faculty–student interactions and collegiality. Given that there is still much to learn about for-profit institutes of higher education and counselor education, future researchers may want to investigate some of these issues.

The Potential Impact of Systemic Factors on Collegiality and Wellness

Although research is just beginning to emerge on systemic factors that have the potential to affect collegiality and wellness, it is still useful to reflect on factors that are not yet supported by research. For example, how might flexibility, or the control over one's own work time, be affected by the type of institution or program in which a counselor educator is employed? In light of what you may know about the different priorities of teaching and research institutions, how might counselor educators need to manage their work time? It is easy to imagine that in a teaching-focused institution, a counselor educator would need to prioritize tasks related to teaching (e.g., preparing for class, creating assignments, spending time with students related to learning), and he or she would know that a significant portion of his or her evaluation would be weighted toward these tasks. This might become a little more complex in an online institution in which teaching is evaluated in nontraditional manner. In a research-oriented institution, a counselor educator would need to prioritize his or her time to focus on tasks that relate to research (e.g., collecting data, writing grants, publishing manuscripts on his or her findings).

Furthermore, given some of the things that are known to be challenges to counselor education and supervision faculty wellness (see below), it is easy to imagine how various types of institutional and organizational priorities and work environments may affect counselor educators. For example, knowing that student conflicts are an established challenge to faculty wellness, it might be important for faculty to know the process for dealing with these events in any type of work or organization. In addition, isolation is known to be a challenge to faculty wellness. How might counselor educators who work in online institutions negotiate the relational demands of a position in which they are required to work in cyberspace with their colleagues? You are encouraged to think about the following contributors and challenges to counselor education and supervision faculty wellness and how each might be affected by institution/organization type:

Snapshot of Contributors to Counselor Education
and Supervision Faculty Wellness
- Control over one's own work time (flexibility)
- Control over research agenda topics
- Congruence of work with personal beliefs
- Control over course assignments
- Professional support (department chair, mentors)
- Personal support (family, friends; adapted from Leinbaugh et al., 2003; Myers et al., 2016; Trepal & Stinchfield, 2012)

Snapshot of Challenges to Counselor Education
and Supervision Faculty Wellness
- Flexibility of roles in an academic position
- Negative departmental racial climate
- High workload
- Student conflicts
- Isolation
- High expectations
- Discrimination related to parenting status (adapted from Shillingford et al., 2013; Trepal & Stinchfield, 2012)

Best Practices for Cultivating Collegiality and Wellness in Counselor Education

In the face of the aforementioned pressures, faculty need to practice self-care. When counselor education faculty have been surveyed and interviewed, they have reported engaging in cultivating their spirituality, developing and maintaining boundaries, appreciating the autonomy of a faculty position, contributing to the profession, forming growth-fostering relationships with students and colleagues, and cultivating a strong support system as wellness strategies (Hill et al., 2005; Shillingford et al.,

2013). Many personal characteristics such as spirituality and sociability are considered what experts call *career-saving behaviors* when they are used to cope with stress (Lawson, 2007). In addition, given the importance that most faculty in the studies reviewed placed on mentorship and support systems, counselor education programs may want to invest in various mentorship models presented in the literature (e.g., Borders et al., 2011; Hammer, Trepal, & Speedlin, 2014).

Despite using strategies to support their wellness, counselor educators still have to persevere in their work environment. According to Baporikar (2015), "Collegial environments do not just happen. They have to be created and cultivated in order to thrive" (p. 60). However, this can be a test in academia, where sometimes ideas that are new, progressive, or innovative need to challenged to make progress. Furthermore, in a discipline such as counselor education and supervision, in which faculty are focused on student growth—even if that growth is slow in coming or challenging—valuing diversity and multiple perspectives is imperative.

However, there have been some suggestions aimed at improving collegiality in a department. These include faculty having a shared vision and goals, taking equal responsibility for their share of the workload, and working to promote a trusting environment (Baporikar, 2015). Furthermore, Baporikar (2015) suggested that department chairs take on the responsibility of engaging faculty in discussions regarding the definition and parameters of collegiality in the department, including what happens when disagreements arise. In addition, it is recommended that when a faculty member's collegiality becomes an issue, he or she be addressed in periodic reviews that include observations of specific problems and behaviors (e.g., what is happening and how the faculty member's behavior is contributing). It is also recommended that the department chairperson engage students, alumni, and stakeholders in the department's vision for continued engagement and the enhancement of relational capital (Baporikar, 2015).

Although it is important to focus special attention on pretenured faculty members' needs related to collegiality and wellness (Hill, 2004; Magnuson, 2002), it should be noted that tenured faculty also continue to face personal and professional challenges. For example, Alexander-Albritton and Hill (2015) reported that female counselor educators who were associate professors were less satisfied with the intrinsic rewards of their careers than they had been before receiving tenure. Conversely, Stinchfield and Trepal (2010) reported that senior female faculty reported feeling a greater sense of balance between work and family obligations than did mothers who were pretenured or at the associate professor level. It seems as though attention should be paid to these topics throughout one's career as a counselor educator.

In addition, given some of the research reviewed in this chapter, it is important for counselor education programs to continue to increase their representation of diverse faculty members. Concerns related to racialized departmental climates, microaggressions, and isolation persist (Brooks &

Steen, 2010; Constantine et al., 2008; Holcomb-McCoy & Addison-Bradley, 2005; Shillingford et al., 2013). Institutions and departments are encouraged to dialogue about racial issues (Bradley & Holcomb-McCoy, 2004). In addition to increasing the representation of diverse faculty members, attention must be paid to retention, acknowledgment, and support. Brooks and Steen (2010) recommended that universities focus on creating opportunities for networking among diverse faculty members on campus to increase support and decrease feelings of isolation. In addition, they also recommended the establishment of centers for racial and ethnic minority faculty support that include mentoring and professional development.

A Word About Adjunct Faculty and Doctoral Students

Adjunct faculty are key components of any counseling program. These professionals work alongside full-time tenured and tenure-track faculty to meet the needs of students and the department. Often students may not even realize the difference in their employment status or departmental contributions. However, adjunct faculty may be marginalized because of their lack of face time in the department. They may have other full-time jobs and thus may not be on campus as often as others in the department. Thus, it is especially important to be good colleagues with adjunct faculty. Small acts of kindness such as emails, lunch invitations, and invitations to graduation may mean a lot to adjunct faculty members. Remember that adjunct faculty are colleagues and part of the team. Late in my doctoral program, I worked as an adjunct faculty member in a local counseling program. I remember feeling removed from the happenings and informal culture of the department. I was extremely grateful for the tenured and tenure-track colleagues who reached out to me. Although collegiality and congeniality are different, tenured and tenure-track faculty should be reminded to include adjunct faculty in departmental life to the greatest extent possible.

Doctoral cohorts can provide a good petri dish for learning how to develop and maintain collegial relationships in academia. Doctoral programs can also serve as testing grounds for the development and maintenance of wellness practices. Thus, it is important to begin to cultivate wellness strategies and collegiality while still in one's doctoral program to enhance personal growth and development. As students contemplate pursuing a career as a counselor educator, they can be encouraged to keep both collegiality and wellness in mind because both will have an impact on their future job satisfaction. Yager and Tovar-Blank (2007) provided 10 concrete suggestions for promoting wellness during counselor preparation: (a) Introduce wellness directly; (b) associate the self-growth, self-awareness emphasis of counselor education with wellness; (c) model wellness; (d) communicate that perfection is not the goal; (e) present wellness as a lifestyle choice; (f) encourage (personal) counseling; (g) review ethical standards as they relate to wellness; (h) promote wellness across the curriculum; (i) develop innovative approaches to reinforce wellness; and (j) focus less on the pathology of human nature amid counselor education (p. 142). These suggestions can be modified to work within any counselor education program at the student or faculty level.

Conclusion

Both collegiality and counselor wellness are important variables in the counselor education context. Both of these important constructs can have positive or negative impacts on the work lives of counselor educators. Given the increasing diversity of faculty and counselor education work environments, it is paramount to keep these issues at the forefront of research and professional dialogue, as the profession has much to learn regarding barriers and best practices in these areas. It is imperative to continue to enact strategies to promote both collegiality and wellness in counselor education.

Additional Online Resources

American Association of University Professors
   www.aaup.org
American Association of University Women
   www.aauw.org
National Center for Faculty Development and Diversity
   www.facultydiversity.org

References

Alexander-Albritton, C., & Hill, N. R. (2015). Familial and institutional factors: Job satisfaction for female counselor educators. *Counselor Education and Supervision, 54,* 109–121. doi:10.1002/ceas.12008

Alvarez, I., Guasch, T., & Espasa, A. (2009). University teacher roles and competencies in online learning environments: A theoretical analysis of teaching and learning practices. *European Journal of Teacher Education, 32,* 321–336. doi:10.1080/02619760802624104

Ambrose, S., Huston, T., & Norman, M. (2005). A qualitative method for assessing faculty satisfaction. *Research in Higher Education, 46,* 803–830. doi:10.1007/s11162-004-6226-6

American Association of University Professors. (2016). *On collegiality as a criterion for faculty evaluation.* Retrieved from https://www.aaup.org/report/collegiality-criterion-faculty-evaluation

Baporikar, N. (2015). Collegiality as a strategy for excellence in academia. *International Journal of Strategic Change Management, 6,* 59–72. doi:10.1504/IJSCM.2015.069522

Borders, L. D., Young, J. S., Wester, K. L., Murray, C. E., Villalba, J. A., Lewis, T. F., & Mobley, A. K. (2011). Mentoring promotion/tenure-seeking faculty: Principles of good practice within a counselor education program. *Counselor Education and Supervision, 50,* 171–188. doi:10.1002/j.1556-6978.2011.tb00118.x

Bradley, C., & Holcomb-McCoy, C. (2004). African American counselor educators: Their experiences, challenges, and recommendations. *Counselor Education and Supervision, 43,* 258–273. doi:10.1002/j.1556-6978.2004.tb01851.x

Brooks, M., & Steen, S. (2010). "Brother where art thou?" African American male instructors' perceptions of the counselor education profession. *Journal of Multicultural Counseling and Development, 38,* 142–153. doi:10.1002/j.2161-1912.2010.tb00122.x

Brown-Rice, K., & Furr, S. (2015). Gatekeeping ourselves: Counselor educators' knowledge of colleagues' problematic behaviors. *Counselor Education and Supervision, 54,* 176–188. doi:10.1002/ceas.12012

Constantine, M. G., Smith, L., Redington, R. M., & Owens, D. (2008). Racial microaggressions against Black counseling and counseling psychology faculty: A central challenge in the multicultural movement. *Journal of Counseling & Development, 86,* 348–355. doi:10.1002/j.1556-6678.2008.tb00519.x

Dollarhide, C. T., & Granello, D. H. (2012). Humanistic perspectives on counselor education and supervision. In M. B. Scholl, A. S. McGowan, & J. T. Hansen (Eds.), *Humanistic perspectives on contemporary counseling issues* (pp. 277–303). New York, NY: Routledge.

Goss, H. B., Cuddihy, T. F., & Michaud-Tomson, L. (2010). Wellness in higher education: A transformative framework for health related disciplines. *Asia-Pacific Journal of Health, Sport and Physical Education, 1,* 29–36.

Hammer, T., Trepal, H., & Speedlin, S. (2014). Five relational mentoring strategies for female faculty. *Adultspan Journal, 13,* 4–14. doi:10.1002/j.2161-0029.2014.00022.x

Haskins, N. H., Daigle, J., Sewell, C., Crumb, L., Appling, B., & Trepal, H. (2016). The intersectionality of African American mothers in counselor education: A phenomenological examination. *Counselor Education and Supervision, 55,* 60–75. doi:10.1002/ceas.12033

Hatfield, R. D. (2006). Collegiality in higher education: Toward and understanding of the factors involved in collegiality. *Journal of Organizational Culture, Communication and Conflict, 10,* 11–19.

Healey, A. C., & Hays, D. G. (2012). A discriminant analysis of gender and counselor professional identity development. *Journal of Counseling & Development, 90,* 55–62. doi:10.1111/j.1556-6676.2012.00008.x

Hill, N. R. (2004). The challenges experienced by pretenured faculty members in counselor education: A wellness perspective. *Counselor Education and Supervision, 44,* 135–146. doi:10.1002/j.1556-6978.2004.tb01866.x

Hill, N. R., Leinbaugh, T., Bradley, C., & Hazler, R. (2005). Female counselor educators: Encouraging and discouraging factors in academia. *Journal of Counseling & Development, 83,* 374–380. doi:10.1002/j.1556-6978.2005.tb00358.x

Holcomb-McCoy, C., & Addison-Bradley, C. (2005). African American counselor educators' job satisfaction and perceptions of departmental racial climate. *Counselor Education and Supervision, 45,* 2–15. doi:10.1002/j.1556-6978.2005.tb00126.x

Huston, T. A., Norman, M., & Ambrose, S. A. (2007). Expanding the discussion of faculty vitality to include productive but disengaged senior faculty. *Journal of Higher Education, 78,* 493–522.

Keashly, L., & Neuman, J. H. (2010). Faculty experiences with bullying in higher education: Causes, consequences, and management. *Administrative Theory & Praxis, 32,* 48–70. doi:10.2753/ATP1084-1806320103

Keashly, L., & Neuman, J. (2013). Bullying in academia: What does current theorizing and research tell us? In J. Lester (Ed.), *Workplace bullying in higher education* (pp. 1–22). New York, NY: Routledge.

Keashly, L., & Wajngurt, C. (2016). Faculty bullying in higher education. *Psychology and Education, 53,* 79–90. Retrieved from www.psychologyandeducation.net/pae/2016/04/26/faculty-bullying-higher-education-loraleigh-keashly-clara-wajngurt/

Komarraju, M., Musulkin, S., & Bhattacharya, G. (2010). Role of student–faculty interactions in developing college students' academic self-concept, motivation, and achievement. *Journal of College Student Development, 51,* 332–342. doi:10.1353/csd.0.0137

Lawson, G. (2007). Counselor wellness and impairment: A national survey. *The Journal of Humanistic Counseling, 46,* 20–34. doi:10.1002/j.2161-1939.2007.tb00023.x

Lechuga, V. M. (2008). Assessment, knowledge and customer service: Contextualizing faculty work at for-profit colleges and universities. *Review of Higher Education, 31,* 287–307. doi:10.1353/rhe.2008.0004

Leinbaugh, T., Hazler, R. J., Bradley, C., & Hill, N. (2003). Factors influencing counselor educators' subjective sense of well-being. *Counselor Education and Supervision, 43,* 52–64. doi:10.1002/j.1556-6978.2003.tb01829.x

Magnuson, S. (2002). New assistant professors of counselor education: Their 1st year. *Counselor Education and Supervision, 41,* 306–320. doi:10.1002/j.1556-6978.2002.tb01293.x

Moate, R. M., Gnilka, P. B., West, E. M., & Bruns, K. L. (2016). Stress and burnout among counselor educators: Differences between adaptive perfectionists, maladaptive perfectionists, and nonperfectionists. *Journal of Counseling & Development, 94,* 161–171. doi:10.1002/jcad.12073

Myers, J. E., Sweeney, T. J., & Witmer, J. M. (2000). The wheel of wellness counseling for wellness: A holistic model for treatment planning. *Journal of Counseling & Development, 78,* 251–266. doi:10.1002/j.1556-6676.2000.tb01906.x

Myers, J., Trepal, H., Ivers, N., & Wester, K. (2016). Wellness of counselor educators: Do we practice what we preach? *Journal of Counselor Leadership and Advocacy, 3,* 22–30.

Ray, D. C., Huffman, D. D., Christian, D. D., & Wilson, B. J. (2016). Experiences of male counselor educators: A study of relationship boundaries. *The Professional Counselor, 6,* 107–120. doi:10.15241/dr.6.2.107

Roach, L. F., & Young, M. E. (2007). Do counselor education programs promote wellness in their students? *Counselor Education and Supervision, 47,* 29–45. doi:10.1002/j.1556-6978.2007.tb00036.x

Salazar, C. F., Herring, R. D., Cameron, S. C., & Nihlen, A. S. (2004). Experiences of counselor educators of color in academe. *Journal of Professional Counseling, Practice, Theory, & Research, 32*, 42–57.

Sangganjanavanich, V. F., & Balkin, R. S. (2013). Burnout and job satisfaction among counselor educators. *The Journal of Humanistic Counseling, 52*, 67–79. doi:10.1002/j.2161-1939.2013.00033.x

Shillingford, M. A., Trice-Black, S., & Butler, S. K. (2013). Wellness of minority female counselor educators. *Counselor Education and Supervision, 52*, 255–269. doi:10.1002/j.1556-6978.2013.00041.x

Stinchfield, T., & Trepal, H. (2010). Academic motherhood for counselor educators: Navigating through the pipeline. *International Journal for the Advancement of Counseling, 32*, 91–100. doi:10.1007/s10447-009-9086-0

Trepal, H., & Stinchfield, T. (2012). Experiences of motherhood in counselor education. *Counselor Education and Supervision, 51*, 112–126. doi:10.1002/j.1556-6978.2012.00008.x

Wester, K., Trepal, H., & Myers, J. (2009). Wellness of counselor educators: An initial look. *The Journal of Humanistic Counseling, 48*, 91–110. doi:10.1002/j.2161-1939.2009.tb00070.x

Yager, G. G., & Tovar-Blank, Z. G. (2007). Wellness and counselor education. *The Journal of Humanistic Counseling, 46*, 142–153. doi:10.1002/j.2161-1939.2007.tb00032.x

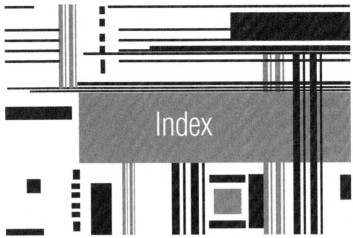

Index

Figures are indicated by "f" following the page number.

(continued)